Party Politics and Populism in Zambia

Party Politics and Populism in Zambia

Michael Sata and Political Change, 1955–2014

Sishuwa Sishuwa

JAMES CURREY

© Sishuwa Sishuwa 2024

The right of Sishuwa Sishuwa
to be identified as the author of this work has been asserted in accordance with
sections 77 and 78 of the Copyright, Designs and Patents Act 1988

All Rights Reserved. Except as permitted under current legislation no part of this work
may be photocopied, stored in a retrieval system, published, performed in public,
adapted, broadcast, transmitted, recorded or reproduced in any form or by any means,
without the prior permission of the copyright owner

First published 2024
James Currey

ISBN 978 1 84701 392 7

James Currey
is an imprint of
Boydell & Brewer Ltd
PO Box 9, Woodbridge
Suffolk IP12 3DF (GB)
www.jamescurrey.com
and of
Boydell & Brewer Inc.
668 Mt Hope Avenue
Rochester, NY 14620–2731 (US)
www.boydellandbrewer.com

British Library Cataloguing in Publication Data
A CIP record for this book is available from the British Library

The publisher has no responsibility for the continued existence or accuracy of URLs
for external or third-party internet websites referred to in this book, and does not
guarantee that any content on such websites is, or will remain, accurate or appropriate

To my mother, Grace Liswaniso Sishuwa

Contents

	List of illustrations	ix
	Preface	xi
	List of abbreviations	xv
	Introduction	1
1.	Becoming Bemba and a 'Man of Action'	33
2.	Mobilising Urbanites in the One-party State	67
3.	Constructing a Power Base in a Dominant Ruling Party	93
4.	Building an Alternative Political Force	135
5.	Winning the Prize	173
	Conclusion	191
	Bibliography	199
	Index	211

Illustrations

Map
    Map of Zambia   xvii

Figures

1. The front page of *The Post*, 23 September 2011, showing people's reaction to Sata's presidential victory — 2
2. Sata's first National Registration Identity Card, obtained in 1965, showing his date of birth — 42
3. Sata's personal details in the *Africa Yearbook and Who's Who 1977* — 42
4. Sata's sworn statement for the Zambian presidential election of 2008 — 44
5. Sata's sworn statement for the Zambian presidential election of 2011 — 45
6. Sata's response to public calls for him to quit politics, *The Post*, 26 October 2001 — 133
7. President Levy Mwanawasa's response to rebel MMD MPs, *Sunday Post*, 9 March 2003 — 149
8. PF campaign advert in *The Post*, 10 April 2003 — 152
9. Sata's declaration of himself as 'the redeemer for Zambia', *The Post*, 15 June 2006 — 163
10. Media portrayal of Sata's 2011 campaigns in Western Province, *Sunday Post*, 22 May — 181

Photographs

1. An example of typical turnout at Sata's public rallies. © Sishuwa Sishuwa — xii
2. Author with President Sata at State House after an interview in 2012. © Sishuwa Sishuwa — 29

3. President Sata serving as a pallbearer at Oliver Irwin's burial.
   © Sishuwa Sishuwa 85
4. Sata travelling to a campaign rally in rural Zambia while in opposition.
   © Sishuwa Sishuwa 164

Tables

1. Results of the Kabwata parliamentary election, 1983 84
2. Results of the Kabwata parliamentary election, 1988 87
3. Results of the presidential election, 2001 146
4. Results of the presidential election, 2006 171
5. Results of the presidential election, 2011 187
6. Sata's results in the 2008 and 2011 presidential elections by province 187
7. Rupiah Banda's results in the 2008 and 2011 presidential elections by province 188

The author and publisher are grateful to all the institutions and individuals listed for permission to reproduce the materials in which they hold copyright. Every effort has been made to trace the copyright holders; apologies are offered for any omission, and the publisher will be pleased to add any necessary acknowledgement in subsequent editions.

Preface

MY INTEREST in the political career of Michael Sata was sparked in late 2010 when I happened to come across a radio discussion on the BBC World Service. The speaker was remembering a harsh-tongued and unpredictable politician, with a rude and aggressive style of politics seen by some as brilliant and by others as a disaster. Though uneducated, this man was described as an organically intelligent politician who had a natural campaigning ability and whose public rallies attracted thousands. I thought to myself, 'They must be referring to Sata. Is he dead?' In fact, I was way off the mark. It turned out that the subject was not the (still living) leader of Zambia's main opposition party, the Patriotic Front (PF), but rather George Alfred Brown, a British politician who served as Deputy Leader of the Labour Party in the 1960s and who died in 1985. Yet it struck me how Brown's rise to political prominence bore an uncanny resemblance to Sata's.

Both Brown and Sata had little formal education but had a 'man of the people' common touch and a talent for making mincemeat of their more educated opponents on the campaign trail. Both cut their teeth in trade unions, were elected as members of parliament in urban constituencies, and rose rapidly within party hierarchies. Brown held several Cabinet positions under Prime Minister Harold Wilson during the 1960s. These positions included Foreign Secretary and First Secretary of State, which effectively made Brown the second in command. Brown and Sata could have crossed paths in these years, on the street or the railway platform, as, at the time, Sata was living and working in England as a porter at London's Victoria Station. Thereafter, their career trajectories went in opposite directions. Sata returned to Zambia and held several Cabinet positions under Presidents Kenneth Kaunda and Frederick Chiluba in the 1980s and 1990s, including latterly Minister without Portfolio, a role that gave him free rein and, it turned out, a little too much power for his own good.

However, the duo had starkly contrasting fortunes following their exits from government. After resigning as Foreign Secretary in 1968, Brown's fortune was a drink-fuelled slide into political oblivion. He lost his seat in 1970 and left the Labour Party in 1976. Announcing his resignation, he tripped and fell into a gutter, glass in hand – a literal fall from grace. He became president of the newly

Photograph 1 Opposition Patriotic Front leader Michael Sata addressing a public rally in Kitwe, Copperbelt Province, a week before Zambia's 2011 election.

formed Social Democratic Alliance in 1980 only to see it quickly swallowed by a stronger rival grouping, which he never joined.

Sata, by contrast, saw his political career recover and eventually flourish. Even allowing for the fact that he was operating in a more fluid and forgiving party system than Brown was (i.e. leaving one of the big parties in the UK's political system spells doom in a way that it does not in Zambia), Sata had a dramatic change in fortune. By the time he resigned from the governing Movement for Multiparty Democracy (MMD) to form the PF in 2001, his political appeal had taken a severe beating, largely because he had been the public face of President Chiluba's attempts to secure an unconstitutional third term. As MMD National Secretary, Sata was the leading light behind the unpopular campaign to change Zambia's constitution, and sometimes even seemed to be dragging a reluctant Chiluba in tow. Following the collapse of the bid and Chiluba's subsequent decision to name Levy Mwanawasa as his successor, Sata struck out on his own. His reputation was in tatters, and most Zambians – me included – did not think he stood a chance. His 2001 election campaign was an abject failure. Yet over the next ten years, he rediscovered his common touch or populist talents.

In early 2011, I wrote to Roy Clarke, a friend, prominent newspaper satirist, and white British national who had been a permanent resident in Zambia since the early 1960s, mentioning my desire to study Sata's political career.[1] I said that I could not understand how a tainted politician who had long been close to the levers of power had recast himself as a 'man of the people', attracting huge crowds at his public rallies. Clarke's response, one that renewed my interest in pursuing the study of Sata, is worth quoting at length.

> I am puzzled and aghast in wonderment at Sata's ability to reassemble himself. I thought the Third Term Fiasco should have finished Sata for ever and for good, and I was very much of the opinion that the last sensible thing Chiluba did, of the few sensible things he did, was to avoid giving us Sata as the next president. Sata was the architect of the absurd MMD national convention which elected Chiluba as party president for a third term, and used chicanery, skulduggery, and thuggery to keep out all who opposed, party leaders and ministers included. So how did he recover?

In attempting to answer this question, I argue that Sata's resurrection after 2001 – as indeed with several of his previous comebacks – owes much to what he learnt over the course of his long career, starting from his trade union days in the early 1960s. This includes an ability to promise people what they want, to identify with people and their needs, and to play the part of the ordinary citizen speaking up for his peers. This is the stock-in-trade of politics everywhere but perhaps even more so in Zambia after the return to multi-party politics in the early 1990s, when most of Sata's political opponents were educated elites – socially awkward university graduates displaying no sign of the humble origins they claimed to have. Given that Sata succeeded in mobilising voters across different periods and party systems, I decided to use the prism of his political life to examine the long history of party politics and political change in Zambia.

In Zambian culture, the raising of a child is the collective responsibility of an entire community. Although this book bears my name, it has been born of the collective contributions and effort of a wider circle. I hold the view that knowledge is a public good, and does not belong to any single entity or person. In truth, without the involvement of so many people in their different roles, I would not have been able to write *Party Politics and Populism in Zambia*. I have been very fortunate to have had great intellectual guides and mentors at every step of the way. Those who stand out include Walima Kalusa and Webby Kalikiti at the University of Zambia; Nic Cheeseman and the late Jan-Georg Deutsch at the University of Oxford; Jeremy Seekings at the University of Cape

---

[1] Clarke had earlier in January 2004 narrowly survived deportation to the United Kingdom after he wrote a satirical article that the authorities interpreted as an insult to President Levy Mwanawasa. For a close discussion of this incident, see S. Sishuwa and D. Money, 'Defamation of the President, Racial Nationalism, and the Roy Clarke Affair in Zambia', *African Affairs*, Vol. 122, Issue 486 (2023), pp. 33–55.

Town, and Sandra Swart at Stellenbosch University. Others are Miles Larmer at the University of Florida, Mary Eaton at Rhodes House in Oxford, and Neo Simutanyi in Lusaka.

I am also indebted to my family, especially my brother, Fred M'membe, who has supported and inspired me in equal measure. My sincere gratitude also goes to the administrators of the Beit Fund in Oxford, who provided the grant that financed the fieldwork for the research that culminated in this book. I am equally grateful to Aaron Griffiths, Patience Mususa, Duncan Money, M'zizi Kantini, Clement Chipokolo, Cleopas Sambo, and Maka Tounkara for their unfailing friendship.

And, lastly, thank you to Sampa Kangwa-Wilkie who has always been there, and to Michael Sata for sharing a very particular version of his life with me.

Stellenbosch, South Africa
28 October 2023

Abbreviations

ADD	Alliance for Democracy and Development
ANC	African National Congress
AG	Agenda for Zambia
BFM	Barotse Freedom Movement
BPF	Barotse Patriotic Front
BRE	Barotse Royal Establishment
BSAC	British South African Company
CRC	Constitution Review Commission
DA	District Administrator
FFTUZ	Federation of Free Trade Unions of Zambia
FDD	Forum for Democracy and Development
HP	Heritage Party
HIPC	Highly Indebted Poor Country
ICFTU	International Confederation of Free Trade Unions
IFIs	International Financial Institutions
IMF	International Monetary Fund
LSE	London School of Economics
LUDC	Lusaka Urban District Council
MP	Member of Parliament
MUZ	Mineworkers Union of Zambia
MMD–PF	Movement for Multiparty Democracy–Patriotic Front
MMD	Movement for Multiparty Democracy
NAREP	National Restoration Party
NCC	National Constitutional Conference
NEC	National Executive Committee
NMP	National Movement for Progress
NP	National Party

NUBWMW	National Union of Building, Wood, and Metal Workers
NUECGW	National Union of Engineering, Construction and General Workers
NLD	National Leadership for Development
PF	Patriotic Front
PS	Permanent Secretary
SDP	Social Democratic Party
SITET	State Investigations Team for Economy and Trade
SAPs	Structural Adjustment Programmes
ULP	United Liberal Party
UNIP	United National Independence Party
UNIPA	United National Independence Party Archives
UPND	United Party for National Development
UPP	United Progressive Party
UNZA	University of Zambia
ZANC	Zambia African National Congress
ZCTU	Zambia Congress of Trade Unions
ZDC	Zambia Democratic Congress
ZED	Zambians for Empowerment and Development
ZRP	Zambia Republican Party
ZANU–PF	Zimbabwe African National Union – Patriotic Front

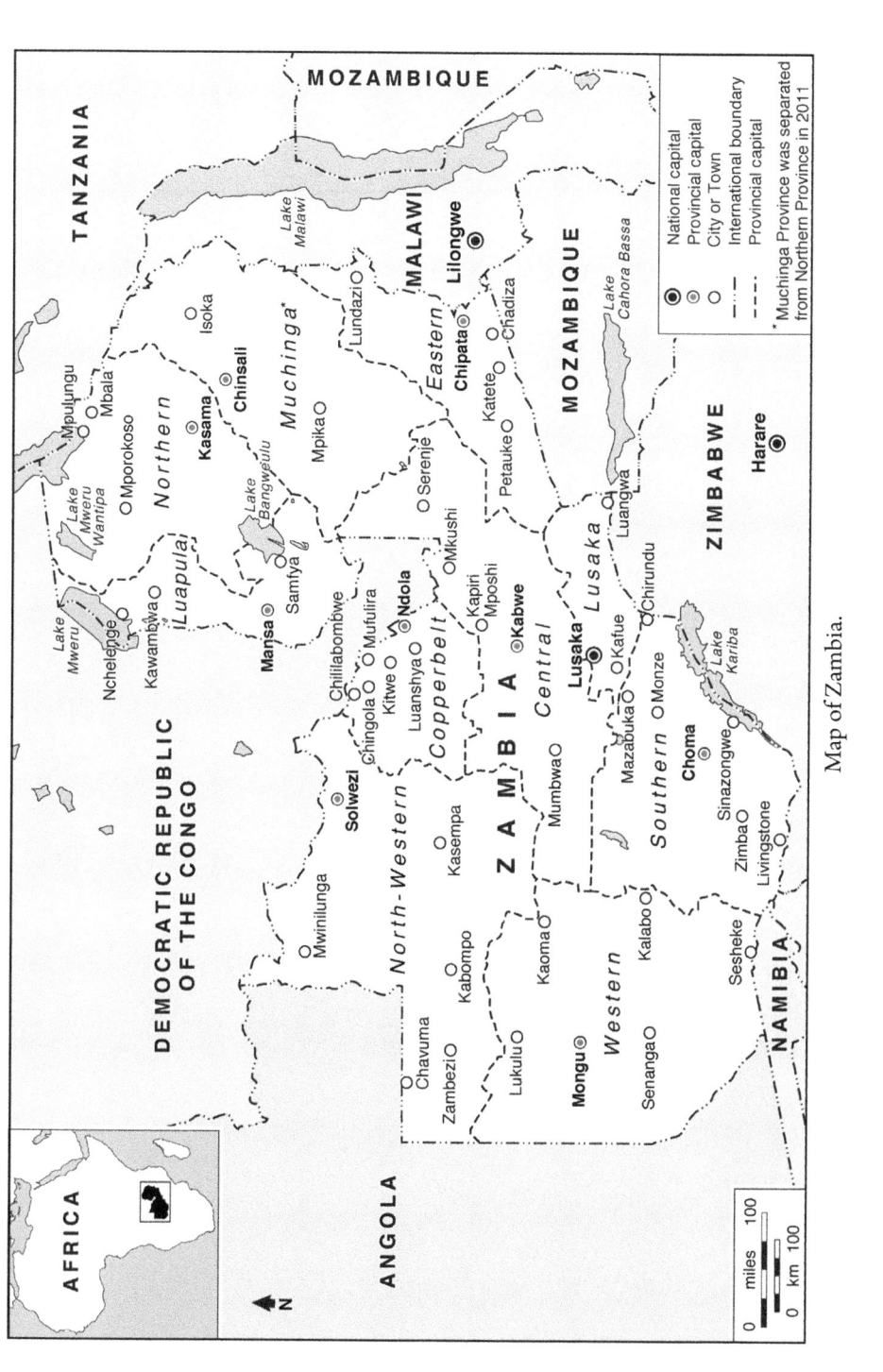

Map of Zambia.

Introduction

ON 23 September 2011, Michael Sata, leader of the opposition Patriotic Front (PF) party, was inaugurated as the fifth elected President of Zambia since independence from Britain in 1964. This followed his victory against incumbent Rupiah Banda of the ruling Movement for Multiparty Democracy (MMD). After a decade in opposition, and at the fourth attempt, Sata, 74, overcame strong competition from Banda, 75, and nine other opposition presidential contenders. He obtained 42 per cent of the vote, ahead of the sitting president, who polled 35.6 per cent. In the early hours of the same day, soon after being declared winner, Sata addressed the media: 'How do I receive this victory? Well, this is the beginning of a long journey.'[1] In fact, it was the exact opposite. At the formation of the PF ten years earlier, Sata had indicated a single-minded focus on becoming President of Zambia, a focus that could be traced back to his days in the grassroots structures of the United National Independence Party (UNIP) in the early 1960s. 'I am coming from grassroots politics to rule', he said in October 2001. 'I will retire from politics after being President [of Zambia] in State House.'[2] In this sense, his generally unexpected victory in the 2011 election was not the beginning of a long journey, but the end of one.

This book explores that historical journey, which began before the achievement of independence and therefore cuts across many supposed divides in Zambian political history, such as the colonial, post-colonial, one-party state, and multi-party eras. In this way, the book addresses a major gap in contemporary academic accounts of Zambian history, which tends to get segmented into different periods and to downplay the importance of individual leaders in the broader processes of political change. It demonstrates that the successful process of political mobilisation and the history of individual leadership that led Sata to victory in the 2011 election had deep roots. The leadership that he provided, the grievances that he articulated and played on, the policy appeals around which he rallied support and the language with which he expressed those appeals,

---

1   George Chellah, 'It's the beginning of a long journey – Sata', *The Post*, 23 September 2011, p. 4.
2   Webster Malido, 'I will retire after being President, says Sata', *The Post*, 26 October 2001, pp. 1–4.

Figure 1 The front page of *The Post*, the country's main private newspaper, on the day when Sata was declared winner of Zambia's 2011 election around 2 am local time.

the constituencies he targeted and mobilised, and the nature and style of his political strategy, all had their origins in much earlier phases of Zambian history, starting from the late-colonial period. This is not to say that the situation in the early 2000s had reverted to that of the late 1950s and early 1960s, but does indicate that these themes are consistent and continuous from the late-colonial period (1945–1964) through the years of one-party rule (1973–1991) and into the era of multi-party democracy (since 1991), and that these continuities can profitably be understood through a critical political biography of one individual whose experiences cut across these apparent divides. In exploring the broad continuities between these different periods through the case study of Sata, this book departs from those studies that have tended to identify and examine Zambia's political history through several supposed turning points and disruptions, or the institutions that have come and gone with them.

A central theme of the book is the evolution of party politics and political change in Zambia and the effectiveness of populism as a strategy of mobilising support across different periods and party systems. Existing scholarship on party politics – be it from the late-colonial to the post-colonial period, or from the one-party era to multi-party democracy – has focused largely on ethnicity, which has taken attention away from the fact that most ethnic politics has had, as I show in this book, a populist component.[3] Populism as a subject has boomed exponentially over the last decade in response to the emergence of purportedly anti-establishment political actors and movements on both the right and left of the political divide. The rise of Donald Trump in the United States and the meteoric emergence of populist leaders in Europe, in the mould of Hungary's Viktor Orbán and France's ultra nationalist Jean-Marie Le Pen, have brought the study of populism to the centre of academic debates. Although a shared definition of populism remains elusive, the concept has been used to describe a political language or style, a means of achieving electoral success, an ideology, and/or a tool of protest in unequal societies.[4]

Our understanding of populism, historically and in the current period, has been continually hampered by a general lack of comparative analysis between periods and wider places. In the United States and much of Western Europe, for example, populism is often equated with a right-wing, anti-immigrant politics that constructs 'the people' in ethno-nationalist terms, marginalising 'non-

---

[3] A good example is Daniel Posner, *Institutions and Ethnic Politics in Africa*, Cambridge: Cambridge University Press, 2005.

[4] See for instance, Benjamin Moffitt, *The Global Rise of Populism*, Palo Alto: Stanford University Press, 2016 and Cas Mudde, 'Populism: An Ideational Approach', in C. Rovira, P. Taggart, P.O. Espejo, and P. Ostiguy (eds), *The Oxford Handbook of Populism*, Oxford: Oxford University Press, 2017.

native' populations and setting itself against liberal elites.[5] In Latin America, the phenomenon is often thought of as inherently left-wing, opposed to globalisation and US imperialism, and defined by class and trade union ties.[6] In Africa, where non-native populations are tiny and ethnicity defines rural political organisation, populism is usually applied to urban spaces where labour-based politics has broken down.

In this book, populism is used in the sense described by Laclau, who interpreted it as a distinctive mode of political articulation constructed around a coalition of social demands or claims that have not found satisfaction within the institutionalised framework in which they were originally conveyed.[7] Even more relevant to the book are the key characteristics of populist leaders as understood by Weyland and well summarised by Cheeseman, Ford, and Simutanyi: they represent a highly personalised politics, are impervious to institutionalisation, and 'communicate with the electorate on an emotional rather than logical level'. Their 'campaigning relies on mass public rallies in which the candidate meets the faithful'.[8] They claim the status of redeemers, who will deliver power into the hands of 'the people'.

In a way, the Global South – led by Latin America and Africa – is a point of origin for work on populism rather than a place where ideas from the Global North are applied. This explains why historians and analysts in other parts of the world are increasingly correcting the presentation of populism as something relatively new by drawing useful comparisons between contemporary populists like Trump and some of the late nineteenth- or early twentieth-century populists in Latin America.[9] In Africa, such approaches to the study of populism are yet to

---

5   See Paul Taggart, 'Populism in Western Europe', in C. Rovira, P. Taggart, P.O. Espejo, and P. Ostiguy (eds), *The Oxford Handbook of Populism*, Oxford: Oxford University Press, 2017 and Joseph Lowndes, 'Populism in the United States', in C. Rovira, P. Taggart, P.O. Espejo, and P. Ostiguy (eds), *The Oxford Handbook of Populism*, Oxford: Oxford University Press, 2017.

6   Carlos de la Tore, 'Populism in Latin America', in C. Rovira, P. Taggart, P.O. Espejo, and P. Ostiguy (eds), *The Oxford Handbook of Populism*, Oxford: Oxford University Press, 2017, pp. 260–84.

7   Ernesto Laclau, 'Populism: What's in a Name?', in Francisco Panizza (ed.), *Populism and the Mirror of Democracy*, London, Verso, pp. 34–49. I provide much detail around this definition later in this chapter.

8   See Kurt Weyland, 'Clarifying a Contested Concept: Populism in the Study of Latin American Politics', *Comparative Politics*, 34, 1 (2001), pp. 1–22; and Nic Cheeseman, Robert Ford, and Neo Simutanyi, 'Is there a "Populist Threat" in Zambia?', in Christopher Adam, Paul Collier and Michael Gondwe (eds), *Zambia: Building Prosperity from Resource Wealth*, Oxford: Oxford University Press, 2014, pp. 339–65.

9   A good example on this score is Carlos de la Torre, 'Trump's populism: lessons from Latin America', *Postcolonial Studies*, 20:2 (2017), 187–98.

take root, but there exists a large body of Africanist literature that has explored the phenomenon under the era of multi-party politics in the 2000s.

Studies by Larmer and Fraser,[10] Cheeseman and Larmer,[11] Resnick,[12] Paget,[13] and Melchiorre[14] have all employed Laclau's conception of populism to provide insights into how it has been applied as a political strategy across the continent. Their works have shown how political, mainly opposition, leaders like Sata in Zambia, Abdoulaye Wade in Senegal, John Magufuli in Tanzania, Julius Malema in South Africa, and Robert Kyagulanyi (aka Bobi Wine) in Uganda have, over the course of the last twenty years, mobilised electoral support through the discursive construction of the categories of 'the people' and 'the elite'. The major limitation of this literature is that it largely focuses on the supply side (including detachment from traditional parties, linking populism to multi-party democracy) and demand-side (including economic grievances) drivers of populism, to the neglect of individual agency. As these studies themselves show, populism in Africa ultimately relies on a charismatic leader who taps into socio-economic grievances. But for many researchers, the individual is seen as performative rather than taken seriously as a unit of analysis. This approach is comparable to the study of religion in Africa. Researchers look at churches as organisations of influence, but what is often not taken seriously within this is actual religious beliefs, partly because most liberal Western social scientists analysing it are not themselves highly religious people. As a result, what is really going on inside religion is not captured. This is analogous to most writings on populism. What constitutes charisma, populism, or populist movements is studied, but what is neglected in such analyses is the personality and origins of the individual leader. How does such a leader emerge? This is where this book comes in, by providing insight into political personalities. What the study of Sata shows is that in essence, three factors – the structural, the economic, and, importantly, the personal – are needed to understand when and how populism emerges and evolves.

---

10 Miles Larmer and Alastair Fraser, 'Of Cabbages and King Cobra: Populist Politics and Zambia's 2006 Election', *African Affairs*, 106, 425 (2007), pp. 611–37.

11 Nic Cheeseman and Miles Larmer, 'Ethnopopulism in Africa: Opposition Mobilisation in Diverse and Unequal Societies', *Democratisation*, 22, 1 (2015), pp. 34–36.

12 Danielle Resnick, *Urban Poverty and Party Populism in African Democracies*, New York: Cambridge University Press, 2014; Daniel Resnick, 'Populism in Africa', in C. Rovira, P. Taggart, P.O. Espejo, and P. Ostiguy (eds), *The Oxford Handbook of Populism*, Oxford: Oxford University Press, 2018, pp. 140–64.

13 Dan Paget, 'Again, making Tanzania great: Magufuli's restorationist developmental nationalism', *Democratization*, 27:7 (2020), pp. 1240–60.

14 Luke Melchiorre, 'Generational Populism and the Political Rise of Kyaluganyi – aka Bobi Wine – in Uganda', *Review of African Political Economy* (forthcoming).

A related weakness of some of the literature on populism in Africa is the tendency to look for unifying patterns of 'African populism', emanating from a generalised view that populism on the continent works in a certain way. This is not the way to understand specific instances of populism in practice because the contexts and outcomes are so demonstrably different. There is also a tendency, especially among political scientists, to say that African politics is relatively less institutional than European politics and therefore the capacity for populism is stronger. This assumption may have seemed true once, but not anymore. If we look at European politics now, or indeed politics almost anywhere in the world – Argentina, Italy, France, India, and the US – populism is thriving. It is therefore more helpful to think about populism as global and local rather than African-wide.

In other words, while there is a certain respectability in trying to draw generalisations, delineation is important. The most instructive and interesting aspects, precisely because populism is about local context, are specifically local. There is only a limited amount of transferability and therefore comparability, and hardly anything specifically *African* that can be said about populism. What may be helpful is thinking about broader instances of comparison, such as what gives populism purchase in specific eras, rather than looking for an African pattern of populism. Copper-producing Zambia, for instance, might have more in common with Venezuela, where oil provides a vehicle for a certain kind of populism, than it would have with, say, Kenya or Uganda. One possible explanation for the lack of these broader comparisons, in both Zambia and Africa more generally, is the absence of serious research work that locates contemporary political developments in a historical context. Another is the neglect of methodological approaches – such as political biography – that enable the study of the interaction between recent democratic politics and earlier practices of it in the early post-colonial and even late-colonial periods through a context-shaped analysis of the careers of individual politicians who straddle these divides. It is precisely this dearth of scholarship examining these useful linkages between the present and the past that *Party Politics and Populism in Zambia* seeks to address.

The main argument of the book is that populism in Africa emerged in the late-colonial period of the 1950s and early 1960s, not the era of multi-party politics in the 2000s or late 1980s, as presented in the literature on African politics. This argument is developed through a case study of Michael Sata, one of Africa's most well-known populist figures of recent times. Like many of the studies on populism in Africa, studies on Sata have focused on his populist mobilisations in the 2000s when he led his political party to State House after only a decade in opposition politics. Set against this scholarship, this book traces the rise of Sata's populism to the late-colonial era in the 1950s and early 1960s when nationalist campaigning, as part of the process by which popular support was generated, laid the seed for the populism that became a staple of African politics in the post-colonial era. A common feature of the utopian futures that nationalist leaders across the continent envisaged was the lack of detail about their political policies and the structural factors underlying economic inequality in their societies. As Larmer has argued, colonists were criticised not because of identified weaknesses in their policies, but because they did not have the nation's interests at heart:

> African nationalist campaigning sought to portray colonial administration not only as dysfunctional and unpopular, but also to depict colonial officials as inherently unable to reflect the wishes of African people. Whereas previous generations of moderate African leaders, both chiefly authorities and educated elites, had appealed to the colonial administration's better nature and ability to intervene to improve people's lives, late-colonial nationalists asserted that foreigners were incapable of understanding African grievances, which could only be effectively addressed by an authentic government of indigenous rulers. This continued right up to the moment of independence and was not incompatible with the fact that nationalist leaders such as Kwame Nkrumah and Kenneth Kaunda took up senior positions within late colonial administrations, operating as ministers and working alongside colonial civil servants. ...
>
> All this was possible because many nationalist parties existed primarily as electioneering vehicles, rather than as institutions capable of debating and agreeing policies. Leaders were frequently not held to account for the positions they adopted and adapted for particular purposes. The lack of national media and the limited penetration of literacy in English or French meant that both local and national leaders were able to tailor their electoral message for mostly rural constituencies, utilising local idioms and discourses and making locally specific promises, thereby raising expectations of rapid post-independence development that were un-costed and, in retrospect, unrealistic. Such promises were ... vital to the success of nationalist parties in mobilising popular support, made at electoral rallies held in the 1950s and early 1960s, which raised expectations of socio-economic change and linked these to the prospect of national independence.[15]

The sources of many of the thwarted expectations of independence in several African countries, and the populist figures that emerged in the wake of independence, are to be found in the unrealistic promises that were made by nationalists during the late-colonial era.

Following the achievement of independence, people in many African countries, such as Ghana, Kenya, and Zambia, had big expectations, which gradually changed into the kind of disappointment that paved the path for a second wave of populist mobilisations in the first decade of the competitive multi-party political system inherited from the departing colonists. Here, the

---

15 Miles Larmer, 'Historicising populism in late-colonial/post-colonial sub-Saharan Africa', paper presented to the Comparing Populism workshop, University of Sheffield, United Kingdom, 8–9 February 2013.

nascent opposition parties, whose leaders had only recently been allies with those now in power, sought to present the governing elites as failing to meet the popular expectations of independence. As was the case with the late-colonial nationalists, the content of the campaign messages of the opposition was marked by a lack of emphasis on the structural factors underlying economic inequality, but it was enough to generate popular support. In response, the ruling elites, presenting opposition parties as agents of foreign interests, imposed one-party states in several African countries including Zambia, starting in the early 1970s and lasting up to the early 1990s. By the 1980s, many of the expected real improvements in people's lives had been frustrated, allowing populism – the third wave – to be used by political entrepreneurs as an effective strategy for mobilising support within the one-party state. As the book's central subject did in Zambia, aspiring and incumbent members of parliament (MPs) built coalitions with businesspeople and used public office to win elections and deliver the long-awaited fruits of independence, such as new houses and even beer.

All these waves predate the populism of the era of multi-party politics in the early 2000s, centred around economic inequality, one that has received much scholarly attention. Taken together, these waves provide two significant lessons about populism in Africa. The first is that populism on the continent is a political phenomenon whose origins are to be found in the content and nature of the nationalist campaigns of the 1950s and early 1960s. This is not to say that all African nationalists were populists; rather, it is to acknowledge the roots of the strategies that political actors have employed to mobilise electoral support in recent times. The reappearance of populism in the early 2000s reflects a deeper connection with the past and demonstrates the long shadow of late-colonial influences on contemporary African politics.

The second lesson relates to the golden thread of populism in Africa that cuts across party systems, different historical eras, and the four identified waves. This populism is characterised by an aversion to complex policy making, a reliance on slogans, and an assumption that the replacement of existing government or state personnel will bring about immediate and significant improvements. Existing governments and political opponents are often identified and construed as in alliance with external actors. Wider populists present themselves this way to gain political support, not from deep-rooted political convictions. It is a cynical exercise to take advantage of a political mood. One key distinguishing issue is that the first three waves were mostly about the structure and control of political institutions. The fourth wave was less about this, as multi-party politics was already established across the continent, and in a way, it was more about economic issues, suggesting that populist mobilisation is possible even outside the nationalist struggle or in the absence of a common enemy.

The value of *Party Politics and Populism in Zambia* lies in its analysis of populism and its associated techniques across two time periods that are often treated separately in the literature on African political history: late-colonial and post-colonial eras. Written at a time when there is increased scholarly interest in the re-emergence of populism across the world, the book is the first close study that offers the explanatory capacity of populism as a theme in African political history since the 1950s and explores the broad continuities in the strategies that individual leaders have employed to mobilise political support across different party systems. It will engage closely with these themes by historicising populism in Zambia through an examination of the life of Sata.

Zambia represents a fascinating study because it has experienced the cited waves of populist mobilisations that have emerged at specific times. The earliest appeared in the late-colonial period, when organised labour and UNIP led the struggle for independence. There has been much work on the mass mobilisation of nationalist parties in the late 1950s, but very little on the political content of these mobilisations and the forms they took.[16] Like elsewhere in Africa, many nationalist parties in Zambia did not formulate detailed policy proposals. Their concerns, not unreasonably, were on the injustices of colonialism. These often provided a unifying force for emerging political elites. As a result, UNIP inherited colonial state structures without having a clear political programme. Much of the populist rhetoric of this period rested on the assumption that removing colonial oppression would result in immediate and widespread material gains for the indigenous populations of the newly independent state. Every Zambian would have an egg for breakfast, promised Kaunda, a pledge that must have resonated among Africans in the early 1960s. Kaunda's former political advisor recalled the campaign of his former boss: 'KK would often tell us that the removal of the British who are uncaring and unresponsive to the grievances of Africans would automatically improve the livelihoods of Zambians once we were free.'[17] As noted by Larmer above, the focus of these nationalist campaigns was on discrediting the colonial state and its officials, notwithstanding the fact that many first-generation African nationalists, including Kaunda himself, worked for the colonial state. Arguably, their experience helped to reproduce those structures following the achievement of independence in 1964, but with new personnel.

Like elsewhere in Africa, political independence did not result in great economic change for the lives of many Zambians. This quickly fed into resentment of UNIP and Kaunda. Disaffection prompted the formation of new

---

16 See for instance, David C. Mulford, *Zambia: The Politics of Independence, 1957–1964*, Oxford: Oxford University Press, 1967.

17 Interview with Mark Chona, Lusaka, 12 September 2016. Chona participated in Zambia's independence struggle and served as Kaunda's political advisor after the attainment of independence.

political parties and a split in the governing party when then vice-president Simon Kapwepwe formed a breakaway opposition in 1971. Kapwepwe's party, the United Progressive Party (UPP), was founded on disaffection with economic developments and the alleged political marginalisation of certain ethnic groups but offered no real policy programme to overcome these problems. Its appeal rested almost entirely on populist mobilisations – the second wave – on the industrial Copperbelt and ethnic appeals to Kapwepwe's Bemba-speaking rural communities.[18] The central message was that Kaunda and UNIP had failed, but without an analysis of how and why they had failed other than alleged incompetence and personal failings. The implications were that replacing UNIP with the UPP would result in greater changes. The UPP never got a chance. The party, which represented a threat not so much on its own but because of the possibility that it could ally with an older opposition party, the African National Congress, to wrestle power from UNIP, was soon banned as Zambia became a one-party state in 1973.

Political life continued under the one-party state. Here, many observers have noted the lack of national level and cross-party political competition, implying a kind of monolithic politics where things were decided by the ruling party.[19] This was not the case. Elections were held and, counter intuitively, these were competitive. Even if the party remained the same, MPs could lose their jobs. Individual political actors took advantage of these polls. By the 1980s, Zambia was experiencing significant economic problems, and enterprising figures used this context to launch their political careers. They claimed that, by replacing incumbent MPs, they could bring out economic developments and satisfy socio-economic grievances. Again, this did not involve a particular political programme beyond the replacement of personnel. Individual political actors would get into power this way, paving the way for the third wave of populist mobilisations that lasted from the early 1980s to the end of that decade.

More broadly, populist politics were also evident in the 1980s in the trade union movement and civil society. Anger over economic decline and structural adjustment policies prompted increasing waves of protests, especially in urban areas. Blaming external actors for the country's economic plight, those opposed to Kaunda and angered by Zambia's economic plight had no real specific policies on how to rectify this. Kaunda and his alleged external socialist backers were blamed, and it was assumed that removing him and changing to a multi-party

18 For a full study of the UPP, see Miles Larmer, '"A Little Bit Like a Volcano": The United Progressive Party and Resistance to One-Party Rule in Zambia, 1964–1980', *International Journal of African Historical Studies*, 39, 1 (2006), pp. 49–83.

19 See, for instance, Carolyn Baylies and Morris Szeftel, 'Elections in the one-party state', in Cherry J. Gertzel (ed.), Carolyn Baylies, and Morris Szeftel, *The Dynamics of the One-Party State in Zambia*, Manchester: Manchester University Press, 1984, pp. 58–78.

political system would result in great economic gains, wider employment opportunities, and political freedom. There was no clearly articulated programme to achieve these changes. In another parallel with the colonial state, many of the leaders of this new movement towards democracy had been senior figures in UNIP. The opposition MMD, a coalition of broad interest groups that was formed out of this movement in July 1990, trumped UNIP at the 1991 elections after promising jobs, significant improvements in the lives of ordinary Zambians, and an end to shortages of basic commodities.[20] Subsequently, there was not much delivery of these promised benefits. Zambia entered an even more painful episode in the 1990s, and the economy only recovered in the early 2000s with a new mining boom. The effect of this boom was felt unevenly, and this situation gave rise to the most recent and well-known emergence of populism.

The motivating factor behind the re-emergence of populism in the 2000s was a widespread feeling that the economic benefits were uneven. The opposition PF were the leaders of this latest wave. They promised that this economic inequality would be rectified by the removal of the MMD and their alleged backers in the form of Chinese foreign investors and Western financial institutions. This message was well received, especially on the Copperbelt, even though leading figures in the PF, including Sata himself, had previously been in the MMD. In fact, Sata had also been involved with UNIP and previously with the nationalist movement. His political life, around which the book is structured, best exemplifies these evolving waves of populist politics in Zambia's party system over a nearly sixty-year period. His political career, like those of several other Zambian politicians, also bridges the main divides in the country's political history: the late-colonial period (1945–1964), the era of the one-party state (1973–1991) and the advent of democratisation (since 1991). Sata's personal experiences further cut across several political organisations that won power over this period and served as his base. These include UNIP (1960–1991, with a brief interruption in the early 1970s when he was a member of the short-lived opposition UPP), the MMD (1991–2001) and the PF (2001–2014).

Educated in rural Northern Rhodesia, Zambia's colonial name, by Catholic European missionaries, Sata started his career as a constable in the colonial police in the 1950s before he went on to become a populist trade union nationalist on the eve of the country's independence. After spending a few years in the United Kingdom in the early 1970s, he returned home and was twice elected as an MP in the one-party state in the 1980s. President Kaunda also appointed him governor of the capital city, Lusaka, during this period. As pressure mounted on Kaunda to return Zambia to multi-party politics, Sata jumped ship to join the MMD, the

---

20   Carolyn Baylies and Morris Szeftel, 'Democratisation and the 1991 Elections in Zambia', in J. Daniel, R. Southall, and M. Szeftel (eds), *Voting for Democracy: Watershed Elections in Contemporary Anglophone Africa*, Aldershot: Ashgate, 1999, pp. 83–109.

Chiluba-led opposition party that unseated UNIP in the 1991 elections. Over the course of the next decade, Sata served as a minister in different portfolios and as the MMD National Secretary. When President Chiluba, barred from running for office by the constitution, overlooked him as his successor, Sata quit both his government and party positions to form the PF, less than two months before he unsuccessfully contested the 2001 general election. After a decade in opposition politics, a populist and ethnic campaign delivered him to State House in September 2011, three years before he died in office in October 2014.

If Zambia has been a site of populist mobilisations since the 1950s, Sata was a key and continuous actor in these mobilisations. A study of his political career, one that deals with both the man and his times, could provide a clear understanding of the major themes of Zambian political history over time and how they intersect with the life of an individual. To achieve this outcome, I have adopted the use of political biography as the framework of analysis, for three main reasons. First, larger historical processes can be illustrated through the lives of individuals who play key roles in the processes. 'The proper subject of biography', Handlin wrote, 'is not the complete person or the complete society, but the point at which the two interact. There, the situation [or the times] and the individual illuminate one another.'[21] Second, focusing on key actors helps us to understand the significance and limits of agency in history, particularly in relation to the choices that such actors make, their consequences, and the forces that constrain or shape their agency. History is not made by 'Great Men' alone, but they certainly play a role in it. Some of the arguments for oral history overlap with arguments for biography: It is not just that individuals have evidence on historical processes and events that might not be reflected in the archive or other written sources; they also have insights into why things unfolded the way they did, through the choices they made based on their understanding of their contexts. The great sociologist Max Weber emphasised the importance of '*verstehen*', i.e. of understanding how key actors understood the choices open to them and the choices they made. Biography is one form of presenting an understanding of history that emphasises *verstehen*. Taking individuals seriously means taking seriously the ideas that animated them, including nationalist and populist ideologies. Hence the connection to these topics.

Third, non-academic readers seem to have an infinite appetite for biographies because they provide an understanding of the historical period, the human challenges facing the biographical subject, and the possibility that we can transform our own lives and make a difference. The writing style – as is the language – in this book is intentionally designed in a way that would appeal to both a specialist and an ordinary reader. By placing emphasis on the relationship between structure and agency, the book offers more depth and objectivity to the unveiling of the past, as

---

21 Oscar Handlin, *Truth in History*, Cambridge: The Belknap Press of Harvard University Press, 1979, p. 276.

it avoids an over-emphasis on individual achievements, but does not downplay the importance of the role of such individuals in a relatively non-institutional political environment. By taking a wider chronological approach and examining the life of an individual who straddles historical periods previously considered somewhat separate and hitherto studied through snapshot or episodic approaches, the book provides a clear lens of disentangling continuities in ways that other frames of references do not, and is a way to fully understand the similarities across transitions.

The approach to historical enquiry used in this book does not privilege the individual whose life is being examined, but equally does not deal only with overarching processes and movements to the exclusion of the lived experience. Although the book is concerned with Sata's political life, and traces both the subjectivity and agency of that life, it also treats him as historically inscribed, born into a particular social stratum, and constantly shaped by the specific historical contexts he inhabited. The tension in biography is often between individual biography and identity as history and as performance. For instance, it is possible for someone from an incredibly elite background such as a Donald Trump to self-present as a man of the people. There is also tension between Sata's own biographical life, that is the things he did in the past and the experiences he lived through, and his later characterisation of these things in the public sphere. This creates tension between life study and self-presentation. The added value of the political biography in this instance is that it allows us to examine the relationship between the two.

The use of the biographical method adopted here also helps to provide a new and instructive analysis of Zambian political history, approached from the perspective of the study of a single prominent individual politician whose career spans both the late-colonial and post-colonial eras and the single-party and multi-party systems. By examining how non-institutional factors such as individual leadership have shaped the country's political and economic changes since independence, the book builds on established literature that has sought to explain political change in Zambia through the prisms of the abstract role of institutions such as trade unions and political parties, to the exclusion of the concrete role of individual political leaders in these institutions. Studying the political life of such an individual also challenges the dominant periodisation in Zambian political history by drawing significant connections between different historical eras and showing how lessons learnt in one period were replicated in recognisable forms in later periods.

Political biography has not generally been the frame of analysis in the literature on understanding broader processes of political change in Zambia from independence to the present. This is somewhat surprising considering the many ways in which the biographical method might be used to explore several understudied themes in both Zambian and African political history. These include the roots of the strategies that political actors employ to mobilise electoral support in recent times, the significant mileage in understanding the evolving patterns or nature of populism across late-colonial and post-colonial African politics, and the competitiveness of parliamentary elections in single-party regimes and the role of patronage politics within this theme. Other themes are the relevance of intra-party competition in explaining succession outcomes in dominant political parties, and the importance of individual political leadership to the success of opposition parties in electoral campaigns. A review of studies on party politics and political change in Zambia since the late-colonial period shows the inattention paid to these themes and the bias towards institutional topics.

The Individual and Political Change in the 1950s and Early 1960s

There exists a set of older scholarship that employed biography to explain political developments and change during the late-colonial era in Zambia. For example, studies by Hall,[22] Macpherson,[23] and Morris[24] focus on the pre-independence politics of Kaunda. These works emphasise Kaunda's supposedly militant leadership in breaking from Harry Mwaanga Nkumbula's African National Congress and forming the Zambia African National Congress, the forerunner to UNIP. Soon after publication of these works, another wave of biographical writings emerged that set out to provide a counter narrative to the exclusive focus on Kaunda, by highlighting the role of other leaders of the nationalist movement. This later strand of literature is exemplified by Mwangilwa's work on Nkumbula that stresses the centrality of Nkumbula's leadership to the achievement of independence, to the extent that it trivialises the contribution of other figures, including that of Kaunda.[25]

The publication of Rotberg's 1978 biography of Stewart Gore-Browne, a white settler politician in late-colonial Zambia, provided a welcome alternative to the hitherto prevailing trend of focusing on leaders of nationalist parties.[26] Rotberg argues that, contrary to the arguments of earlier historians that the leadership of Kaunda and Nkumbula secured Zambia's independence, there were other individual figures, including non-Zambians, who played a key role. He identifies Gore-Browne, a close advisor to Kaunda in the early 1960s, as one such individual who was involved in the negotiations around independence, but one whose contribution does not fit into the traditional narratives of liberation

---

22 Richard Hall, *Kaunda: Founder of Zambia*, Lusaka: Longmans, 1964.
23 Fergus Macpherson, *Kenneth Kaunda of Zambia: The Times and the Man*, Oxford: Oxford University Press, 1974.
24 Colin Morris, *Black Government? A Discussion between Colin Morris and Kenneth Kaunda*, Lusaka: Rhodesian Printers, 1960.
25 Godwin Mwangilwa, *Harry Mwaanga Nkumbula: A Biography of the Old Lion of Zambia*, Lusaka: Multimedia Publications, 1982.
26 Robert I. Rotberg, *Black Heart: Gore-Browne and the Politics of Multiracial Zambia*, Berkeley: University of California Press, 1978.

struggles. Close to the leading members of the nationalist government, and highly respected for his contributions to the transition from colonial rule to independence, Gore-Browne remains the only non-Zambian politician from the colonial period to be granted a state funeral in post-colonial Zambia.[27]

The works cited above demonstrate the importance and influence of individual leaders in the broader processes of political change. The problem is that these biographical studies were conducted in the late-colonial era or the early years of independence; far fewer are being produced today, at least as serious and rigorous scholarship. Most importantly, a major limitation of these early works is that they neglect the extent to which their individual subjects were constrained by their institutional context. The biographies of Kaunda and Nkumbula, for instance, discuss the duo's political strategies, actions, and achievements outside their wider historical context, and fail to demonstrate how their institutional environment and, as Rotberg shows, other individual leaders, aided their successes. Even Rotberg's own biography of Gore-Browne does not pass the context limitation. Apart from mentioning that Gore-Browne was Kaunda's ally and political consultant, Rotberg's work is more of a straightforward life history that makes little attempt to situate or integrate Gore-Browne's life into the wider political developments of Zambia at the time. As a result, these studies can be viewed as no more than hagiographies that fall within the nationalist history literature that celebrates the people who liberated Africa from colonial rule, and that sees men like Kaunda or Ghana's Kwame Nkrumah as the embodiment of their new nation states. A methodological approach that locates the individual within the changing socio-political and economic dynamics of their time would go beyond this limitation.

Indeed, more recent studies of individual figures have employed this biographical approach. An example is Vickery's work on Dixon Konkola, a leading trade-union-cum-political leader in late-colonial Zambia.[28] Vickery locates Konkola's brief but quite successful career within the broader political developments of the 1950s and early 1960s. The major limitation of Vickery's study is that it does not trace developments beyond the late-colonial era, probably because Konkola played no major role in the post-colonial period. A more useful work in this regard is Larmer's work on Valentine Musakanya, a leading civil servant in late-colonial Zambia who also went on to become the head of the country's post-colonial public service, an MP, and the Governor of the Central Bank.[29] Larmer does not show how Musakanya mobilised political

---

27   Interview with Mark Chona, Lusaka, 12 September 2016.
28   Kenneth P. Vickery, 'Odd Man Out: Labour, Politics and Dixon Konkola', in Jan-Bart Gewald, Marja Hinfelaar, and Giacomo Macola (eds), *Living the End of Empire: Politics and Society in Late Colonial Zambia*, Leiden: Brill, 2011, pp. 111–37.
29   Miles Larmer (ed.), *The Musakanya Papers: The Autobiographical Writings of Valentine Musakanya*, Lusaka: Lembani Trust, 2010.

support in independent Zambia, but his work is helpful because, like that of Vickery, it offers an alternative approach to the hagiographic one of earlier historians by demonstrating that individual actions and achievements can be explored without downplaying the extent to which they were constrained by their context. This is also the methodology adopted by Macola's biography on Nkumbula, the African National Congress (ANC) leader whose political career cuts across the colonial and post-colonial divide.[30] Through an examination of Nkumbula's contribution to decolonisation, nationalism, and post-colonial political change, Macola deconstructs the framework of political analysis that saw UNIP and Kaunda as the overriding and central subjects of Zambia's post-colonial narratives.

Granted, a focus on an individual whom Macola refers to as 'the father of Zambian nationalism' perpetuates the concentration of historical research on well-known leaders of nationalist parties and overlooks those figures like Sata who, despite a lack of strong nationalist credentials, found their way into a political system that was heavily weighted against such individuals. What Macola's work does show, though, is the extent to which Nkumbula's career was both helped and constrained by the institutions through which he operated, and the changing political context of his time. In the introduction to his book, the first serious historical work on post-colonial Zambia that employs a biographic approach to analyse political developments, Macola invites researchers to consider utilising this methodological framework to explore the country's complex political past. This book is a response to that call, building on his efforts and those of Vickery and Larmer.

Patronage Politics and Electoral Competition in the One-party State

In contrast to the literature on decolonisation, most later writers of Zambia's political history downplay the role of individual leaders and emphasise structural factors in influencing political change. Studies by Tordoff,[31] Bates,[32] and Burawoy,[33] for instance, reject a focus on central leaders. They instead place emphasis on the periphery or the masses, or on institutional subjects such as parliament, trade unions, the patrimonial power of the presidency, the

---

30   Giacomo Macola, *Liberal Nationalism in Central Africa: A Biography of Harry Mwaanga Nkumbula*, New York: Palgrave Macmillan, 2010.
31   William Tordoff (ed.), *Politics in Zambia*, Berkeley: University of California, 1974.
32   Robert Bates, *Unions, Parties and Political Development: A Study of Mineworkers in Zambia*, New Haven: Yale University Press, 1971.
33   Michael Burawoy, *The Colour of Class on the Copperbelt: From African Advancement to Zambianisation Mines*, Lusaka: University of Zambia Institute of African Studies, 1972.

dominance of UNIP and the multifaceted nature of opposition to Kaunda's authoritarianism, or economic decline. Indeed, this was and remained the dominant mode of analysis in the 1970s and 1980s. Ironically, even during the years of one-party rule when Kaunda had assumed the position of presidency for life, the same period saw the importance of political biography diminish. Researchers working on the one-party state concluded that the party in power was so dominant that political events like elections were effectively meaningless, as they did not provide for a constitutional means of removing the party in power. This bias towards non-electoral topics is perhaps well illustrated in *The Dynamics of the One-Party State in Zambia*, the most comprehensive work on the subject.[34] Of the book's six chapters, only one is devoted to the study of elections.

Indeed, a focus on structural factors like economic decline, presidentialism, and the centralisation of power sheds significant light on the operations of the one-party state. The corollary, however, is that it ignores the role of individual actors in a political system characterised by relatively weak institutions. This is a particularly important point considering the prevailing assumption that elections in one-party regimes, for instance, were insignificant because they did not result in political change.[35] While this interpretation may be true of presidential elections, it was hardly the case at parliamentary level, where, because of a competitive democratic environment, several non-performing lawmakers lost their seats, sometimes to little-known challengers. Institutional analyses have tended to obscure these frequent high turnovers of incumbent candidates, which demonstrate that the one-party state was more complicated than previously understood.[36] Although there was autocracy above, a degree of democracy certainly existed below – especially in the 1980s, a period that has not received much attention from researchers of party politics in independent Zambia. As I demonstrate in this book using the example of Sata, individual case studies can help explain how competing parliamentary candidates mobilised political support within the constraints of a party-controlled electoral campaign. They can also aid our understanding of the several instances within the one-party state where MPs were able to carve out a constituency of support for themselves or to build patronage support networks in a political system heavily weighted against

---

34   Cherry J. Gertzel (ed.), Carolyn Louise Baylies, and Morris Szeftel, *The Dynamics of the One-Party State in Zambia*, Manchester: Manchester University Press, 1984.

35   Peter Wanyande, 'Democracy and the One-Party State: The African Experience', in Walter O. Oyugi, E.S. Atieno Odhiambo, Michael Chege, and Afrika K. Gitonga (eds), *Democratic Theory and Practice in Africa*, Nairobi: Heinemann Educational Books, 1988, p. 78.

36   See, for instance, Baylies and Szeftel, 'Elections in the one-party state', pp. 58–78. Another example of a study that dismisses elections in Africa's single-party systems as 'meaningless' and 'uncompetitive' is Wanyande, 'Democracy and the One-Party State', p. 78.

such practices. What this illustrates is that, although it offers useful insights that contribute to our understanding of political change, the institutional approach of analysis, conversely, neglects the agency of the individual in those institutions, thereby impoverishing that understanding.

In sum, this book rejects the limitations of both the linear individual methodology and the institutional approach as frames of political analysis. It instead encourages a middle-way approach that allows the interaction between structure and agency, or between the individual and their times. A context-driven political biography of this kind offers more depth and objectivity to the unveiling of the past, as it avoids an over-emphasis on individual achievements while at the same time not downplaying the importance of the role of such individuals in a relatively non-institutional political environment.

The Resumption of Multi-party Democracy, Internal Party Politics, and Succession

After the successful transition from the one-party state to multi-party rule at the beginning of the 1990s, researchers' interest focused on Zambia's 'founding' elections and the optimism generated by these competitive and unprecedented contests. Following the lead of international and local civic actors at the time, the first wave of the literature covering the 1990s hailed the country as 'a model of democracy' that was starting over again.[37] This narrative remained dominant throughout the MMD's first term in office. Caught in this soaring optimism, scholars only gave cursory glances at the important political developments that were taking place within the governing party, such as its gradual implosion, starting as early as 1992, not least because of leadership and succession-driven intra-party machinations. However, they brought another dimension to the hitherto existing frames of political analysis by suggesting that political mobilisation and change in Zambia is best understood through a series of major dividing lines such as the resumption of multi-party democracy. Unsurprisingly, these studies are generally uninterested in the political developments of the preceding one-party era, and treat the end of one-party rule as the termination of one form of politics and the advent of multipartism as a blank slate on which a new style of political engagement followed.[38] This book challenges this view

---

37 See, for example, Carolyn Baylies and Morris Szeftel, 'Democratisation and the 1991 elections in Zambia', pp. 83–109; B. Chikulo, 'End of an Era: An Analysis of the 1991 Zambian Presidential and Parliamentary Elections', *Politikon*, 20, 1 (1993), pp. 87–104; Michael Bratton, 'Zambia Starts Over', *Journal of Democracy*, 3, 2 (1992), pp. 81–94; and Richard Joseph, 'Zambia: A Model for Democratic Change', *Current History*, 91, 565 (1992), pp. 199–201.

38 It is worth noting that Bratton, and Baylies, and Szeftel wrote extensively about the one-party era. See, for instance, Michael Bratton, *The Local Politics of Rural*

and argues that the beginning of one-party rule in 1973 and the resumption of multi-party democracy in 1991 were not the turning points that they have been imagined to be in many of the existing studies.[39] As the case of Sata demonstrates, the careers of many of Zambia's successful political actors cut across the eras of one-party rule and democratisation. A critical biography that focuses on the political intentions, actions, strategies, and lives of such individual figures allows us to understand how they have been able to traverse these perceived divides. It also enables us to trace the broad continuities and changes in Zambian politics from one political system to another.

The second wave of academic writings that cover political life during the MMD's first decade in power began appearing in the late 1990s and focused on the 1996 elections and the extent to which the MMD had institutionalised democracy.[40] Chiluba's manipulation of the constitution to exclude Kaunda from electoral competition in 1996 formed much of the backdrop to the conclusion that political change had been frustrated by enduring practices of the one-party state. Neglected by this focus on institutional aspects in explaining political change were other equally important developments, such as the continuing break-up of the broad MMD coalition, which had wrested power from UNIP. There was, for instance, no serious discussion and analysis of what happened between 1991 and 1996, such as the several by-elections held during this period and the strategies employed both by the MMD and opposition parties to mobilise electoral support. The nature of political engagement and mobilisation during this period has thus not been captured. Also overlooked was the fierce

---

Development: Peasant and Party-Sate in Zambia, New Hampshire: University Press of New England, 1980; and Baylies and Szeftel, 'Elections in the One-Party State', in Cherry J. Gertzel, Carolyn Baylies, and Morris Szeftel (eds), *The Dynamics of the One-Party State in Zambia*, Manchester: Manchester University Press, 1984, pp. 58–78. What they exaggerate in their later writings referred to above is the extent of the change that took place after 1991.

39 For instance, Chikulo and Bratton see the 1991 elections as the end of patronage long used by Kaunda and UNIP before and during the era of the one-party state to purchase political support. Yet as I demonstrate using Sata's case, the practice continued even under the new multi-party system, demonstrating enduring similarities between the two divides.

40 Examples of these studies include Jan Kees van Donge, 'Kaunda and Chiluba: Enduring Patterns of Political Culture', in John A. Wiseman (ed.), *Democracy and Political Change in Sub-Saharan Africa*, London: Routledge, 1995, pp. 193–219; Michael Bratton and Daniel N. Posner, 'A First Look at Second Elections in Africa, with illustrations from Zambia', in Richard Joseph (ed.), *State, Conflict and Democracy in Africa*, Boulder, CO: Lynne Rienner Publishers, 1999, pp. 377–408; and Carolyn Baylies and Morris Szeftel, 'The 1996 Zambian Elections: Still Awaiting Democratic Consolidation', *Review of African Political Economy*, 24, 71 (1997), pp. 113–28.

contestation of succession within the MMD even though three of Chiluba's four opponents in the 1996 election were founding members of the party, which illustrates the lack of unity within the government, and the early campaign to succeed Chiluba. Sata, this book's central subject, played a significant role in both the elections and the succession contests of this period, demonstrating the utility of studying internal party dynamics and political change through the lens of an individual.

It is ironic that, despite the centrality of succession-driven intra-party politics during the MMD's decade-long tenure, even later studies that cover this period generally focus on what was happening outside the ruling party rather than inside it. Unrivalled academic attention has been given, for instance, to subjects on which democracy is contingent, such as the strength of formal institutions, the power of civil society, the importance of conducting regular elections, and the role of international actors. The exception is Rakner's book, which appeared at the turn of the century and was the first work to devote attention to the internal dynamics of the MMD.[41] However, Rakner does not discuss the subject in depth, as her primary concern was the extent to which the decade-long economic and political liberalisation reforms were implemented, and the role of interest groups in those processes. Her concluding characterisation of the Zambian experience as a failure to reform, rather than of reform, suggests the need to pay attention to individual agency. While themes like economic reform, donors and even the 'unrealised democratic prospects'[42] of the 1991–2001 period are undoubtedly important, they do not tell us much about the overall period of Chiluba's rule, in which succession-driven internal party dynamics took centre stage.

Succession is particularly important within the study of political parties, and in particular dominant parties, because it is often a major source of instability and, in some cases, regime change. Yet it is rarely the subject of study, in part because it is often very hard to look inside the 'black box' of organisations that tend to be secretive and lack transparency. As such, when the autobiographies of some of the key political figures who played significant roles between 1990 and 2001 began appearing at the turn of the century, students of Zambian political change welcomed them as important primary sources.[43] Indeed, the memoirs of Mbikusita-Lewanika and Chitala (the MMD's two principal organisers), for instance, provide significant insight into the contradictory, if opportunistic,

---

41 Lise Rakner, *Political and Economic Liberalisation in Zambia 1991–2001*, Uppsala: Nordic Africa Institute, 2003.

42 David J. Simon, 'Democracy Unrealised: Zambia's Third Republic under Frederick Chiluba', in Leonardo A. Villalon and Peter VonDoepp (eds), *The Fate of Africa's Democratic Experiments: Elites and Institutions*, Bloomington: Indiana University Press, 2005, pp. 199–220.

43 See, for instance, Miles Larmer, 'What went Wrong? Zambian Political Biography and Post-colonial Discourses of Decline', *Historia*, 51, 1 (2006), pp. 235–56.

nature of the MMD coalition and the waves of political desertions and internal power struggles that characterised the ruling party throughout the 1990s.[44] However, these writings should be understood for what they really are: memoirs, notorious for their authors' tendency to overdramatise their role in historical events and processes, to describe rather than analyse, to sanitise 'the truth', and to present a highly selective view of what they supposedly know or remember.

More recent studies, focusing on the twilight of the MMD's first decade in power, give relative importance to internal party dynamics and focus much more on civil society, which is credited with the collapse of Chiluba's plans to change Zambia's constitution and stand for a third term in 2001.[45] Yet as I have demonstrated elsewhere, opposition to Chiluba's plans within the MMD was far more significant than civil society's role.[46] In other words, the failure of Chiluba's third term was a triumph of intra-party democracy and had important implications for both competitive politics and the growth of the Zambian party system. Here, it is worth pausing to note that, until the start of the early 2000s, the MMD had remained the dominant political force since 1991. The broad-based nature of the alliance meant that, following the transition to multi-party politics, opposition to the MMD was concentrated within the party rather than outside it. Although a few opposition parties existed, most were poorly funded and institutionally weak, and consequently did not pose any significant threat to its hold on power. The fact that Chiluba was elected on a popular mandate and went on to run in the second round of multi-party elections in the mid-1990s made budding successors shelve their ambitions to a later date. Many such political elites – one of whom is the book's central subject – nevertheless chose to remain in the ruling party where they attempted to build power bases over the course of the 1990s.

Thus, when Chiluba tried to amend the constitution to run for a third term, several ambitious MMD figures, who had established constituencies of support within the party, opposed him because he threatened their ambitions. This

---

44 Akashambatwa Mbikusita-Lewanika, *Hour for Reunion: Movement for Multi-Party Democracy: Conception, Dissension and Reconciliation*, Mongu: African Lineki Courier, 2003; Mbita Chitala, *Not Yet Democracy: The Transition of the Twin Process of Political and Economic Reform in Zambia, 1991–2001*, Lusaka: Zambia Research Foundation, 2002.

45 Bizeck J. Phiri, *A Political History of Zambia: From the Colonial Period to the 3rd Republic*, Asmara: Africa World Press, 2006, p. 207; Jeremy Gould, 'Subsidiary sovereignty and the constitution of political space in Zambia', in Jan-Bart Gewald, Marja Hinfelaar, and Giacomo Macola (eds), *One Zambia, Many Histories: Towards a History of Post-colonial Zambia*, Lusaka: Lembani Trust, 2009, pp. 275–93.

46 Sishuwa Sishuwa, 'Surviving on Borrowed Power: Rethinking the Role of Civil Society in Zambia's Third-term Debate', *Journal of Southern African Studies*, 46, 3 (2020), pp. 471–90.

clearly illustrates how studying political change through the lens of internal party dynamics can help us understand the trajectory of political developments, such as succession, in contemporary Africa. Researchers who focus on the moment of political succession, rather than the process and consequences of a poorly managed succession, miss this point. Using the example of Sata, who was one of several MMD leaders who attempted to build a power base in the ruling party over the course of the 1990s, this book demonstrates that succession outcomes in African political parties are best understood as the result of complex and protracted processes of intra-party competition, as aspiring leaders seek to position themselves and win the right to be the next incumbent president. The internal politics of the MMD is thus of great import not just for the fate of Chiluba's presidency, but also for the future of the Zambian party system.

Ethno-populism, Opposition Parties, and Political Change in the 2000s

The latest scholarship on political life and competition in Zambia focuses on the MMD's second decade in power during the 2000s. By almost remarkable consensus, this scholarship stresses the role of populism and ethnicity when explaining political change and one of the main political developments of this period – the rise of Sata and his opposition party, the Patriotic Front (PF). This literature has two broad strands to it. The first emphasises the critical role played by populist worker mobilisations in explaining Sata's appeal in the capital, Lusaka, and the politically important Copperbelt region.[47] The protagonists of this strand see Sata's populist strategy as one that was constructed within Zambia's dire socio-economic situation of the early 2000s and in response to the growing impatience of Zambians with the governing MMD to bring about the promised economic growth that would translate into improved living standards for the majority of the population. The wider context is crucial to understanding the importance of this point.

The MMD had defeated UNIP in 1991 on a promise of revitalising Zambia's economy. The key instrument of economic revival was a large-scale privatisation programme, initiated at the behest of the World Bank and the International Monetary Fund, that would result in the transition from state capitalism to free market enterprise. Over the course of the first decade of the MMD's two decades in power, large parts of the economy, previously run by the state, were quickly sold off, including, crucially, the strategic mining sector in the year 2000.[48] The privatisation of the mining industry to European, Canadian, Indian, and Chinese

---

47   See, for instance, Resnick, *Urban Poverty and Party Populism*, and Miles Larmer and Alastair Fraser, 'Of Cabbages and King Cobra: Populist Politics and Zambia's 2006 Election', *African Affairs*, 106, 425 (2007), pp. 611–37.
48   Rakner, *Political and Economic Liberalisation*, p. 77.

investors proved to be a huge blow for the Copperbelt Province in particular, as employment fell sharply.

In addition, when the industry went under private ownership, Copperbelt residents expected the mines to continue providing the welfare and social services, such as education and health, that they had provided under state ownership.[49] However, the new investors soon made it clear that they had no intention of doing so. This was a development that generated, over the course of the early 2000s, mounting frustration that investment had not brought the kind of improvements that people had anticipated and that it had, in fact, made life more difficult for many.[50] Criticism also arose that the government was favouring new mine owners, mostly Indian and Chinese nationals, while ignoring local employees' concerns about unsafe and poor working conditions. This situation was exacerbated by the absence of a more radical or militant labour movement that could check the excesses of the employers and the government, and scrutinise the relationship between the two. It did not help that Presidents Levy Mwanawasa, who succeeded Chiluba in 2002, and Rupiah Banda, who took over from Mwanawasa after the latter died in office in 2008, identified themselves closely with the mining companies.[51]

In Lusaka, whose economic base does not rest on the fortunes of the copper industry, the context for populist mobilisations was provided by widespread unemployment resulting from the privatisation of approximately 250 state enterprises and the existence of a large population of urban poor, 100,000 of whom had migrated from the Copperbelt in search of opportunities over the course of the 1990s.[52] By 2010, at least 70 per cent of the city's 2.5 million residents lived in high-density, poorly serviced informal settlements commonly known as shanty compounds, where they attempted to eke out a living in the informal economy.[53] Many took to retail trade, which was, however, hampered by the influx of cheap Chinese goods and the government's 'Keep Zambia Clean' campaign, which saw the removal of thousands of vendors from the streets on the basis of sanitary concerns.[54] For the relatively few who were able to find employment in

---

49   Patience Mususa, *There Used to be Order: Life on the Copperbelt after the Privatisation of the Zambia Consolidated Copper Mines*, Michigan: University of Michigan Press, 2021.
50   J. Lungu, 'Copper Mining Agreements in Zambia: Renegotiation or Law Reform?', *Review of African Political Economy*, 35, 117 (2008), p. 404.
51   Ibid.
52   M. Hinfelaar, D. Resnick and S. Sishuwa, 'Cities and Dominance: Urban Strategies for Political Settlement Maintenance and Change – Zambia Case Study', *ESID Working Paper No. 136*, Manchester: University of Manchester, 2020, p. 5.
53   Ibid.
54   Resnick, *Urban Poverty*, p. 71.

the formal sector, repeated complaints of higher taxes and poor salaries from public sector unions fed newspaper headlines throughout the early 2000s.[55]

Taken together, this context created a groundswell of discontent that Sata skilfully exploited using a populist strategy. Starting around 2003, the opposition leader presented himself as the authentic representative of Zambians who would increase workers' salaries, create more jobs, lower taxes, ensure effective management of street vending, and deport recalcitrant foreign investors. He further presented his political competitors, represented by the incumbents Mwanawasa and subsequently Banda, as colluding with mining companies to exploit ordinary workers. In their impressive study of Zambia's 2006 election,[56] Larmer and Fraser most notably made the argument that Sata's rise in Lusaka and Copperbelt provinces rested on his use of a populist message that resonated with urban voters who, disillusioned by the economic performance of the party in power, sought an alternative. When Sata first ran for office in 2001, he obtained only 3 per cent of the total vote, with his party winning only one of the possible 150 seats in parliament – a seat in a rural constituency in his home area. This tally is particularly striking when we consider that, five years later, in the 2006 general elections, he finished second to Mwanawasa (who polled 42.98 per cent) by a 13.61 per cent margin. The PF, which rose to become the largest parliamentary opposition, captured forty-three seats in parliament and won all the urban constituencies in Lusaka and on the Copperbelt.[57]

Taking populism as 'a political impulse removed from any particular ideological persuasion or policy programme', Larmer and Fraser attributed Sata's remarkable rise in urban popularity to his ability to engage in mobilisations that were populist in character.[58] Echoing Laclau's argument that 'a movement is not populist because in its politics or ideology it presents actual contents identifiable as populistic, but because it shows a particular logic of articulation of those contents',[59] the duo argued that

> Sata's logic of articulation accords with Laclau's definition, involving the identification of particular unmet demands of distinct social groups, and their representation to those groups not only as legitimate but also as aspects of a wider set of linked and unmet demands, sharing few characteristics beyond their frustration. The suggestion is then made that the frustration of these demands results from a disconnection between a newly imagined 'people' (those whose demands are being frustrated) and 'power' (those on

---

55 See for instance, Speedwell Mupuchi, 'Gov't is killing its own people through high taxation, says Sata', *The Post*, 18 November 2002; Larry Moonze, 'Trade unions have let down workers, says Sata', *The Post*, 27 August 2003, pp. 1 and 4; and Webster Malido, 'Stage countrywide protests over high tax, urges Sata', *The Post*, 27 February 2003, p. 3.
56 Larmer and Fraser, 'Of Cabbages and King Cobra'.
57 Ibid.
58 Larmer and Fraser, 'Of Cabbages and King Cobra', p. 613.
59 Laclau, 'Populism: What's in a Name?', p. 2.

whom demands are made). The aim of the populist is thus to construct a set of symbols and arguments that unify the demands and construct a popular subjectivity around them. In the Zambian case, Sata intimates that 'power' consists of a corrupt alliance between domestic political and business networks and a set of international sponsors (including foreign businesses, foreign states, and international financial institutions).[60]

Larmer and Fraser's argument has since been reiterated by other researchers, who also credited the PF's electoral success among the urban poor to Sata's ability to mobilise support using a populist strategy.[61]

The second strand of literature that attempts to explain the growing popularity of Sata and the PF in the early 2000s is made up of research that, in addition to emphasising the conclusions of the first strand, focuses on how Sata successfully exploited Bemba ethnic-language identities to mobilise political support in Bemba-speaking Northern and Luapula provinces. Cheeseman and Hinfelaar provided perhaps one of the most illuminating examples of the fusion of ethnic and populist strategies of mobilisation in a study of the 2008 Zambian presidential by-election that was occasioned by the death of President Mwanawasa, three years before the next scheduled general election.[62] Going beyond earlier conclusions, the pair argued that Sata's appeal during the early 2000s must be understood as a result of his ability to 'mobilise a diverse support base – by employing a 'populist' message in urban areas at the same time as receiving the support of their ethno-regional community in rural areas'.[63]

As an ethnic group, Bembas constituted only 21 per cent of Zambia's population, according to official figures from the 2010 census. When measured as a language group, incorporating Bisa, Lungu, Mambwe, Namwanga, Ushi, and Senga ethnic and linguistic communities from Northern and Luapula provinces, however, the number rose to 41 per cent, the largest in the country.[64] In particular, the exponents of this strand take Sata as an ethnic entrepreneur who successfully presented himself as the presidential candidate for the Bembas, particularly in

---

60   Larmer and Fraser, 'Of Cabbages and King Cobra', p. 613.
61   For example, see Resnick, *Urban Poverty*, p. 60.
62   Nic Cheeseman and Marja Hinfelaar, 'Parties, Platforms and Political Mobilisation: The Zambian Presidential Election of 2008', *African Affairs*, 109, 434 (2010), pp. 51–76.
63   Ibid.
64   See Central Statistical Office, *Census of Population and Housing – National Analytical Report*, Lusaka, 2012, p. 66. The linguistic landscape of Zambia consists of four major language groups: the dominant Bemba, Nyanja (spoken mainly in Eastern Province), Tonga (Southern), and Lozi (Western). Even in urban areas such as the Copperbelt, Zambians from these groups identify themselves as Bemba, which partly explains why 83.9 per cent of Copperbelt residents use Bemba as the language of communication – the highest proportion of Bemba language use by province, followed by Luapula (71.3 per cent) and Northern (69.2 per cent) provinces.

constituencies that were increasingly at odds with the ruling party. The MMD had previously drawn much support from these constituencies but progressively lost this support over the course of the 1990s and early 2000s. Voters in Bemba-speaking areas, decrying their marginalisation from the central government and unhappy with Mwanawasa's support for the protracted prosecution on corruption charges of his Bemba-speaking predecessor, Chiluba, realigned themselves to support Sata, who used ethnic-language appeals to win them over.

Both the first and second strands of the literature yield significant insights into the importance of individual leadership for the success of opposition parties within the context of democratisation, weak party machinery, lack of institutionalisation, and continued obstruction from the ruling elites. The strands convincingly demonstrate the centrality of Sata's personality and campaign strategy in eliciting support for the PF. The major limitation of this set of scholarship is that it has tended to place a heavy emphasis on the period between 2001 and 2011 as the foundational moment of the ethnic and populist strategies that Sata employed to mobilise political support. This book shows that this is an inaccurate analysis that arises from taking the reintroduction of multi-party democracy in the early 1990s as the starting point for understanding the dynamics of party politics in the 2000s, and reflects the weakness of examining political change through institutional, episodic, or snapshot approaches.

As shown in Chapter 1, the ethnic and populist strategies of mobilisation that Sata adopted in the 2000s were not developed during this time. Rather, they were rooted in his experiences on the late-colonial Zambian Copperbelt, where he secured employment as a police constable following appeals to ethnic-language identities, and where he worked as an organiser in the trade union movement, which exposed him to the aspirations of workers and helped him identify the general grievances that affected urbanites. As a result, he was almost always going to mobilise in this way – as he did in the one-party state and after the return to democratisation in the 1990s. What researchers working on multi-party politics in Zambia during the 2000s mistook for a 'new' direction in fact had deeper historical roots. In other words, the ethno-populist strategy that Sata adopted in opposition politics was not simply a response to electoral failure, as existing studies have argued, but represented a return to a long-established form of mobilisation that was familiar to him and that can be uncovered through in-depth historical case studies.

This is not to say that the wider conditions that enabled Sata to employ his methods in these very different periods were the same. On the contrary, there were profound differences. For instance, the economic boom era of anti-colonialism and labour struggles in the late 1950s and early 1960s was clearly not the same as that of the 2000 to 2011 period, where multi-party democracy was operational, and the economy was only gradually recovering from a calamitous, decades-long crisis. The commonality between the late-colonial period and the 2000s is to be found in the weak institutional nature of Zambian political and civic life.

This similar institutional environment in these two otherwise very different eras enabled political leaders and union activists to move between parties and other organisations with relative ease. The same was not entirely true during the lengthy one-party state period, when there were considerably greater constraints on the agency of individual leaders. Even in the one-party state, however, skilful individuals still found a way to exercise greater individual agency than many political leaders. For instance, Sata, as shown in the Chapter 2, restyled himself particularly successfully, embodying the role of the individual leader.

Although the existing scholarship of the rise of Sata and the PF undoubtedly contributes to our understanding of the mobilisation strategies of opposition parties, the nature of political campaigning, and the importance of individual leadership in explaining political change in Zambia during the 2000s, it also demonstrates the limitations that the absence of serious historical work on the subject has generated. The importance of historical influences to recent Zambian politics is a significant theme, one that has been made more generally by Cheeseman and Larmer, who were the first to explicitly apply the 'ethnopopulism'[65] label to PF, to situate the opposition party and Sata in Zambian political history starting from the late-colonial period, and to suggest continuities between the discourse of Bemba-speaking urbanites in the opposition UPP, which rose to challenge UNIP in the early 1970s, and the discourse of the PF.[66] This book applies a biographical approach to build on the brief historical explanations contained within these works, by demonstrating in greater detail how Sata, who straddled these historical periods and institutions, personally embodied these continuities. It provides a sustained analysis of how Sata as an individual was, in very different time periods, able to situate himself in relation to defining political and socio-economic grievances, and to embody political change in the way that populists typically seek to do. In so doing, the book simultaneously presents an accurate biography of Sata and uncovers the wider specific conditions that shaped his political ideas and actions. By exploring his political life through the main trends in Zambian politics, the book historicises the evolution of political strategies such as populism, provides fresh insights into the country's complex post-colonial history, and contributes to the utility of biography in understanding political change in post-colonial Africa more generally.

65   Nic Cheeseman and Miles Larmer, 'Ethnopopulism in Africa: Opposition Mobilisation in Diverse and Unequal Societies', *Democratisation*, 22, 1 (2015), pp. 34–36. The authors define ethnopopulism as 'the ethnic appeal of party leaders to their own communities in addition to a more overarching populist message that is usually most effective in more cosmopolitan urban constituencies', p. 23.
66   Ibid., pp. 34–36.

Sources

The major sources that are at the core of the methodological approach employed in this study and justified above are interviews, newspapers, archives, personal correspondence, and participant observation. I conducted six separate wide-ranging interviews with the study's central subject, Sata. I began interviewing him in 2011 while he was leader of his opposition party. I also conducted two separate interviews with him at State House after he became President of Zambia. Sata subsequently died in October 2014, making the sources I have unique.

In addition to Sata, I managed to identify and locate forty individuals from across Sata's life, such as his former school and work friends in late-colonial Zambia, his political allies and opponents in UNIP and the MMD and under the PF, and journalists from both the print and electronic media who worked closely with him. I conducted wide-ranging interviews with these informants, some more than once, which yielded valuable insights into certain aspects of Sata's political life.

I went to all the major provinces of Zambia including Lusaka, Copperbelt, and Northern where Sata had either worked or lived at one time or another, and interviewed people who knew or were close to him. Their insights illuminate my study, and it is hoped that my utilisation of their views does some justice to their efforts.

Many people associated with Sata no longer live in Zambia. I therefore also travelled to interview such informants in the United Kingdom, South Africa, and Zimbabwe. For instance, I went to Bulawayo in Zimbabwe to interview Phineas Makhurane, who worked with Sata on the Copperbelt in late-colonial Zambia. I also travelled to Johannesburg, South Africa, to interview Joan Irwin, the widow of Sata's business associate Oliver Irwin, who helped finance Sata's electoral campaigns in the one-party state.

Newspapers constitute another important source for the study of Sata. They shed light on very different times in his life. I utilised different newspapers for different times. I used the *Northern News*, a mouthpiece for white settlers that covered the industrial developments on the Copperbelt, for the late-colonial period, as it was the only daily paper at the time. For the subsequent post-colonial period, I used the state-owned *Zambia Daily Mail* and the *Times of Zambia*, which had the most coverage of Sata from independence up to 1991. In the multi-party period, I utilised both the state-owned newspapers and *The Post*, an independent daily that gave considerable coverage to Sata, especially during his time in opposition.

Alongside newspapers and interviews, I also used archival sources. But these were restricted to the late-colonial archives of UNIP, which provided valuable insights on Sata's activities as a trade unionist on the Copperbelt. Archival sources after the 1970s in Zambia are relatively poor, demonstrating the significance of utilising other sources. I also used private correspondence made available through

Photograph 2 I interviewed Sata several times including on 13 January 2012 at State House after he was elected President of Zambia.

interviews, and these were particularly useful for understanding Sata's transition from UNIP to the MMD and from the MMD to PF. Finally, I also employed participant observation. For instance, in the run-up to the 2011 general elections, I frequently attended several of Sata's rallies in different parts of Zambia, which helped me identify the people who attended his political gatherings and observe his campaign message and tactics.

All these sources clearly have their shortcomings. Interviews permit us to gain some insights from living voices and fill lacunae in existing works, but they are far from perfect. Informants' view of Sata may be affected by their relationship to him. Just as those on the opposite end of the political spectrum may vilify him, people on the side of Sata may focus only on his virtues. Sata himself was very accommodating, possibly because he wanted to ensure a favourable portrayal of his life in my research. Interviews can also be unreliable. As I discovered, many things that Sata told me in interviews were not true. This uncovers a danger of relying on interviews alone. I have tried to address this weakness by crosschecking information gained through interviews with other sources.

Newspapers have their weaknesses too. Unlike in interviews, one cannot ask newspapers questions. It is also possible that many things that Sata said were not captured in newspapers, demonstrating that newspapers are limited as a historical source. I hope that, by employing a diversity of sources and triangulating between them, I have succeeded in addressing the shortcomings of each source and in presenting a historical truth of Sata's long political career in ways that strengthen the biographic method as a frame of historical analysis.

Structure of the Book

The arguments advanced in this book, which revolve around the ways in which Sata's individual experiences illustrate the broader themes of Zambian history, are put forward in five chapters that are presented in a chronological order. Following this introduction, which has explained the methodological approach and the use of source materials, Chapter 1 deals with Sata's early life, beginning with his birth in Northern Province in the mid-1930s – the precise date of his birth itself being a matter of historical dispute. Sata migrated to the industrial Copperbelt in 1955, when the anti-colonial struggle was gaining considerable momentum. There, he worked in the late-colonial administration as a police constable before reinventing himself as a radical trade unionist and nationalist in the early 1960s. Chapter 1 shows that the lessons that Sata learnt early in life on the late-colonial Copperbelt went on to shape his political strategies in later life, demonstrating the ways in which the past shapes the present.

Chapter 2 deals with how Sata mobilised urbanites in Lusaka. After being away from Zambia in the years following the achievement of independence in 1964, Sata returned home in 1973, the same year that President Kaunda declared the country a *de jure* one-party state. Sata initially refrained from active involvement in politics. Instead, he tried to establish himself in business, founding a company that specialised in constructing low-cost housing units for the city's rapidly increasing urban population. In line with the general policy at the time, the government nationalised his firm in 1975, a development that was prompted in part by Sata's increasing criticism of the policies of the one-party state. With his business ambitions frustrated, Sata made a decisive entry into mainstream Zambian politics in the late 1970s, joining UNIP, the sole legal political party. Over the course of the 1980s, he rose through the ranks of UNIP and government, serving as a councillor, an elected MP, the governor of Lusaka, and a minister in Kaunda's Cabinet. Chapter 2 demonstrates how Sata successfully built links with leading business elites in Lusaka and used these ties to launch his political career, a move that illustrates a broader argument that populism and business interests are not necessarily opposed. It also shows Sata's use of patronage politics during parliamentary elections under the one-party state. This is a dynamic missing from the literature, which has generally overlooked these elections or assumed that they were non-competitive.

Following the reintroduction of multipartism in December 1990, Sata jumped ship to the newly formed opposition MMD, the party that went on to defeat Kaunda and UNIP at the polls in October 1991. Sata, meanwhile, retained his former parliamentary seat on the MMD ticket, and trounced his UNIP rival by a huge margin. Over the next ten years, Sata was appointed to various ministerial positions, re-elected as an MP, and played a leading role in the ruling MMD, serving in several key party posts such as National Secretary. It is against this background that Chapter 3 focuses on the era of multi-party politics from 1991 to 2001. As shown earlier, the relevant literature has an inadequate account of political life in Zambia during these years. The focus has been on relatively small-scale opposition movements and civil society groups, rather than on internal dynamics within the MMD. Chapter 3 provides a much-needed corrective to these studies by covering the considerable internal struggles within the MMD over the succession to President Chiluba.

By examining internal MMD politics through the lens of Sata, who was a central participant, Chapter 3 foregrounds the internal succession within the MMD, which was the real focus of Zambian politics in the 1990s. It demonstrates Sata's efforts to build a power base within the MMD, by broadening his appeal from urban constituencies in Lusaka to rural areas, where he made ethno-language appeals to Bemba speakers. His activities, in this regard, were only part of a wider succession struggle within the MMD that started as early as 1992, as several figures positioned themselves to succeed Chiluba after the expiry of his second and, according to the Zambian constitution, final term in office. After finding himself on the losing side of the succession struggle, Sata quit the MMD in protest at the end of 2001 to form his party.

Chapter 4 examines Sata's efforts to establish the PF as an alternative political force in Zambia. The chapter shows that, in doing so, he sought to mobilise the same constituencies of support that he had mobilised under the MMD, in the one-party state, and during the late-colonial period on the Copperbelt. This strategy was almost successful: Sata and the PF quickly emerged as the major political competitors to the MMD and President Mwanawasa, who succeeded Chiluba in 2001. Having obtained a paltry 3 per cent of the presidential vote five years earlier, Sata increased his vote share to 29 per cent in 2006, losing only to Mwanawasa who secured 43 per cent. His party, meanwhile, increased its share of parliamentary representation from one to forty-six out of the available 150 seats over the same period. Chapter 4 concludes that Sata ultimately fell short because of the narrowness of his support base, highlighting the limits of his campaign strategy.

Chapter 5 explores Sata's reaction to electoral failure and discusses his political activities between 2006 and 2011. It describes and analyses Sata's efforts to broaden his support base by reaching out to civil society groups with whom he established coalitions aiming for constitutional reform. He also took up national political issues, such as decentralisation, which enabled him to build alliances with non-Bemba ethnic groups that found the policy particularly appealing. Chapter 5 argues that these efforts were successful and enabled Sata to secure the prize he had long sought when he won the 2011 presidential elections – the point at which this introduction began.

In conclusion, I draw together the key themes of this book, offering reflections on Sata's achievements and legacy, the interaction between populism and political change, and the main input of the book in revising our thinking on Zambian history and politics. I also restate the central arguments linked to the significant mileage in understanding the evolving nature of populism across late-colonial and post-colonial African politics and the role and utility of biography in understanding the broader processes of political change.

1

Becoming Bemba and a 'Man of Action'

THE PERIOD between 1953 and 1964, generally described by researchers working on Zambia as the late-colonial era, was dominated by the rapid expansion of the colonial state and the push for better wages on the industrial Copperbelt.[1] It also witnessed the intensification of the drive towards independence, led initially by the African National Congress (ANC) and later by the United National Independence Party (UNIP). This phase of Zambian history is important because it coincides with Michael Sata's migration from Northern Province to the Copperbelt, where he began work as a constable in the colonial police – a role that put him in direct conflict with African nationalists – before joining the trade union movement on the eve of independence in 1964.

In trekking to the Copperbelt, Sata followed well-trodden labour migration routes that had been established in the 1920s. By the 1950s, thousands of Africans had travelled between Northern Province and the Copperbelt and back again.[2] Thus, at this time, Sata was one body in a great human tide. As well as being

---

1 This chapter is derived, in part, from an article published in the *Journal of Southern African Studies* on 28 June 2021: <https://doi.org/10.1080/03057070.2021.1940602> (2 November 2023). A recent publication that adequately covers the period discussed in this chapter is Jan-Bart Gewald, Marja Hinfelaar, and Giacomo Macola (eds), *Living the End of Empire: Politics and Society in Late Colonial Zambia*, Leiden: Brill, 2011. Historians widely consider the year 1953 as the start of the late-colonial period in Zambia mainly because that is when the Central African Federation, which turned out to be the most significant catalyst for nationalist organisation in the country, was established. The pre-eminent political organisation was the African National Congress (ANC) led by Harry Mwaanga Nkumbula, which remained the only nationalist party from its inception in 1949 until October 1958, when a more radical faction of the ANC broke away to establish the Zambia African National Congress (ZANC), the short-lived forerunner to the United National Independence Party (UNIP).

2 Daniel Posner, *Institutions and Ethnic Politics in Africa*, Cambridge: Cambridge University Press, 2005, p. 69. Also see James Ferguson, *Expectations of Modernity: Myths and Meanings of Urban Life on the Zambian Copperbelt*, California: University of California Press, 1999, p. 1; and R.L. Prain, 'The Stabilisation of Labour on the Rhodesian Copperbelt', *African Affairs*, 55, 22 (1956), pp. 305–12.

the economic powerhouse of the country, the Copperbelt also represented a training ground for political education for many Africans. A variety of prominent figures who were actively involved in the labour movement during the terminal stages of colonial rule subsequently took up leading political roles in the post-independence era.³ Despite the striking continuities between these eras, including the individual actors whose careers cut across these divides, few studies on Zambian history bridge the late-colonial and post-colonial periods.⁴ Most historical works take 1964 as either the end point or the start point.⁵ This may be due to researchers seeing the date of Zambia's achievement

3   Notable examples of prominent trade unionists who assumed key ministerial roles in Zambia's founding and later Cabinets include Jonathan Chivunga and Wilson Chakulya, both from the United Trade Union Congress, John Chisata and Mathew Nkoloma from the African Mineworkers Union, Justin Chimba from the African General Workers' Union, and Basil Kabwe of the Northern Rhodesia Union of Teachers. Others, like Alfred Chambeshi, Gabriel Mushikwa and Timothy Kankasa, were appointed into the foreign diplomatic service.

4   A clear illustration of these continuities is the indigenisation of the Zambian economy and civil service in the early years after independence, which effectively represented an expansion of the Africanisation policies initiated by the colonial state and mining firms in the 1950s. For a work that discusses the Africanisation policies of the colonial period, see Prain, 'The Stabilisation of Labour'. Another example of continuity relates to how an agreement brokered in late-colonial Zambia between nationalists, the departing British authorities and traditional leaders of a semi-autonomous kingdom known as Barotseland, which was effectively administered as a protectorate throughout colonial rule, still crops up regularly as a contentious political issue in the post-independence era, highlighting the long shadow cast by decolonisation politics. I discuss this point in detail in Chapter 5. A third example is that several of the leading political actors of the late-colonial period, many of whom worked in one form of colonial institution or another, went on to become key leaders in the post-colonial era, straddling through the First to Third Republics when Zambia transitioned from a multi-party state (1964–1972) to a one-party state (1973–1991) before reverting to multipartism again. Prominent examples of leaders include Kenneth Kaunda, Mark Chona, and Sikota Wina. Other leaders are Valentine Musakanya, Arthur Wina, Vernon Mwaanga, and Humphrey Mulemba. Focusing on such individual political actors may yield fresh insight into the endurance of not just the institutions of the late-colonial period but also of its practices carried through these individuals. For recent works that attempt to do exactly this – showing how these continuities became apparent and real in the everyday decisions and practices of individual lives – see Miles Larmer (ed.), *The Musakanya Papers: The Autobiographical Writings of Valentine Musakanya*, Lusaka: Lembani Trust, 2010.

5   See, for instance, David C. Mulford, *Zambia: the Politics of Independence, 1957–1964*, Oxford: Oxford University Press, 1967; Henry S. Meebelo, *African Proletarians and Colonial Capitalism: The Origins, Growth and Struggles of the Zambian Labour Movement to 1964*, Lusaka: Kenneth Kaunda Foundation, 1986; Robert I. Rotberg,

of formal independence as a historical demarcation that needs no additional justification. By drawing such a divide, however, they miss the connections in the subjects and interactions of relationships that cut across the transition, and the result is the production of a chopped-up national history that fails to capture narratives of continuity, such as how late-colonial influences manifest in the politics of the post-colonial period.

This chapter draws on Sata's experiences on the Copperbelt to illustrate the interaction between late-colonial influences in Zambia and the strategies that political leaders adopted to mobilise electoral support in the post-colonial period. An examination of this interactive influence contributes to better understanding of continuity and change between these eras that are usually treated as separate, in both Zambian and African history. While a number of studies have demonstrated profound continuities between these periods when it comes to the relationship between state, society, and economic trends,[6] there has been little academic discussion of the political linkages, particularly of how individual figures drew lessons from one era and attempted to apply them in the next.[7] An examination of the political life of an individual who straddles through this transition provides a clear lens of disentangling these continuities in ways that other frames of references do not. By drawing on the historical case of Sata, this chapter builds on existing scholarship by demonstrating how his post-colonial political strategy of mobilising electoral support drew heavily on his experiences

---

The Rise of Nationalism in Central Africa: The Making of Malawi and Zambia, 1873–1964, Cambridge: Cambridge University Press, 1965; L.J. Butler, *Mining and the Colonial State in Northern Rhodesia, c. 1930–1964*, London: Palgrave Macmillan, 2007; and Elena L. Berger, *Labour, Race and Colonial Rule: The Copperbelt from 1924 to Independence*, Oxford: Oxford University Press, 1974. In instances where there are exceptions to this divergence, the focus of such studies is usually on institutions and broad national trends rather than individual actors. For instance, see Bizeck J. Phiri, *A Political History of Zambia: From the Colonial Period to the Third Republic*, Asmara: Africa World Press, 2006; Guy C.Z. Mhone, *The Political Economy of a Dual Labor Market in Africa: The Copper Industry and Dependency in Zambia, 1929–1969*, London: Associated University Press, 1982; Mathew Mwendapole, *A History of the Trade Union Movement in Zambia up to 1968*, Lusaka: Institute of African Studies, 1977; and Andrew Roberts, *A History of Zambia*, London: Heinemann Educational Books, 1976.

6   See, for instance, Frederick Cooper, *Africa since 1940: The Past of the Present*, Cambridge: Cambridge University Press, 2002; Mahmood Mamdani, *Citizen and Subject: Contemporary Africa and the Legacy of Late-Colonialism*, Oxford: James Currey, 1996; and Walter Rodney, *How Europe Undeveloped Africa*, London: Bogle-L'Ouverture Publications, 1972.

7   For an impressive study that tries to do exactly this, see Daniel Branch and Nicholas Cheeseman, 'The Politics of Control in Kenya: Understanding the Bureaucratic-Executive State, 1952–78', *Review of African Political Economy*, 33, 107 (2006), pp. 11–31.

on the Copperbelt in late-colonial Zambia. A focus on an individual figure who, for the most part, was on the wrong side of the nationalist movement during the era of decolonisation – but who, as the subsequent chapters demonstrate, still became a major political player in the post-independence period – also helps explain how post-colonial developments in Zambia diverged from other African countries such as Mozambique, Namibia, Tanzania, South Africa, and Zimbabwe, where political success remains closely tied to one's ability to don the uniform of nationalist struggle.[8]

Following this introduction, the second section of this chapter sketches an overview of the political economy of the late-colonial era within which Sata's actions are better understood. In the third section, I discuss the early years of Sata in colonial Northern Province, from his birth in the mid-1930s to September 1955, when he moved to the late-colonial Copperbelt. The final section focuses on the main thrust of the chapter and shows how the late-colonial period on the Copperbelt was the formative influence on Sata's post-independence political strategy.

The Political Economy of the Late-colonial Era, 1953–1964

The political economy of the late-colonial era in Zambia was characterised by the gradual rise of a relatively long post-war copper boom, the consequent expansion of the colonial state, and the apparent strengthening of white settler rule. It also saw the emergence and radicalisation of the African nationalist movement. Below, I provide an overview of the 1953–1964 period, focusing on the main political and economic trends.

Economic Developments

The economic background of this chapter can be traced in the story of the copper boom. From 1949, copper prices in colonial Zambia, like elsewhere in the world, started to rise, having experienced a sharp slump prior to that year. This positive turnaround was triggered in part by post-Second World War demand for new consumer goods in advanced economies, the devaluation of the pound sterling, and the outbreak of the Korean War in 1950. The rising demand resulted in a bigger industrial expansion in capacity and supply, leading to the opening of two new mines, Chibuluma and Bancroft (renamed Chililabombwe in 1968), on the Copperbelt in the early 1950s. By 1953, the value of minerals produced in colonial Zambia had sharply increased to £95 million from £13 million in 1945. Meanwhile, the price of copper rose dramatically from £180 per long ton in 1950 to a record high £420 in March 1956.[9]

8   For an excellent example of a study that draws this parallel between Zambia and Zimbabwe, see Blessings Miles-Tendi, 'Zimbabwe's Third Chumurenga: The Use and Abuse of History', DPhil Thesis, University of Oxford, 2008.
9   This section relies on Roberts, *A History of Zambia*, p. 212.

This boom underpinned the economic growth in the newly created Central African Federation, bringing ever-increasing revenue for both the colonial Zambian government and the Federal administration in Harare, Zimbabwe (then known as Salisbury, Southern Rhodesia). It also spurred the creation of tens of thousands of jobs on the Copperbelt, both in the mining sector and in related service industries or trades. Sata arrived on the Copperbelt in the mid-1950s at the height of the copper boom and this spectacular economic advance. He was among the many thousands of Africans who sought the greatly expanded opportunities there. An increase in the colonial police force, where Sata enlisted as a constable, provided openings.

In July 1956, the boom ended abruptly when copper prices on the international market fell to £264 per ton, mainly due to a general disconnect between supply and demand.[10] A short recession followed on the Copperbelt, worsened by huge waves of industrial unrest. The African Mineworkers Union, for instance, initiated a series of successful strikes that lasted from July to September 1956, constantly halting production.[11] What followed was a declaration of a State of Emergency, which was only lifted in January 1957, and the arrest of several leaders of the African trade union movement.[12]

Copper prices reached their lowest in February 1958, causing huge disruption to the political economy of colonial Zambia. They continued to be low until the early 1960s when another boom emerged, one that lasted for almost a decade of uninterrupted production and fairly high prices into the 1970s. Sata, having by now reinvented himself as a radical trade unionist, sought to exploit the disconnection between the nationalist parties and trade unions by railing against so-called moderate trade union leaders who were not performing their duties (ascribed to them by political actors) in the struggle for independence.[13]

By 1964, the economy was growing steadily though it was highly vulnerable to fluctuations in copper prices. A major hurdle that threatened to delay Zambia's march to independence – the hugely profitable mineral royalties owned by the British South African Company (BSAC) – was overcome when the new Zambian government, supported by Britain, agreed to buy the royalties from the BSAC at a total cost of £4 million.[14]

10   Ibid.
11   Meebelo, *African Proletarians*, p. 300.
12   Ibid., p. 326.
13   M. Larmer, *Mineworkers in Zambia: Labour and Political Change in Post-colonial Africa*, London, I.B. Tauris, 2007, p. 29.
14   Roberts, *A History of Zambia*, p. 222.

Political Developments

Nationalist organisations emerged later in colonial Zambia than in other countries in the region. For instance, by the early 1940s, nationalist associations had already been formed in colonial Zimbabwe and Malawi (then called Nyasaland).[15] In Zambia, however, it was not until July 1948 that the first African nationalist party, the Northern Rhodesia African Congress (renamed the African National Congress in 1951), was formed from a coalition of welfare societies under the leadership of Godwin Mbikusita-Lewanika.[16] The ANC underwent distinct radicalisation in the early 1950s when white settlers began to press for the creation of a federation of colonial Zambia, Malawi, and Zimbabwe 'predicated on the redirection of copper mining revenues to the benefit of white settlers', primarily in the last territory.[17] Faced with the prospect of a settler-dominated government being imposed on colonial Zambia, and attempting[18] to inject fresh urgency in its leadership, the party replaced its founding president in 1951 with Nkumbula. The new leader was 'an ex-teacher who had studied at Makerere College in Uganda and also in London where he had discussed politics with students from other parts of Africa'.[19] Over the next two years, Nkumbula and the Congress 'worked hard to unite the whole territory in a sense of common purpose: opposition to the Federation'.[20]

Despite vehement resistance from the reconstituted ANC and strong protests from Africans, the Central African Federation was created in 1953, though the dominion status desired by white settlers was not realised.[21] The anti-Federation campaign was seriously hampered by the trade union movement's reluctance to support the ANC-sponsored protests with industrial action. For instance, the leadership of the largest component of the labour movement in the country, the African Mineworkers Union, refused to exert pressure on the government and, more generally, to accompany the nationalist movement on this path of growing political radicalisation. Instead, it chose to direct its ire and strength against the mining companies in a series of disputes over wages and working conditions.[22] When Nkumbula and the ANC called for a Day of National Prayer on 1 April 1953, during which no African was to report for work, in an effort to register their opposition to the planned Federation, the leadership of the mineworkers union urged their members to ignore the call.[23] This disclamation of the anti-

---

15   Rotberg, *The Rise of Nationalism in Central Africa*, p. 194.
16   Ibid.
17   Larmer, *Mineworkers in Zambia*, p. 34.
18   Roberts, *A History of Zambia*, pp. 210–11.
19   Ibid.
20   Ibid., p. 211.
21   Simon Zukas, *Into Exile and Back*, Lusaka: Bookworld Publishers, 2002, p. 109.
22   Roberts, *A History of Zambia*, p. 211.
23   Ibid.

Federation campaign was to be a start of a widening gulf between the labour leaders and the nationalist parties, one that lasted until the early 1960s.[24]

The increasing militancy of the trade union movement was directed primarily at white employers, not at the structures of the colonial state. This nevertheless produced a hostile response from the colonial state. For instance, at the height of the chaotic waves of industrial strikes that occurred in mid-1956, the colonial authorities declared a State of Emergency during which virtually the entire leadership of the African Mineworkers Union was arrested and restricted to different parts of the country.[25] Amidst brewing internal dissatisfaction with Nkumbula's leadership, attempts by the ANC to convert this heightening discontent amongst workers into political capital were generally unsuccessful. It came as no surprise that, in October 1958, a more radical and better-educated faction of the party, led by Kenneth Kaunda (ANC Secretary General since 1953), broke away to establish the Zambia African National Congress (ZANC). Nkumbula's less effective leadership, and his decision to consent to taking part in the 1958 general elections based on a recently enacted controversial constitution, were cited by the breakaway group as the reasons for their departure.[26]

Kaunda was subsequently elected President of ZANC's executive council, which included Dixon Konkola (Deputy President), Munukayumbwa Sipalo (Secretary General), and Simon Mwansa Kapwepwe (Treasurer). The new party immediately declared its objective – 'independence now' – and went on a sustained campaign in pursuit of this demand before it was banned for alleged violence in March 1959, as part of a Federation-wide declaration of a State of Emergency. Nearly all its leaders were arrested and restricted to different rural parts of the country, and Kaunda was sent to the Federal prison in Harare following his conviction for an unlawful meeting later in June.[27] In their absence, as anti-colonial agitation grew, a series of small parties came together to form a coalition, UNIP, under Konkola's leadership.[28] Kaunda and his colleagues took over the leadership of UNIP on their release from prison in 1960, giving the party a new lease of urgency in the continuing struggle for independence.

24 From as early as the late 1940s when the African Mineworkers Union was formed, mining companies strongly discouraged trade unions from taking political action, which partly explains why the latter were so wary of forming an alliance with the nationalists. When the unions voted to reject 'tribal leadership', in 1953, class-consciousness was effectively asserted. See, for details, Arnold Leonard Epstein, *Politics in an Urban African Community*, Manchester: Manchester University Press, 1958, pp. 246–47.
25 Meebelo, *African Proletarians*, p. 326.
26 Roberts, *A History of Zambia*, p. 220.
27 This section relies on Wittington Sikalumbi, *Before UNIP*, Lusaka: National Educational Company of Zambia, 1977, pp. 129–36.
28 Mulford, *Zambia: The Politics of Independence*, p. 114.

By 1961, the Federation was disintegrating. The growing strength of the African nationalist movement, the inability of Britain to retain its Empire in the face of opposition, and the apparent unwillingness of white settlers in colonial Zambia to engage in the kind of violent resistance to decolonisation evident elsewhere in the region, coupled with the settlers' lack of inclination and resources to act independently, put the Federation on course for a demise that arrived eventually in 1963. Earlier, in August 1961, the nationalist campaign reached its highest tempo with the declaration of *Cha Cha Cha*, a series of relatively violent protests, spearheaded by UNIP and its rank-and-file activists, demanding immediate independence. These protests resulted in the destruction of public infrastructure such as bridges and schools, and the obstruction of roads, especially in the rural provinces of Luapula and Northern.[29] As argued by Rasmussen, this active involvement of rural areas in the national independence movement 'demonstrated conclusively that anti-colonial sentiment was not the monopoly of a discontented, urban minority but was deeply felt by many rural Africans'.[30]

What followed were complex constitutional arrangements and negotiations in London that culminated in the 1962 elections, which none of the three main political parties – UNIP, ANC, or the settler-dominated United Federal Party – won decisively. The ANC and UNIP, however, agreed to form a coalition government, effectively heralding the end of colonial rule. All that remained was the rapid working out of the consequences of the ANC–UNIP coalition coming to power. The coalition came to an end following UNIP's sweeping victory in the January 1964 elections. Kaunda's party won 70 per cent of the votes, against the ANC's nine, and fifty-one of the sixty-five seats in parliament.[31] A few months later, on 24 October 1964, Zambia was declared a Republic with Kaunda as president.

Sata's Early Years

There are few aspects of Sata's life that can be stated as fact, or with certainty. In other words, large areas of his life story are contestable. Sata routinely changed important aspects such as his name, ethnic identity, profession, principles, and personal history, depending on the prevailing circumstances. Even his date of birth, an aspect of life that one would ordinarily consider unalterable, was, for him, subject to change.

---

29   Miles Larmer, *Rethinking African Politics: A History of Opposition in Zambia*, Surrey: Ashgate, 2011, p. 40.
30   Thomas Rasmussen, 'The Popular Basis of Anti-colonial Protest', in William Tordoff (ed.), *Politics in Zambia*, Berkeley: University of California Press, 1974, p. 43.
31   Larmer, *Rethinking African Politics*, p. 49.

A Changing Date of Birth: An Expression of Sata's Fond Memories of Colonial Rule?

If the Copperbelt in late-colonial Zambia was the training ground for Sata in political strategy, the contradictions in his date of birth demonstrate an important lesson that he appears to have taken from that era – that his past was a malleable resource to be changed, emphasised, or ignored, depending on prevailing circumstances. In an interview on 26 April 2011, Sata stated, 'I was born on 6 July 1937'.[32] He maintained this date four months later when entering his personal details on the nomination papers for Zambia's presidential election of 2011 (see Figure 4).[33] Following his election as president in September 2011, Sata – and Zambians more generally – celebrated his birthday on 6 July every year.

It is, however, reasonable to conclude that, despite what he argued later in life, Sata was born on 6 January 1936. This is the date that appears on his first National Registration Identity Card (see Figure 2), which he obtained in 1965, a year after Zambia's independence.[34] It is also the date that he reported in the *Africa Year Book and Who's Who 1977* (see Figure 3) and that appears in the various electoral records from 1983, when he first ran for election to public office, to the early 2000s, when he was leader of his opposition Patriotic Front (PF) party. Even as recently as September 2008 (see Figure 4), when indicating his personal details on the nomination papers for that year's presidential election, Sata wrote that he was born on '6th January 1936'.[35]

These contradictions in Sata's date of birth are better understood with a brief analysis of the historical context of the early 2000s, when he changed his birthday. Around 2008, at the height of the protracted constitution-making process (a subject discussed in Chapter 5), the governing Movement for Multiparty Democracy (MMD) considered introducing an age limit of 75 for the Zambian presidency. The proposal was a constitutional manoeuvre specifically meant to exclude Sata from running for presidency. In December 2007, a senior MMD leader, George Mpombo, who was also Minister of Defence in President Levy Mwanawasa's Cabinet, appealed to the National Constitutional Conference (NCC) to set an age limit for presidential candidates:

> Some people become mentally tired when they reach a certain age and in the process service delivery to the nation is [adversely] affected. We really need to put in place safeguards. For example, Mr Sata has demonstrated that at his

---

32 Interview with Michael Sata, Lusaka, 26 April 2011.
33 Electoral Commission of Zambia, 'Nomination Papers for the 2011 Presidential Elections', August 2011.
34 Ralph Uwechue (ed.), 'Sata, Michael Chilufya', *Africa Yearbook and Who's Who 1977*, London: Africa Journal Limited, 1976, p. 1319.
35 File, 'Nomination Papers for the 2008 Presidential Election', Electoral Commission of Zambia, September 2008.

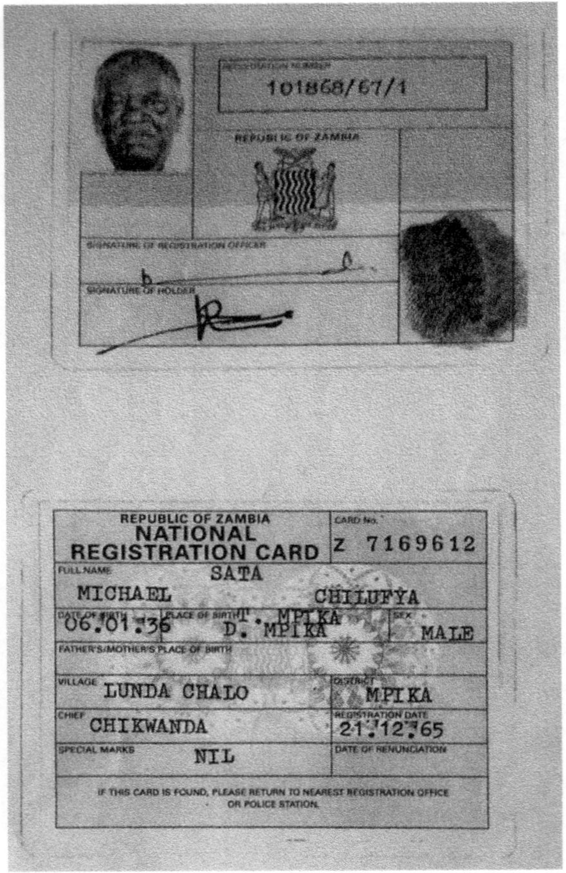

Figure 2
Sata's first National Registration Identity Card, obtained in 1965, one year after Zambia formally achieved independence, showing his date of birth.

Figure 3
Sata's personal details in the *Africa Yearbook and Who's Who 1977.*

Who's Who in Africa

High School, 1938–40; High Commissioner to Senegal and Sierra Leone, Ambassador to Liberia, Guinea, Mali, Mauritania and Guinea-Bissau, February 1971–September 1974; foreign honour: Member of the British Empire (MBE); member, People's Progressive Party; recreations: tennis, cricket; office address: Gambia High Commission, 162 Awolowo Road, PO Box 8073, South-West Ikoyi, Lagos. Telephone 24632; home: Plot 868, Victoria Island, Lagos.

SATA, Michael Chilufya, Zambian businessman, managing director, Tanners and Taxidermists (Zambia), executive chairman, Ndola Inn Ltd, Project director, Avondale Housing Estates Limited, director, Delta Electrical Contractors, director, Trans-Africa Safaris Ltd since 1964; born January 6, 1936, Mpika, Zambia; married December 28, 1968, Margaret Manda, one daughter, two sons; educated: Mpika Local Education Authority School, 1941–47, Katibunga Seminary, 1947–48, Kantensha, 1948–51, Lubushi Seminary, 1951–56, London School of Economics and Political Science, 1970–73; Director of Publicity and Research, United Trades Union Congress, Northern Rhodesia, 1962–63, member, Executive Council, United Trades Union Congress, 1962–64, general secretary, National Union of Engineering Construction and General Workers of Northern Rhodesia, 1962–64, chairman, Young Trade Union Movement, United Trades Congress, 1963–64, Chimwemwe branch treasurer, United National Independence Party (UNIP), associate, Institute of Personnel Managers, 1964–66; recreations: flying, target shooting; office address: Room 135, Farmers House, Cairo Road, Lusaka. Telephone 75719; home: 37 Serval Road Kabulonga, Lusaka. Telephone 52413.

SAVIMBI, Dr Jonas, Angolan politician, founder-president, União Nacional para a Independência Total de Angola (UNITA), since March 1966; educated: University

age (71), he is incapable of providing fresh ideas. There are certain fellows who could be very bright, like [Republican] Vice President Rupiah Banda. He is full of mental drive. He is an intellectual dynamite, but for Mr Sata … the problem is his age … mental capacity … coupled with his [low] level of education. He is woven from a different material mentally.[36]

Mpombo's recommendation met virulent disapproval from civil society groups, opposition parties, and Zambians more generally. The most vociferous opposition, however, came from Sata, who, in February 2008, argued that:

> the NCC wants to use my age against me … to pass a clause in the Constitution that would … block me from standing as a presidential candidate in 2011 on account of old age.[37]

In June 2008, President Mwanawasa, then 59 years old, overruled his Minister of Defence and other MMD leaders by stating that:

> The MMD government has no intentions of blocking Sata from participating in the 2011 presidential election by inserting an age limit in the new constitution. Mr. Sata is not a factor for us in 2011 because we are ready to face him and we will defeat him. Now if we start putting age limits, we will be giving Mr. Sata an excuse. He will say 'I could have beaten the MMD if they did not stop me contesting' … If anyone wants to put an age limit, let them put 140 years so that no one is disadvantaged.[38]

Mwanawasa, with whom Sata had earlier reconciled and whom he had pledged not to reproach publicly, died in office a few weeks after making the above assurance, triggering the 2008 election that was won by Vice-President Rupiah Banda. Since the NCC was still in session under the new MMD administration, Sata, who by then had consolidated his position as the most plausible opposition candidate, was uncertain that Banda, who had taken over the presidency of the ruling party, would follow Mwanawasa's lead on the proposal to limit the age of a presidential candidate. If the recommendation was approved by the NCC, and the NCC had consequently enacted it into law by parliament ahead of the 2011 elections, the PF leader, who was set to turn 75 on 6 January 2011, would have been ineligible to seek presidential office, unless the elections were to be held before his birthday. Seeking to neatly dodge this prospect of disqualification,

---

36 Patson Chilemba, 'NCC should look at age limit for presidency, says Mpombo', *The Post*, 17 December 2007, p. 4.

37 Bivan Saluseki, 'NCC wants to use my age against me, says Sata', *The Post*, 18 February 2008, p. 3.

38 Amos Malupenga, 'We have no intention of blocking Sata – Levy', *The Post*, 21 June 2008, pp. 1 and 4.

REPUBLIC OF ZAMBIA

OATH/AFFIRMATION OF ZAMBIAN CITIZENSHIP OF PRESIDENTIAL CANDIDATE AND PRESIDENTIAL CANDIDATE'S PARENTS

I, (full names) MICHAEL CHILUFYA SATA of
(residential address) NO 3 OMELO MUMBA, Rhodes Park, LUSAKA of
(postal address) P.O. BOX 30885 LUSAKA and holder of
National Registration Card No. 101868/67/1 Being a candidate for election to the office of President of the Republic of Zambia.

1. I was born on 6th JANUARY 1936
   Village/Township/Town CHITULIKA, CHIEF CHIKWANDA
   District MPIKA Country ZAMBIA

2. That I have attained the age of thirty five years:

3. That I am a Zambian Citizen;

4. That both my parents are Zambian citizens by birth/descent*
   That my father (full names) LANGFORD MUBANGA SATA
   Was born on 1904
   Village/Township/Town LUNDACHULO, CHIEF CHIKWANDA,
   District MPIKA Country ZAMBIA
   And that my mother (full names) HENRIETA KABUSWE BUKALI
   Was born on 1909
   Village/Township/Town KAMUTI, Chief CHIKWANDA
   District MPIKA District MPIKA ZAMBIA

5. That I am qualified to be elected as a member of the National Assembly

6. That I have bee domiciled in Zambia for a period of at least twenty years and

7. That I have not twice been elected as President

The above information has come to my knowledge by from Chilonga Mission
Date 23rd Sept 2008 Signature

SWORN/AFFIRMED BY THE SAID:
At:
This 23rd day of SEPTEMBER 2008

BEFORE ME:
Notary public
*delete which ever is not applicable
(as amended by Act No. 23 of 1996)

[Stamp: REPUBLIC OF ZAMBIA JUDICIARY 23 SEP 2008 REGISTRAR OF THE HIGH COURT NOTARY PUBLIC PO BOX 50067, LUSAKA]

E. L. Sakala
CHIEF JUST

Figure 4 Sata's sworn affidavit for the Zambian presidential election of 2008.

REPUBLIC OF ZAMBIA

OATH/AFFIRMATION OF ZAMBIAN CITIZENSHIP OF PRESIDENTIAL CANDIDATE AND PRESIDENTIAL CANDIDATE'S PARENTS

I, (full names) MICHAEL CHILUFYA SATA .... of
(residential address) NO 5 ONELD MUMBA, RHODES PARK, LUSAKA .... of
(postal address) P.O. BOX 30885 LUSAKA .... and holder of
National Registration Card No. 101868/67/1 .... Being a candidate for
election to the office of President of the Republic of Zambia.

1. I was born on 6TH JULY 1937
   Village/Township/~~Town~~ CHITULIKA
   District MPIKA   Country ZAMBIA

2. That I have attained the age of thirty five years:

3. That I am a Zambian Citizen;

4. That both my parents are Zambian citizens by birth/descent*
   That my father (full names) JULIANO MUBANGA SATA
   Was born on 1904
   Village/~~Township/Town~~ LUNPA CHALO
   District MPIKA   Country ZAMBIA
   And that my mother (full names) HENRETA KABUSWE BUKALI
   Was born on 1909
   Village/~~Township/Town~~ KAMUTI
   District MPIKA   Country ZAMBIA

5. That I am qualified to be elected as a member of the National Assembly

6. That I have been domiciled in Zambia for a period of at least twenty years and

7. That I have not twice been elected as President

The above information has come to my knowledge by CHILONGA CATHOLIC MISSION
Date 9th August 2011 Signature

SWORN/AFFIRMED BY THE SAID: MICHAEL CHILUFYA SATA
At: LUFALA
This 9TH day of AUGUST 20 11

BEFORE ME:
Notary public
*delete which ever is not applicable
(as amended by Act No. 23 of 1996)

E.L. Sakala   *Egispo Mwansa*
CHIEF JUSTICE   REGISTRAR

Figure 5 Sata's sworn affidavit for the Zambian presidential election of 2011.

Sata altered his date of birth in early 2009.³⁹ Originally born on 6 January 1936, Sata's new birthday was eighteen months later, on 6 July 1937. In 2011, he insisted that he would turn 74, not 75.⁴⁰

As it turned out, the proposal to introduce a presidential age limit was omitted from the final Constitution of Zambia Amendment Bill, which also fell through in March 2011 after lawmakers belonging to Sata's party vetoed it in parliament.⁴¹ By that time, however, Sata was already enjoying the renewed youthful vigour of his revised date of birth. The choices of 6 July and 1937 for his birthday may not have been entirely random ones: 6 July was in fact the birthday of Colin Dunn, a British-born colonial police officer whom Sata, many years later, spoke warmly of as 'my first boss'.⁴² Dunn was born on 6 July 1934. The possibility that Sata, seeking to make himself younger, may have adopted the same date for 1937 is reinforced by the fact that he met Dunn a few days before he altered his date of birth:

> I arrived in Northern Rhodesia in December 1955 and was posted to Mufulira police in April 1956. Sata joined me there a few weeks later in May ... and we subsequently became very close ... He knew my birthday as early as July 1956 when I turned 22. I celebrated it by unofficially taking a day off and asked him to stand in for me. He was on my shift that day. His English, education was far better and ahead of other constables. As a result, I often asked him to stand in for me when it was my shift because he could write and record things clearly. He also accompanied me on several patrols in the communities of Mufulira ... I came to know Sata's birthday after he became President and have sometimes thought he probably adopted mine. We remained close. For instance, in May 2012, he invited me to attend African Freedom Day at State House. Earlier, in early February 2009 when he was still in opposition, I was driving on Luanshya Road in Lusaka near his party's secretariat. Sata, who was also driving on the same road in a motorcade, saw me. He immediately stopped in the middle of the road, called everyone in his entourage and said 'Come and see my first boss', causing a huge traffic jam.⁴³

It is therefore likely that in picking 6 July, Sata was honouring his 'first boss' in working life and drawing from his experiences on the Copperbelt in late-colonial Zambia. This is another good indication that the late-colonial period remained a constant reference point for Sata in post-colonial Zambia.

---

39   Records from the Department of National Registration, Passport and Citizenship shown to me in confidence on 19 April 2016, by a highly placed source in the Ministry of Home Affairs, revealed that Sata altered his date of birth on 9 February 2009.
40   Interview with Michael Sata, Lusaka, 20 March 2011.
41   Bright Mukwasa and Ernest Chanda, 'MMD loses vote on Constitution', *The Post*, 20 March 2011, pp. 1 and 4.
42   Interview with Colin Dunn, Lusaka, 28 November 2015.
43   *Ibid.*

The choice of year was no accident, either: 1937 was the year in which the then incumbent, Rupiah Banda, was born. Banda, who publicised his desire to seek re-election around the same time that Sata was amending his date of birth, was born on 13 February 1937. By changing his year of birth, Sata changed from being thirteen months older than Banda to being the younger candidate going into the presidential election of 2011. Appearing on a phone-in popular radio programme in Lusaka on 4 January 2011, Sata rejected callers' suggestions that he should leave politics to younger people:

> The previous caller is MMD. He is saying I should retire because I am old. But Rupiah Banda is far much older than me, so why don't you ask him to retire first? ... Abbdoulaye Wade was 74 years when he was [first] elected President of Senegal [in the year 2000], but the people said 'we want this one' even when there were much younger candidates on the ballot. ... In 2007, Wade was re-elected as President when he was over 81 years old. Today, he is governing Senegal much better than some of the younger presidents in Africa ...[44]

Family and Educational Background

According to official record, Sata was born in Mpika, Northern Province, to Langford Juliano Mubanga Sata, a cook for a District Commissioner in colonial Zambia, and Henrietta Kabuswe Bukali, a housewife.[45] Sata's place of birth, according to the details of his National Registration Identity Card cited earlier, was Lunda Chalo village, Mpika district. However, Sata, in the several entries he made for the electoral record and in an interview, later stated that his place of birth was Chitulika village.[46] Further investigation during field research, however, revealed that there has never been any village known as Lunda Chalo in Mpika, while Chitulika emerged only in the early 1950s, and thus did not exist when Sata was supposedly born.[47]

These contradictions about Sata's place of birth have led to suggestions that he was probably not born in what is known today as Zambia. For example, in 2001, Sata sued Patrick Katyoka, a Mpika-born Bemba political opponent, for claiming that he (Sata) was born in neighbouring Tanzania.[48] During the subsequent court trial, Sata argued that he was born at Chilonga, a Catholic-run

---

44 Radio Phoenix Zambia, *'Let the People Talk Radio Program'*, Lusaka, 4 January 2011.
45 Interview with Michael Sata, Lusaka, 13 January 2013; Sata's sworn statement for the Zambian presidential and general elections of 2011; Sata's sworn statement for the Zambian presidential election of 2008.
46 *Ibid.*
47 Interview with Chief Chikwanda, Mpika, 24 March 2016. Chikwanda, who presides over Sata's Bisa ethnic group, is the most senior traditional leader in Mpika district and the custodian of the history of the area.
48 Sheikh Chifuwe, 'Sata sues Katyoka', *The Post*, 4 December 2001, p. 3.

mission hospital in Mpika, and even called the priest in charge to testify in his defence.⁴⁹ In the absence of definitive evidence, Sata's actual place of birth, like much else of his life story, remains ambiguous.

Sata was the sixth of his parents' nine children.⁵⁰ Both his parents were Bisa from Mpika district, under chief Chikwanda, the traditional leader of the area's Bisa ethnic group. Sata was named Michael Langford at his birth and retained this identity until the early 1960s when, on his release from prison (a subject that I discuss later in this chapter), and attempting to make a fresh start, he dropped the Langford name to become Michael Chilufya Sata instead.⁵¹ Sata attended Mpika Local Education Authority Native School in the late 1940s for his elementary education (standards 1 and 2) before he proceeded to Katibunga in 1951 for Standards 3 and 4.⁵² Located in Mpika, Katibunga was a lower preparatory seminary meant for the training of Africans seeking to become Catholic priests. It was run by the Missionaries of Africa, also known as the White Fathers, who arrived in the region in 1891 before the establishment of British colonial rule.⁵³

In August 1953, Sata, alongside twenty-one other pupils from the surrounding areas, enrolled at Kantensha, a recently opened upper primary Catholic seminary in Isoka District (about 200 kilometres from Mpika), for his Standards 5 and 6.⁵⁴ He successfully completed primary education in July 1955, and obtained his Standard 6 certificate (equivalent to a Grade 9 or Junior School Certificate in Zambia today) the following month.⁵⁵

Sata distorts his educational record after his education at Kantensha. His 2011 curriculum vitae indicates that he proceeded to Lubushi Seminary in Kasama (the headquarters of Northern Province) for his secondary education before completing a degree in political science and economics at the London School of Economics (LSE) in 1973.⁵⁶ This is also what Sata told me in an interview and what he indicated in his entry in the 1977 Africa yearbook.⁵⁷ Subsequent research, however, has revealed that both claims he made are calculated fabrications.

---

49   Sheikh Chifuwe, 'Court orders police to arrest Katyoka', *The Post*, 21 December 2001, p. 1; Editor, 'Katyoka's hour has come', *The Post*, 1 October 2002, p. 12.
50   Sata's parents and eight siblings all died before the commencement of my fieldwork research in 2012. *Ibid.*
51   Interview with Michael Sata, Lusaka, 13 January 2013.
52   *Ibid.*
53   Hugo Hinfelaar, *History of the Catholic Church in Zambia*, Lusaka: Bookworld Publishers, 2004, pp. 147–49.
54   Interview with Emmanuel Chikopela, Lusaka, 5 April 2016. Chikopela was one of Sata's classmates at Kantesha Seminary.
55   *Ibid.*
56   Michael Sata's curriculum vitae, April 2011.
57   Interview with Michael Sata, Lusaka, 13 January 2013; Uwechue (ed.), *Africa Yearbook 1977*, p. 1319.

Emmanuel Chikopela, one of Sata's classmates at Kantensha who later attended Lubushi Seminary, recalled:

> We completed our upper primary education in July 1955. Sata, who was then known as Michael Langford, did not go to Lubushi [Seminary] but obtained his Standard 6 certificate. We wrote the exams together and finished Standard 6 together. In fact, when we were writing exams, I was seated next to him. We parted in August when I went to Lubushi for my secondary education while he later went to the Copperbelt in September 1955. There, he joined the Northern Rhodesia colonial police together with Moses Soloti, who was also our classmate at Kantensha … I was at Lubushi from August 1956 to December 1959 when I went to Kachebere Major Seminary in Malawi for my senior secondary school.[58]

Additional research carried out at the archives of Lubushi Seminary in Kasama corroborated Chikopela's testimony. A thorough examination of the class lists and records of pupils who attended Lubushi between 1950 and 1960 established that Sata was not among them. Fr Nicholas Kaliminwa, the Rector of the Seminary, expressed great surprise at the discovery, stating that he had hitherto believed Sata's public pronouncements that he had attended Lubushi.[59] Chikopela's account and the finding at Lubushi were also supported by one of the surviving White Fathers who worked in the Northern Province in the 1960s:

> He (Sata) attended Kantensha, a pre-seminary school for preparation for Lubushi … but he was dismissed from the seminary and as a result did not proceed to Lubushi. I cannot divulge the details of what he did because they are confidential, but can confirm that after completing his Standard 6 exams, Sata was asked not to return to the seminary by Fr. Papineau, a Canadian who was in charge of Mbala Diocese [under which Kantensha Seminary fell] at the time. In his confidential notes, Fr. Papineau wrote that 'it is clear that he is not meant to be a priest'.[60]

Archival research at LSE reveals that the claims by Sata that he attended the institution in the early 1970s are also untrue. These frequent and consistent fabrications about his record of education suggest that he was embarrassed about his limited formal education and was attempting to cover it up.[61] Most importantly, as was the case with the changes to his date of birth, these falsehoods are careful and deliberate. Lubushi and LSE occupy important places in the wider historiography of late-colonial Zambia.

58   Interview with Emmanuel Chikopela, Lusaka, 5 April 2016.
59   Interview with Fr Nicholas Kaliminwa, Lubushi, 23 March 2016.
60   Interview with Fr Pierre Lafollie, Lusaka, 4 April 2016.
61   In both late-colonial and early independent Zambia, an African's completion of secondary school or attainment of graduate qualification was generally seen as a measure of success and capacity. For details, see Andrew Sardanis, *Zambia: The First 50 Years: Reflections of an Eyewitness*, London: I.B. Tauris, 2014, p. 21.

Established in 1928, Lubushi was the most prestigious school for Catholic missionary training in the country before independence in 1964.[62] Nearly all the key Catholic leaders in early post-colonial Zambia, certainly all the Bemba figures, received their priestly training there during the late-colonial period.[63] Many other Bembas who obtained a Catholic missionary education from Lubushi, such as Lawrence Katilungu, Pascal Sokota, and Paulo Shikaputo, all left for the Copperbelt in the 1940s where they assumed prominent roles in the trade union and nationalist movements during the late-colonial period.[64] By claiming that he was at Lubushi, Sata was aligning himself with the general formative experiences of many Bembas from the Northern Province in a way that reinforced his ethno-language roots.

Similarly, LSE is a name that resonates with many Zambians because Nkumbula, the ANC leader widely acknowledged as the father of Zambian nationalism, unsuccessfully studied political science and economics there in the late 1940s. By claiming to have read the same course at the same institution as Nkumbula, Sata was placing himself alongside a formidable historical figure who 'commanded mass support in late-colonial Zambia'[65] and retained significant political influence after independence. Ironically, and perhaps unknown to Sata, Nkumbula failed his intermediate examinations and left LSE without any degree.[66]

---

62 Hinfelaar, *History of the Catholic Church in Zambia*, pp. 158; Interview with Fr Pierre Lafollie, Lusaka, 4 April 2016.

63 Archbishop James Mwewa Spaita, *They Answered the Call: Nyasa-Bangweolo Vicariates*, Kasama: Kalebalika Publishers Audio Visual Systems, 2012, pp. 15–22.

64 Katilungu, for instance, led the influential African Mineworkers Union from 1949 to November 1961 when he died in a road traffic accident. He rose from being a primary school teacher in Luwingu District, Northern Province, to becoming the most powerful trade unionist on the Copperbelt in late-colonial Zambia. Sokota, who had been a teacher at Kapatu Mission in Northern Province, was transferred to the Copperbelt in the late 1940s where he subsequently joined the ANC in 1951. He was then elected to the Northern Rhodesia Legislative Council where he advocated the education of Africans, the establishment of a national university, and the appointment of Africans to the rank of District Officer in the same way that Bemba Catholic priests were sharing the same responsibilities as expatriate missionary colleagues. Thereafter Sokota became one of the foremost anti-Federation campaigners in the early 1950s and, over the years, went on to play an important role in the nationalist movement. This footnote draws from Brian Garvey, 'The Development of the White Fathers' Mission among the Bemba-speaking Peoples, 1891–1964', Doctoral Thesis, University of London, 1974, pp. 371–76. Also see Hinfelaar, *History of the Catholic Church in Zambia*, p. 233.

65 Mulford, *Zambia: The Politics of Independence*, p. 75.

66 Nkumbula subsequently returned to Zambia in 1950, a few months before he was elected ANC president, a position he held until 1972 when he dissolved his party to join UNIP. For more details about Nkumbula's education background,

A notable feature of Sata's fabricated educational achievements is that he did not lie about the things he knew nothing about; he lied about the things he knew a bit about. At Kantensha, for instance, he obtained sufficient knowledge of the later educational stages of the seminary passage to claim that he had completed his education at Lubushi. Similarly, having lived in England between 1970 and 1973 and worked at Victoria Railway Station in central London, he certainly knew something about the LSE and could offer comments on what the school was like. This possibly explains why it was hard for many Zambians such as Fr Kaliminwa to believe that he was making things up.

Migration to the Copperbelt

With his education curtailed, Sata returned to Mpika. Like the rest of the territory's rural areas, his birthplace was a relative backwater in late-colonial Zambia. The momentous changes in the territory were, at this time, occurring on the industrial Copperbelt where the rapid expansion of the colonial state, the push for better wages by African employees in the mining industry, and the intensification of the drive towards independence, initially led by the ANC and later UNIP, were in motion. With very little happening in Northern Province in the early 1950s, Sata left for the Copperbelt in September 1955 when the anti-colonial struggle was gaining considerable momentum. What followed was the formative period of what would turn out to be a successful political career in independent Zambia.

Becoming Bemba

By the mid-1950s, the hegemony of the Bemba language group was already well established on the Zambian Copperbelt. This was largely due to the labour recruitment efforts of the colonial government and mining companies, who drew workers mainly from present-day Northern and Luapula provinces, which were home to large numbers of Bemba speakers. In the late 1920s, for instance, the colonial government, responding to growing complaints of labour shortages from mining firms, decided to designate the Northern and Luapula provinces as labour recruiting enclaves for the country's mining companies.[67] Since 1910, many Africans from the region had sought employment in the better-paying Katanga copper mines in neighbouring Belgium Congo or on the Rand in South Africa. With the policy changes, the flow of migrant labour from Northern and Luapula provinces leaving the country for Katanga was stemmed significantly, while recruiters from the Rand were limited to hiring from the Western Province.[68]

---

see Giacomo Macola, *Liberal Nationalism in Central Africa: A Biography of Harry Mwaanga Nkumbula*, New York: Palgrave Macmillan, 2010, p. 20.
67   Posner, *Institutions*, pp. 73–74.
68   Ibid.

By the end of the 1930s and early 1940s, these specific corporate and state policies had led to the establishment of well-defined labour migration routes between the Northern and Luapula provinces and the Copperbelt. It is no surprise, then, that by 1937, 51 per cent of African workers on the Copperbelt's three largest mines came from Northern and Luapula.[69] This is a remarkable figure when one considers that the two provinces contained only about 25 per cent of colonial Zambia's total population.[70] By 1961, this number had risen to 60 per cent, highlighting a consistent increase in migration to the Copperbelt.[71] While migrants from these rural regions came from ethnically and linguistically diverse groups, such as Ushi, Bwile, and Lunda for Luapula, and Bemba, Bisa, Namwanga, and Mambwe for Northern Province, they shared familiarity with the Bemba language, which was the medium of instruction in colonial and missionary schools across the two provinces.[72] Upon arrival on the Copperbelt, migrant workers from Northern and Luapula, who were employed variously in the mining and service industries, also forged bonds around shared economic and social grievances. Bemba became the lingua franca through which they could express these shared concerns.[73]

The conditions on the Copperbelt – large workplaces and densely populated residential compounds, with large numbers of people coming from the same regions – saw the emergence of a collective group identity that coalesced around the Bemba language. In the mining towns, for instance, Bemba became the principal language of communication, notwithstanding the fact that mining companies paid no attention to ethnic identity when recruiting African labour.[74] Urban social events such as the popular Kalela dance also facilitated the growth of a Bemba macro-ethnicity.[75] As a result, a set of previously disparate ethnic groups from Northern and Luapula provinces became Bemba by merging their linguistic and ethnic differences in this new group identity. The Bemba commonality on the Copperbelt was thus constructed not wholly by mining companies but also by African migrants themselves. In other parts of colonial

69 Ibid., p. 75.
70 Ibid.
71 Ibid.
72 Sirarpi Ohannessian and Mubanga Kashoki, *Language in Zambia*, London, International African Institute, 1978, p. 287.
73 Posner, *Institutions*, p. 75.
74 Posner, *Institutions*, p. 75. Although mining companies paid no attention to ethnic identity when recruiting Africans, the colonial state did, especially in relation to employment in the police force. As we shall see, the notion that some groups were hard working or lazy was at the heart of the hiring practices of the colonial state on the Copperbelt in the 1950s.
75 J. Clyde Mitchell, *The Kalela Dance: Aspects of Social Relationships among Urban Africans in Northern Rhodesia*, Manchester: Manchester University Press, 1956.

Zambia, for instance, Bemba and Bisa speakers still retained separate identities.[76] Not so on the Copperbelt. Being Bemba was not defined in narrow ethnic terms: it encompassed a broader language-group identity that extended to non-Bemba African migrants from Northern and Luapula provinces who spoke the language. Identification as Bemba opened up a wide range of social and economic advantages. This then was the wider context that Sata found on the Copperbelt in September 1955.

Sata arrived almost at the peak of the post-war copper boom that began in the late 1940s.[77] Ever-increasing revenue from copper exports facilitated a major expansion of the mining companies and, to a lesser extent, of the colonial state. The burgeoning urban settlements required not only a significant expansion of services but also, for the authorities, expanded means of controlling the African population. The wave of urban unrest led by African mineworkers that gripped the Copperbelt for the first three months of 1955, coupled with the increasing challenge of African nationalists and the need to supervise urban activities such as beer halls and the illegal brewing of beer, underscored the need for an expanded police force.[78] Sata was one of the beneficiaries of the greater opportunities for employment that arose in the colonial police, where he secured employment as a constable a few months after arriving on the Copperbelt.

Explaining why he chose to join the colonial police, Sata noted that:

> At the time, it was much easier to join the Northern Rhodesia Police if you were a Bemba because we are one of the only two tribes in this country who fought against the [imposition of] British [colonial rule]... Although we were ultimately defeated, the colonial masters knew that the Bembas are warriors and can make very good soldiers and policemen and that they would be easier to train. So when I went to the Copperbelt, it was easier for me to join the police because I am Bemba ... I had [also] completed my secondary education with a school certificate, so that also made things easier for me [To join the Northern colonial police, applicants needed to demonstrate, in addition to physical fitness, that they had reached Standard 4 education level – a requirement that Sata satisfied since he was a Standard 6 graduate] ... I went for police training at Lilayi in December 1955. After six months, I passed the training and was posted to Mufulira Police [on the Copperbelt].[79]

---

76 W.V. Brelsford, *The Tribes of Zambia*, Lusaka, Government Printer, 1965, p. 38.
77 Andrew Roberts, 'Northern Rhodesia: The Post-War Background, 1945–1953', in Jan-Bart Gewald, Marja Hinfelaar, and Giacomo Macola (eds), *Living the End of Empire: Politics and Society in Late Colonial Zambia*, Leiden: Brill, 2011, pp. 15–24.
78 Anthony Clayton and David Killingray, *Khaki and Blue: Military and Police in British Colonial Africa*, Athens, OH: Ohio University Press, 1989, p. 49; Tim Wright, *The History of the Northern Rhodesia Police*, Bristol, BECM Press, 2001, p. 266.
79 Interview with Michael Sata, Lusaka, 13 January 2013.

Although we need to be wary about taking his words entirely at face value – his is a retrospective account, and he was constructing a narrative with certain aims in mind – this was one of the last in-depth interviews that Sata gave before his death, so it is certainly of historical significance. In locating his actions within a tradition of Bemba resistance to colonialism, Sata was, in effect, furthering his individual political agency against the backdrop of broader socio-historical changes by exaggerating an aspect of Zambian history that has been understudied: local resistance to the imposition of colonial rule. While it is true that, on a large scale, the Ngonis resisted British occupation until their war machine was crushed,[80] there is no indication that the Bembas did the same. In fact, existing research suggests otherwise. For instance, in *A History of the Bemba*, one of the best known historical works on the subject, Roberts demonstrates that the European occupation of Bembaland was achieved without much local resistance.[81] An earlier work by another historian, Meebelo, produced the same conclusion.[82]

Despite this record, however, the belief that Bembas took up arms against the introduction of colonial rule retains popular appeal in the conventional wisdom of many Zambians.[83] It is also worth noting that Bembas also typically claim to have been the drivers of the earlier noted *Cha Cha Cha* campaign that took place at the peak of decolonisation. Their unproven resistance to the British conquest of Zambia might thus reflect an attempt to read this later claim back into history to justify the broader assertion that they resisted colonial rule in this way from the start. In repeating the earlier claim, Sata was thus framing his decision to join the police within an imagined history of Bemba anti-colonial resistance. As Mulford correctly argued, however, when it came to anti-colonial resistance in Zambia, 'the pen was mightier than the sword'.[84]

Sata's testimony that he found it easier to join the colonial police because he was Bemba is important, however, because it suggests that his recruitment was not based only on his educational qualifications or physique but also his adherence to a well-established colonial stereotype. As in other parts of the British Empire, colonial officials and local settlers believed that certain ethnic groups were particularly martial. In colonial Zambia, this widely held and

---

80   Jan-Bart Gewald, *Forged in the Great War: People, Transport and Labour: The Establishment of Colonial Rule in Zambia, 1890–1920*, Leiden: African Studies Centre, 2015, p. 21.
81   Andrew Roberts, *A History of the Bemba: Political Growth and Change in North-Eastern Zambia Before 1900*, Wisconsin: University of Wisconsin Press, 1973, p. 229; also see Roberts, *A History of Zambia*, p. 168.
82   Henry Meebelo, *Reaction to Colonialism: A Prelude to the Politics of Independence in Northern Zambia, 1893–1939*, Manchester: Manchester University Press, 1971, pp. 27–35.
83   Interview with Neo Simutanyi, Lusaka, 7 April 2011.
84   Mulford, *Zambia: The Politics of Independence*, p. 83.

oversimplified categorisation fell to the Bemba and Ngoni ethnic groups and was evidenced as early as 1910:

> The two most warlike races in this country are the Awemba [i.e. Bemba] and Angoni [i.e. Ngoni]. The Awemba are much the finer race, for, although the Angoni are descended from the Zulu stock that invaded this country, they are now much intertwined with inferior tribes and have been spoiled by civilisation. Both Awemba and Angoni are, as a rule, medium-sized, wiry men but the former are much harder and pluckier.[85]

Following the establishment of the Northern Rhodesia Police in 1912, recruitment to this law enforcement agency and even to the military focused almost exclusively on these two groups. This pattern continued until the 1930s when the authorities began to conscript the Chewas (also from the Eastern Province), the Tongas, and the Ilas (both from Southern Province) owing to the 'large stature' of people from these ethnic groups.[86] By the late 1940s and early 1950s, recruiting Bembas to the security forces became more difficult because of competition from the better-paying Copperbelt mines.[87] This meant that, at the time of Sata's arrival on the Copperbelt, demand for Bembas in the colonial police was much greater. His self-representation to colonial authorities as a Bemba suggests that he was responding to this demand and shows the utility of colonial-era stereotypes. It also shows how Africans in colonial settings adopted ethnic identities for personal advancement. As Ranger discovered in his study on the reinvention of ethnicity in colonial Zimbabwe, many Africans during the colonial era appear to have effectively adopted the view that 'if this is how colonial authorities see us, this is how we must be'.[88] In this sense, Sata's 'invention' of ethnicity is emblematic of a much wider point in the contemporary literature on a subject that has developed subsequent to Ranger's work – the agency of Africans to respond effectively to colonial ethnic stereotyping and turn it to their benefit.[89]

---

85   Dennis Lyell, *Hunting Trips in Northern Rhodesia*, London, Horace Cox, 1910, p. 100. Another notable work that provides a richer contextual account to the emergence of these martial races and patterns of military and police recruitment in nineteenth-century Zambia is that of Giacomo Macola, *The Gun in Central Africa: A History of Technology and Politics*, Athens OH: Ohio University Press, 2016, Chapter 6.
86   Wright, *The History*, p. 170; Clayton and Killingray, *Khaki and Blue*, p. 226.
87   Clayton and Killingray, *Khaki and Blue*, p. 226.
88   Terence O. Ranger, 'Missionaries, Migrants and the Manyika: The Invention of Ethnicity in Zimbabwe', paper presented to the African Studies Institute, University of Witwatersrand, 2 April 1984, <http://mobile.wiredspace.wits.ac.za/bitstream/handle/10539/9582/ISS-356.pdf?sequence=1> (10 May 2020). Also see Terence O. Ranger, *The Invention of Tribalism in Zimbabwe*, Gweru: Mambo Press, 1985.
89   For particularly relevant works, see, for instance, Thomas Spear, 'Neo-traditionalism and the Limits of Invention in British Colonial Africa', *Journal of African History*,

An analysis of oral sources about politicised figures is necessary especially for events that occurred nearly fifty years prior, but gauging their truthfulness is much easier when collaborative substantiation is available. Evidence from one of Sata's former teachers and a former classmate at the seminary allows us to date Sata's 'discovery' that he was a Bemba with some precision. Prior to his migration to the Copperbelt in the mid-1950s, Sata reportedly refused to speak Bemba and thought Bemba speakers should learn his language, Chibisa, instead.

> [Seminary] Pupils came from all over Northern Province. We had Mambwes from Mpulungu area, Bisas from Mpika, Bembas from Kasama and a few Namwangas from Isoka, where the school was [located]. Sata is Bisa from Mpika and I clearly remember that he was very proud of his Bisa identity during our school days. He would always try to speak to us in Icibisa, which is the language of the Bisa. He would often say 'I am not Bemba, so why should I learn or speak Bemba when you [Bembas] are fewer than us [Bisas]? It is you who should speak my language.'[90]

Sata's emphasis on his Bisa background and preference for the use of Chibisa was also confirmed by one of the surviving White Fathers.[91] It is clear, then, that Sata's emergence as a Bemba coincided very closely with his realisation of the economic opportunities that accrued or were available to those who presented themselves as Bembas on the late-colonial Copperbelt. Sata learnt not only the importance attributed to this ethno-linguistic group, but also how arbitrary and instrumental these forms of identification were. If being Bemba opened up wider social networks and group membership, Sata saw no problem in portraying himself as such. In addition, the absence of any objective criteria to determine who was truly Bemba by ethnicity, beyond an ability to speak the language, opened up opportunities for Africans like Sata to assume different, even multiple, ethnic identities.

It is this exploitation of ethnic-language identities for personal economic benefits on the Copperbelt in late-colonial Zambia that would later influence his political strategy of mobilisation in the post-colonial era, as researchers were to discover only in the 2000s under the multi-party era. The kind of Bemba identity that Sata, as leader of the opposition PF, successfully deployed

---

44, 1 (2003), on how 'ethnicity reflected longstanding local political, cultural and historical conditions in the changing contexts of colonial rule' (p. 3), and Benjamin Lawrence, Emily L. Osborn, and Richard L. Roberts (eds), *Intermediaries, Interpreters, and Clerks: African Employees in the Making of Colonial Africa*, Madison: University of Wisconsin Press, 2006, which demonstrates African agency in the construction of colonial-era 'ethnic' and other identities.

90 Interview with Moses Soloti, Kitwe, 12 April 2016. Soloti, like Sata, attended Kantensha Seminary in Northern Province before he migrated, in 1955, to the Copperbelt where he too joined the colonial police.

91 Interview with Fr Pierre Lafollie, Lusaka, 4 April 2016.

between 2001 and 2011 to mobilise political support in Bemba-speaking rural communities of Northern and Luapula provinces (see Chapter 4) was not only an expansion of the uses of that identity and the movement towards Bemba-ness that was set in motion in the 1950s but also reflected the very different political contexts of the two periods. If the 1950s were marked by anti-colonialism in a new urban environment experiencing growth, the 2000s were marked by a formal democracy that was until recently characterised by economic decline. Notwithstanding his Bisa heritage, Sata used his capacity to speak the Bemba language to claim a Bemba identity and portray himself plausibly as the guardian and protector of Bemba interests by speaking to the common grievances or concerns of Bemba speakers.

Here, we see two results that underline the importance of studying the role of individual agency in broader processes of historical change. The first is a clear interaction between the late-colonial and post-colonial periods of Zambian history, illustrated by the changing utility of a strategy (initially for economic and later for political reasons) for personal advancement founded on the exploitation of ethno-language identities. As he had done in the mid-1950s with a view to enhancing his employment opportunities, the Bisa Sata, in the early 2000s, took on a Bemba identity when campaigning in Bemba-speaking rural areas to secure the political benefits that came with identifying himself that way. Even when his Bemba-ness was called into question by his Bemba-by-ethnicity political opponents, he was able to deflect the challenge by pointing to his language group identity.[92] The second is the relationship between nationalism and ethnicity, and the way in which the two are entwined with Zambian politics throughout the post-colonial period, particularly in relation to political leadership and ideology. For the Bemba, the rivalry between President Kenneth Kaunda and his vice-president, Simon Kapwepwe, which started in the late-colonial period and has been discussed in greater detail elsewhere,[93] provides significant insights into our understandings of this nationalism–ethnicity nexus. For inter-ethnic rivalries, these political continuities between the nationalist and the post-colonial eras are represented most convincingly by what Macola calls

> [the] clash between two ill-defined and ill-definable interest blocs structured around both ethno-linguistic criteria (Bemba-speakers vs. Bantu Botatwe) and different regional modes of incorporation in the colonial economy (roughly: waged workforce in the Copperbelt and its vast Northern hinterland vs. rural-based agricultural producers in the Southern and Central Provinces).[94]

92   Christine Chisha, 'Sata is Bisa – Mumbi', *Zambia Daily Mail*, 31 December 2009, p. 2.
93   Sishuwa Sishuwa, '"A White Man Will Never Be a Zambian": Racialised Nationalism, the Rule of Law, and Competing Visions of Independent Zambia in the Case of Justice James Skinner, 1964–1969', *Journal of Southern African Studies*, 45, 3 (2019), pp. 503–23.
94   Macola, *Liberal Nationalism in Central Africa*, p. 71.

Across the decades, these great 'traditions', as Macola called them, have found expression in different parties, and have continued to shape Zambian politics both before and after Sata's rise to the presidency in 2011. The historical context of Sata's experiences on the late-colonial Copperbelt, discussed in this and the next sections, has a place *within* these traditions and perhaps is central to understanding class struggles that take on ethnic forms, a link that Kapesa and McNamara, for instance, explored in relation to the extent to which the Copperbelt's self-conscious cosmopolitanism was itself a 'Bemba' cultural phenomenon.[95]

The Making of a 'Man of Action'

Sata worked in the service of the colonial police for about two years, during which time he was involved in the policing of nationalists and radical trade unionists. Dingiswayo Banda, a national youth leader in UNIP at the time, recalled that Sata was 'among the black police officers that were being used to torture and persecute people who were perceived to be freedom fighters'.[96] Policing nationalist leaders who not only articulated grievances they themselves felt but who would also soon be transformed from 'suspects to their paymasters and political overlords' created a conflict of loyalties for the African police forces, especially those, such as Sata, who were in the mobile and intelligence units.[97] As one informant put it, 'While the nationalists considered Sata to be a 'capricorn' [a code name for a police informer], the colonialists suspected him to be leaking information to the nationalists about their strategies'.[98] This uneasy position appears to have contributed to the end of Sata's policing career, which was abruptly cut short by his own arrest and subsequent imprisonment in August 1958.

Accounts of why Sata was arrested differ. William Banda, with whom Sata shared a prison cell at Bwana Mkubwa in Ndola, stated that the officer-in-charge informed him that Sata was arrested for forgery.[99] The veracity of Banda's testimony could not, however, be substantiated as the person who told him about the nature of Sata's alleged offence died before my fieldwork started. An

---

95 Robby Kapesa and Thomas McNamara, '"We are not just a union, we are a family": class, kinship and tribe in Zambia's mining unions', *Dialectical Anthropology* 44, 2 (2020), pp. 153–72.
96 *Times of Zambia* Reporter, 'Sata was jailed for criminal offence – Dingi', *Times of Zambia*, 20 March 2010, p. 1.
97 David Killingray and David M. Anderson, 'An Orderly Retreat? Policing and the End of Empire', in David Killingray and David M. Anderson (eds), *Policing and Decolonisation: Politics, Nationalism and the Police, 1917–65*, Manchester: Manchester University Press, 1992, p. 10.
98 Email correspondence, Chitimukulu Kanyanta Manga Henry Sosala to the author, 28 May 2016. Sosala lived and worked on the Copperbelt with Sata in the late 1950s.
99 Interview with William Banda, Lusaka, 17 October 2012.

alternative, less flattering account of why Sata ended up in prison came from Simon Zukas, one of Zambia's foremost nationalists. Zukas claimed he had been informed that Sata was imprisoned 'for a monetary misdemeanour or theft', which consequently led to his dismissal from the colonial police.[100] The problem with Zukas's evidence, like Banda's, is that it is based on second-hand information from a source who is no longer alive. At the time of Sata's arrest, Zukas had been out of Zambia for nearly six years, having been deported to the United Kingdom in 1952 for his anti-colonial activities. It was not until 1965 that he returned to Zambia.[101] Sata himself claimed in an interview that he was arrested for openly espousing anti-colonial and violent sentiments.[102] This testimony is weakened by the point that Sata is unlikely to have proposed violence while he remained in the employment of the police.[103]

Whatever the reasons for his dismissal from the police, Sata received two years in prison with hard labour for the offence. Sources on his time in prison are scanty, but by his release in late 1960, the context on the Copperbelt was very different. Independence now appeared much more likely, and it was a question of when, not if, the Federation of Rhodesia and Nyasaland would crumble. Internal dissatisfaction with Nkumbula's leadership of the ANC had, in October 1958, caused a split and given rise to a more formidable political force, UNIP. The increasingly confident and assertive nationalist movement had by this time become estranged from the trade union movement. This split was not helped when the former president of the influential African Mineworkers Union, Lawrence Katilungu, took over as acting president of the ANC in late 1960.[104] Sata, however, sought to take advantage of this greatly altered context.

In November 1960, a few months after his release from prison, Sata secured a clerical job with one of the Copperbelt's largest construction firms, Roberts Construction, a leading civil engineering and building company with over 1,300 workers on the Copperbelt and several outlets across Central Africa.[105] Sata joined the firm at a time of widespread urban discontent among workers

---

100   Interview with Simon Zukas, Lusaka, 8 April 2011.
101   *Ibid.*
102   Interview with Michael Sata, Lusaka, 13 January 2013.
103   Interview with Colin Dunn, Lusaka, 28 November 2015.
104   As leader of the African Mineworkers Union in the late 1950s, Katilungu, supported by other senior leaders of the organisation, advocated close collaboration between his union and the European Mineworkers Union, and between African political leaders and white settlers. He also supported the banning of the ZANC, the forerunner to UNIP, in early 1959. The assumption of the ANC leadership by such a divisive figure threatened to split unions and nationalists further rather than uniting them. For details, see Berger, *Labour, Race and Colonial Rule*, p. 212.
105   Meebelo, *African Proletarians*, p. 497; Interview with Michael Sata, Lusaka, 14 April 2011.

in the construction sector, related to poor working conditions and inadequate representation from their leaders in the National Union of Building, Wood, and Metal Workers (NUBWMW). In April 1961, NUBWMW officials, led by General President Raphael Mubanga, General Secretary Jonas Ponde, and General Treasurer Moses Chama, co-opted Sata into the union as an organising secretary, a role that he combined with his work at Roberts Construction.[106]

As with many other African workers in other industries on the late-colonial Copperbelt, there was great anger in Roberts Construction at the vast wage disparities between white and black workers, the lack of African representation in supervisory and management positions, and the practice of paying workers on a weekly rather than monthly basis.[107] These frustrations coincided with the workers' growing criticism of the ineffectiveness of NUBWMW officials and Sata's personal frustration about his own lack of advancement in the union. Notwithstanding his low position, he began to advocate the elimination of wage differentials based on race, frequently castigating his white South African employers as 'implementing apartheid policies on the Copperbelt'. One of Sata's workmates at Roberts Construction in the early 1960s recalled that this position won Sata support from the workers:

> There were very few blacks in [management positions at] Roberts Construction, a South African company that today operates as Murray and Roberts Construction Limited. A white fellow headed every department. Sata regularly criticised this overly colonial structure at public meetings, saying the company was implementing apartheid policies on the Copperbelt. The senior union leaders quite often overruled him, especially when he would say something against the white workers or the company itself. He was quite a peripheral figure. The rest of us, however, admired Sata for his bravery. He denounced whites and, unlike many of us, lacked any fear for them. Sata was free and he never called any white 'Boss', like many of us used to do.[108]

Arguing that workers in the construction sector were unhappy that the NUBWMW leadership had not subjected itself to another election since the union's founding in 1960, Sata began in mid-1962 to call for a leadership election, a demand that highlighted his desire to assume a senior role in the union. He met strong opposition from the other union leaders, however, and was expelled from the executive, along with two other organising secretaries, in October

---

106 Interview with Michael Sata, Lusaka, 14 April 2011.
107 Interview with Phinias Makhurane, Bulawayo, 24 April 2014. Makhurane worked for Roberts Construction from 1961 to 1962. For a discussion of his time at the company, see Phinias-Mogorosi Makhurane, *Phinias-Mogorosi Makhurane: An Autobiography*, Gweru, Booklove Publishers, 2010, pp. 59–60.
108 Interview with Phinias Makhurane, Bulawayo, 24 April 2014.

1962.[109] Frustrated with the timidity of the existing union leadership and its unwillingness to let him realise his personal ambitions within its ranks, Sata consequently renounced his NUBWMW membership and formed a breakaway union, the National Union of Engineering, Construction, and General Workers (NUECGW). He became General Secretary and was joined by the other two organising secretaries.[110] This experience – the frustration of Sata's personal ambitions in one organisation and the consequent formation of his own to give expression to those ambitions – bears an extraordinary resemblance to his formation of the opposition PF party in 2001. Sata's formation of the PF followed his exit from the governing MMD after his strong desire to succeed Chiluba as the party president – and ultimately Zambia's president – was thwarted.[111]

Sata's former colleagues in NUBWMW responded by trying to discredit him with allegations of financial impropriety and general mismanagement.[112] Similar accusations were used by Roberts Construction and other employers in the construction industry, most of whom refused to recognise or negotiate with the splinter union several months after its formation. This situation was compounded by Sata's dismissal, in May 1963, as a clerk from Roberts Construction on charges of misconduct and insubordination.[113] These developments did not prove to be major barriers to the success of the new union. As a matter of fact, they motivated Sata to take a harder line in disputes with employers and create a formidable challenge to the leadership of the more established union.

Using his astute reading of workers' grievances at Roberts Construction and in the industry generally, Sata embarked on a recruitment drive predicated on a promise to articulate and deliver the key concerns of labour. Most workers demanded monthly pay, something of a status symbol on the Copperbelt at the time. This was a long-running grievance that had not been satisfied by the NUBWMW leadership. Criticising the existing practice as unfair, Sata demanded that workers be paid monthly.[114] He also advocated the introduction of a provident fund with contributions from workers and employers to take care of workers

---

109 Lusaka, United National Independence Party Archives (UNIPA): Letter from Moses Chama, Acting General Secretary of NUBWMW to UNIP National Secretary, 16 May 1963, UNIPA 6/42.
110 Interview with Michael Sata, Lusaka, 14 April 2011.
111 Sishuwa Sishuwa, 'Surviving on Borrowed Power: Rethinking the Role of Civil Society in Zambia's Third-term Debate', *Journal of Southern African Studies*, 46, 3 (2020), pp. 471–90.
112 Letter from Moses Chama, UNIPA 6/42. See also Meebelo, *African Proletarians*, p. 493.
113 Interview with Michael Sata, Lusaka, 14 April 2011.
114 *Northern News* Reporter, 'Striking Africans build bonfire with Union stop-order forms', *Northern News*, 23 October 1963, p. 1.

after retirement.[115] To these demands, he added more general grievances such as the need to provide African workers in the construction sector with free social amenities like houses, as was done in other trades like mining.[116]

In September 1963, Sata, whose organisation now claimed a membership of 20,000[117] (eclipsing the older union in membership size), gave Roberts Construction a one-month ultimatum in which it was to adopt a monthly pay rate, commit to the provident fund and recognise his breakaway union.[118] When Roberts Construction defaulted, he rallied its workers in a strike against his former employers on 22 October. *The Northern News*, the leading daily newspaper in late-colonial Zambia, described the industrial action in detail:

> About 700 strikers gathered outside the offices of their employers, Roberts Construction Co. (Central Africa) Ltd. And for about five hours listened to a series of speeches by Mr Sata, by a company management spokesperson and a labour officer. The strike was confined to Roberts Construction and Mr Sata claimed that all the company's workers responded to the strike call. Construction work in the mines was halted ... Hopes of a settlement faded during the afternoon after the workers acclaimed their support for the breakaway union. Mr Sata declared that the strike would continue tomorrow and another open-air meeting has been called for 9 a.m.[119]

---

115 Ibid.
116 Interview with Michael Sata, Lusaka, 14 April 2011.
117 There is some consideration here of the potential unreliability of these figures, as newspapers simply reported the claims made by trade union leaders. Evidence of trade union membership in the late-colonial period is fragmentary. Some unions submitted membership returns but many did not. Although the available evidence suggests that Sata was successful in winning most of the union members to his new formation, claims of trade union memebrship for the late-colonial period need to be treated with considerable scepticism, as it was part of the modus operandi of unions to claim vastly inflated memberships beyond anything they could document. This potential methodological flaw is not helped by the fact that the other key sources for statistical evidence on late-colonial trade unions, two books written by the historian Henry Meebelo, are problematic. Meebelo's 1971 work *Reaction to Colonialism: A Prelude to the Politics of Independence in Northern Zambia, 1893–1939* (Manchester: Manchester University Press) and his 1986 title, *African Proletarians and Colonial Capitalism: The Origins, Growth and Struggles of the Zambian Labour Movement to 1964* (Lusaka: Kenneth Kaunda Foundation), both written under the auspices of UNIP, are emblematic of the pro-nationalist approach to trade unionism that I highlight in this section. Labour Officer files in the National Archives of Zambia, which could provide a compensatory source that would at least demonstrate the problematic nature of trade union membership claims in the late-colonial period, were withdrawn from consultation for purposes of digitisation at the time this research was conducted.
118 Reporter, 'Striking Africans', p. 1.
119 Ibid.

The response of the older union to Sata's activities was both dismissive and revealing: 'The strikers will learn very soon [that] Mr Sata has promised them many things which he cannot fulfil'.[120] The strike, which lasted for two days, met with overwhelming success. Every demand was finally met, an outcome that had important implications for Sata.

First, he had succeeded in winning recognition for his breakaway union, which meant that employers now acknowledged him and his team, rather than his former union, as the legitimate representatives of workers for collective bargaining. Meebelo noted that membership of Sata's union soared in the wake of the October 'big strike' at Roberts Construction, with 'only 60 of the Company's labour force of 1,300' retaining affiliation with the old union.[121] Of the construction industry's 25,000 national membership, a staggering 90 per cent belonged to the new union by 6 November 1963.[122] Second, Sata had delivered where other trade union leaders had failed. It is possible that the fear of the total shutdown of the company may have persuaded Roberts Construction to concede to workers' demands, but that may have been of little consequence to Sata because the audience and those around him perceived that he was the one who had won the concessions for them, epitomising the 'Man of Action' who gets things done – a self-styled description by which Sata became commonly known in Zambia's urban areas during the early 2000s – in a very public way, in front of 'the masses'.

In other words, the open way in which demands for improved working conditions were presented to employers made it appear that it was Sata who had secured them. As the earlier cited newspaper passage shows, Sata typically put forward workers' grievances at mass meetings, a common feature of industrial disputes on the Copperbelt during the late-colonial era. As shown by Larmer, several trade union leaders presented workers' demands for better conditions publicly to avoid the practice of negotiating deals in secrecy or behind closed doors.[123] In addition to promoting transparency, the advantage of this practice for Sata was that the membership witnessed that it was he who was publicly delivering their demands. Contrary to the expectations of his former colleagues in the rival union, therefore, the strikers in fact learnt that Sata could and did deliver.

Third, and as he had earlier done with the exploitation of ethno-language identities, Sata succeeded in portraying himself as part of a wider group to which he did not, in fact, belong. Notwithstanding the fact that he was not a building worker, he effectively presented himself as one by noting what the construction workers wanted and promising to deliver it. This strategy was one that he was

---

120 Ibid.
121 Meebelo, *African Proletarians*, p. 497. To support his claims regarding membership, Meebelo cites several Labour Office files in the National Archives of Zambia as his source base, but these files were, for the reason stated earlier, not available for consultation at the time of this research.
122 Ibid.
123 Larmer, *Mineworkers in Zambia*, pp. 72–73.

again to deploy successfully nearly five decades later when, campaigning as the leader of his opposition party among mineworkers on the Copperbelt, he claimed to be a mineworker, and no one contradicted him (see Chapter 4).

Taken together, these late-colonial experiences of Sata formed the foundation of his post-colonial political strategy in urban areas. What he did, for instance, when mobilising political support for his opposition party on the Copperbelt in the early 2000s was not simply a response to electoral failure but a return to a form of mobilisation that was very familiar to him, and that can only be uncovered through longer-term historical studies. In other words, Sata's later appeal to urban constituencies as an opposition leader reflects a historical and deeper connection to these support bases, and is in line with the way in which he had operated in his earlier career.

In addition to mobilising workers around prevailing economic grievances, Sata picked up on a general feeling prevalent at the time that the trade union movement had not fully aligned itself with the nationalist movement.[124] Attempting to exonerate himself from this criticism as NUECGW Secretary General, Sata deliberately and specifically aligned his union with UNIP, the more radical component of the nationalist movement, a few weeks after he formed his union.[125] He sharply castigated unionists who refused to emulate him as enemies of the workers and of the nationalist struggle, who were in league with foreign firms.[126] He later reflected that 'My trade union ... played a vital part in the struggle for independence in that our organisation was based on labour movement first and UNIP second'.[127] Sata criticised his former colleagues in NUBWMW for alleged links to foreign capital, arguing that:

> the Chamas, Pondes, etc. are ICFTU [International Confederation of Free Trade Unions] agents ... who are ... afraid of white employers, exploiting workers and holding back the struggle for independence.[128]

This was not simply a public display of support for UNIP. Above all, it was a strategic way of differentiating himself from his previous associates in

---

124 This is discussed in greater detail in Anirudha Gupta, 'Trade Unionism and Politics on the Copperbelt', in William Tordoff (ed.), *Politics in Zambia*, Berkeley: University of California Press, 1974, p. 294.
125 This context may help explain why Meebelo's nationalist history of the union movement is sympathetic to, and uncritical of, Sata's union's membership claims.
126 In straddling the divide between trade unions and political parties, Sata had much in common with several other figures during the late-colonial era. Notable examples include Dixon Konkola from the African Railway Workers Trade Union, who formed several political parties, and John Chisata from the African Mineworkers Union, who aligned himself with UNIP. See more about Konkola in Kenneth P. Vickery, 'Odd Man Out: Labour, Politics and Dixon Konkola', in Gewald, Hinfelaar, and Macola, *Living the End of Empire*, pp. 111–37.
127 Meebelo, *African Proletarians*, p. 445.
128 'Press Release', *Central African Mail*, 1 July 1963, p. 3.

NUBWMW, and marginalising them. The implication was that they had failed both the workers – whose grievances they could not address because they were too timid to take on powerful foreign-owned firms – and the nationalist movement. The latter was a remarkable claim when one considers that the old union had aligned itself with UNIP in 1960, two years before Sata followed suit.

Placing his trade union role ahead of his political involvement represented Sata's way of distinguishing himself from UNIP leaders by pointing out that he was, first and foremost, an advocate for workers' interests, and then a nationalist, and suggesting that the UNIP approach of simply focusing on the fight for independence was inadequate. Overall, Sata portrayed himself as the embodiment of the alliance between labour and the nationalist movement. This kind of populist rhetoric and posture – which could be summarised in the phrase 'politics is about having an enemy' – reappeared in the early 2000s when, as an opposition leader, he presented the ruling elites and Chinese investors in the mining industry as colluding to exploit mineworkers on the Copperbelt. A central tenet of populism includes anti-elitism and cultivating the claim that only an individual leader who is of the common people can articulate their interests or speak effectively on their behalf.

To defuse any potential charge that he was on the wrong side in the nationalist struggle, Sata consolidated his political membership in early 1963 when he became UNIP Treasurer for Chimwemwe branch in Kitwe, the Copperbelt's second largest municipality.[129] UNIP archival documents show that he spoke at several party meetings alongside other trade union leaders who identified with the organisation.[130] Sata was not the only employee of Roberts Construction who later went on to enjoy a prominent role in public life. Phinias Makhurane, a fellow employee and future Vice-Chancellor of the University of Zimbabwe, recalled Sata in this passage, which is worth quoting at length:

> While at Kitwe, I built up a friendship with one very active man who also worked for Roberts Construction. He had completed his Junior Certificate and was regarded as one of the most educated black people in the country. His name was Michael Sata. Besides being a worker, he was also the secretary of the local trade union organisation. The trade union worked closely with the United National Independence Party (UNIP) of Northern Rhodesia, led by Kenneth Kaunda. During weekends, Michael would take me to meetings of his union as well as political rallies organised by UNIP. My exposure to politics continued from where it had started in Salisbury. While I was not an activist in any way politically, nevertheless, I had opportunities to see Kaunda and his senior officers and to appreciate the message that they were putting across. There were many small riots and a lot of teargas thrown around by the police each time a riot occurred. In later life, Michael became a full-fledged politician, rising to the position of government minister and leader of the

---

129 Uwechue (ed.), 'Sata, Michael Chilufya', p. 1319.
130 See, for instance, 'Programme of Unity of Action – Membership Drive Part 1', 13 June 1963, UNIPA/12/1/7–18.

opposition, with the unusual nickname of 'Cobra'. I have not seen Michael in person since I left the Copperbelt in January 1962 and I doubt if he would recognise me the next time we meet.[131]

By the end of 1963, Sata was widely regarded as one of the labour movement's most effective, if populist, leaders. As one of his contemporaries on the Copperbelt recollected,

> Sata was greatly effective especially at 'picketing'. When a strike was declared, for instance, he would go and hide around the entrance to the mines and prevent and harass those who would like to defy the strike and go to report for work.[132]

As colonial Zambia's transition to independence approached, Sata left the country in December 1963 for six weeks' industrial relations training in the Soviet Union, courtesy of a nomination from the United Trade Union Congress. By that time, he had effected his own remarkable transition. From a willing constable in the colonial police, Sata had refashioned a public role for himself within a few years as both a militant trade unionist and ardent nationalist – exactly the kind of people he used to police.

Sata's ability to transition from the wrong end of the nationalist movement to the correct side before the achievement of independence demonstrates the similarity as well as the difference between Zambia and, say, Zimbabwe, when it comes to the importance of nationalism to political leadership. On the one hand, Sata realised the need to cloak himself in nationalism – so in this sense he followed the 'Zimbabwe model' – when he became a union leader and a nationalist. What is different is his ability in later years to somehow persuade people that he had nationalist credentials, something that would have not been possible in Zimbabwe. This is where the real difference lies: organisational affiliations were much weaker in Zambia during this period than they were in Zimbabwe, a factor that enabled shape-shifting in Zambia. The absence of prolonged conflict in Zambia also meant that identities were not as hard, and the cleavage between 'them' and 'us' was not as strictly drawn as in Zimbabwe, allowing someone like Sata to swap sides when it suited him.

Not everyone was convinced by Sata's conversion, however. Many UNIP leaders, including Kaunda, still regarded Sata with some suspicion owing to his service with the colonial police.[133] This mistrust ensured that there was no place for him in the new nationalist government. He would not be able to continue ascending the ranks in the trade union and nationalist movements. However, Sata's ambition was undimmed. Instead, he fought tenaciously to find his way into the political system and secure what he felt was his rightful place in post-colonial Zambia's political life.

131   Makhurane, *An Autobiography*, pp. 59–60.
132   Email correspondence, Chitimukulu Kanyanta Manga Henry Sosala to the author, 28 May 2016.
133   Interview with Kenneth Kaunda, Lusaka, 29 April 2011.

2

Mobilising Urbanites in the One-party State

THE PRE-EMINENT political force in Zambian society from independence in 1964 to 1991 was the United National Independence Party (UNIP) led by its founder, President Kenneth Kaunda.¹ UNIP's dominance of national politics was first highlighted in two competitive multi-party elections: one at the close of the colonial period in January 1964² when the party won an outright majority, and the other in 1968 when it increased its support across the country.³ UNIP consolidated its political hegemony in December 1972 when Kaunda declared Zambia a one-party state. This declaration ushered in a second and longer phase of UNIP's formal grip on power that ended only in 1991 when a popular uprising, spearheaded by a newly formed opposition party named the Movement for Multiparty Democracy (MMD), saw the reintroduction of multi-party politics and the subsequent defeat of Kaunda and his nationalist movement.

It should not be assumed that the one-party state was monolithic. General elections, which were competitive especially at parliamentary level, were held in 1973, 1978, 1983, and 1988. The first two of these have been the subject of detailed research by scholars of Zambian political history. The latter two, in contrast, have not, and are important because they took place after UNIP removed the unpopular restriction that had previously limited the number of candidates who could run for election to the National Assembly to three per constituency. In instances where there were more than three prospective candidates in a constituency, primary elections were held to determine the finalists. Although prospective candidates still had to apply to the party's Central Committee

---

1   This chapter is derived, in part, from an article published in the *Journal of Eastern African Studies* on 9 October 2020: <https://doi.org/10.1080/17531055.2020.1831146> (2 November 2023).
2   See David C. Mulford, 'Northern Rhodesia: some observations on the 1964 elections', *Africa Report*, 9, 2 (1964), p. 13.
3   Robert Molteno and Ian Scott, 'The 1968 general election and the political system', in William Tordoff (ed.), *Politics in Zambia*, Berkeley: University of California Press, 1974, pp. 155–96.

for adoption, the abolition of the primary elections paved the way for greater voter choice and more open electoral contests. Studying electoral contests in this greatly altered political environment can yield significant insights into our understanding of the workings of one-party participatory democracy.

Moreover, the 1983 and 1988 elections are of particular interest to this chapter because they occurred after Sata, who went on to become one of the key political actors in the one-party state until its demise, made his formal entry into Zambian mainstream politics in 1981. He ran for parliamentary office in both elections, defeating nine other contestants including an incumbent Member of Parliament (MP) in the first election before being re-elected five years later. The nature and style of the strategies he employed to mobilise electoral support in both campaigns have much to tell us about political life in Zambia under the one-party state, such as how electoral parliamentary competition in urban areas was conducted. More importantly, Sata's political experiences are representative of those of several other prominent political actors who ran for parliamentary office in the 1980s.

An examination of the strategies that political leaders employed to mobilise electoral support, particularly in a party context characterised by a tight rein on policy and campaign messages, could deepen our understanding of political life in Africa's single-party systems more generally. As will be demonstrated using the example of Sata in Zambia, it was possible under the one-party state to mobilise political support outside the party structures and build patronage networks within them that challenged the logic of centralised control. For the most part, however, these power bases and patronage networks were invisible and can be uncovered only through detailed case studies of the internal politics of single-party systems. The literature that dismisses elections in Africa's single-party regimes as insignificant simplifies the complexity and nature of political competition and change in such systems. Elections in one-party states were, at least at the parliamentary level, highly competitive, with major turnovers in MPs, and should be studied seriously.

Following this introduction, the next section of this chapter provides an overview of the political economy of the period between 1973 and 1991 – the era of one-party rule – as a framework within which to understand Sata's actions. As Sata was either away in the United Kingdom or operating outside active politics in nearly the first twenty years of Zambia's independence, the third section offers a brief discussion of his activities from 1964 to 1983 when he first ran for parliamentary election. The fourth section engages extensively with the main thrust of this chapter, namely the strategies that Sata employed to mobilise electoral support among Lusaka's urban voters in the legislative polls of the one-party state. The final section examines Sata's political activities in relation to Zambia's transition from one-party rule to multi-party democracy in the late 1980s and early 1990s.

The Political Economy of One-party Rule, 1973–1991

Before examining how Sata attempted to mobilise urban voters using pragmatic clientelism and the creation of patronage networks, it is worth looking at Zambia in the 1970s and 1980s to understand how his political ideas and actions were shaped by the wider historical context.

Economic Developments

Zambia attained independence in 1964 with a copper-reliant economy whose fortunes were tied closely to fluctuations in the global economy. Attempting to secure the confidence of foreign investors who retained control of the strategic mining industry, President Kaunda quickly moved to reassure them that his administration had no plans to nationalise the sector.[4] For the first few years after independence, this position brought considerable gains, as copper prices boomed, revenue from mining taxes increased, and average workers' wages rose considerably. The prosperous nation that UNIP had envisaged during the nationalist struggle appeared to be a realistic prospect. The revenue generated from copper enabled the government to make meaningful investments in education, housing, and health, and to encourage diversification into manufacturing.[5]

This began to change in the late 1960s when Kaunda, arguing that Zambia was not enjoying the full fruits of the economic riches within its borders, abandoned his earlier pledge by moving to nationalise sections of the economy. The President introduced a raft of indigenisation reforms that saw the takeover, with compensation, of over twenty-five major foreign-owned companies, and put limits on non-Zambians owning small-scale businesses.[6] The radical switch in the structure of Zambia's economy was completed in 1969 with the government's acquisition of the copper mines, a move justified as a necessary step towards the achievement of economic independence.[7]

The nationalisation of the mines, which provided 90 per cent of Zambia's export earnings, could not have been timed more poorly. The dramatic rise of international oil prices in 1973 and the recession that it generated led to the collapse of the copper price, dragging the Zambian economy down with it. Having peaked in the 1960s and early 1970s at between £1,300 and £1,400 per ton,

---

4   Andrew Roberts, *A History of Zambia*, London: Heinemann Educational Books, 1976, p. 230.
5   Ibid.
6   Miles Larmer, 'Zambia's Mineworkers and Political Change, 1964–1991', PhD thesis, University of Sheffield, 2004, p. 81.
7   Ibid., p. 82.

the price of copper plunged to £500 per ton in 1975,[8] drying up the revenue flows upon which Zambia's development expectations had been built. The downturn in the global mining industry was to last for thirty years and have a decisive impact on the country's economic position and politics.

By the early 1980s, when Sata decided to enter Zambian politics, the country had experienced almost a decade of sustained economic decline and misery. In addition to a US$3.2 billion international debt by 1983, annual growth rates since 1975 averaged minus 0.1 per cent, gross domestic savings fell by 16 per cent, and the country's balance of payments sharply deteriorated to minus US$853 million, highlighting the collapsing value of Zambia's exports.[9] Discontent and social unrest increased, especially in urban areas. The absence of any rival political party meant that UNIP bore sole responsibility for this deepening crisis.

Initially, Kaunda blamed external enemies opposed to Zambia's support for liberation movements in the region for the country's poor economic performance. However, with the independence of Angola and Mozambique (1975) and later Zimbabwe (1980), this argument was no longer plausible. Although South Africa and Namibia remained under white supremacist rule, the aggression of South Africa's apartheid authorities was by this time directed less at Zambia than at Angola and Mozambique.[10] This regional context, alongside a spiralling foreign debt that consumed 65 per cent of foreign exchange earnings and gave donors significant sway in determining the country's economic policy, heightened opposition to UNIP, especially in the urban areas.[11] Eager to find solutions to the country's deteriorating economic environment, the government turned to the International Monetary Fund (IMF) in early 1983.

The implementation of IMF-imposed stabilisation and adjustment measures, a prerequisite for receiving assistance, did little to rescue the collapsing economy.[12] Instead it served mainly to humiliate Kaunda and his co-nationalists, who, having won political independence, were now appealing cap in hand to international financial institutions for economic help. In November 1986, drawing on IMF policies, the government removed subsidies on food prices that had been used to partially compensate urban dwellers for the relative decline

---

8 Miles Larmer, *Mineworkers in Zambia: Labour and Political Change in Post-colonial Africa*, London: I.B. Tauris, 2007, p. 46.
9 World Bank, *Zambia – Country Economic Memorandum: Policies for Growth and Diversification, Volume 1. Main Report*, Washington, DC: World Bank, 2004, p. 73.
10 Stephen Chan, *Southern Africa: Old Treacheries and New Deceits*, New Haven: Yale University Press, 2012, p. 201.
11 Miles Larmer, *Rethinking African Politics: A History of Opposition in Zambia*, Surrey: Ashgate, 2011, p. 242.
12 Carolyn Baylies and Morris Szeftel, 'The Fall and Rise of Multi-Party Politics in Zambia', *Review of African Political Economy*, 19, 54 (1992) pp. 75–91.

in their incomes since the oil shock in the early 1970s.[13] This led to serious food shortages and huge increases in the price of essential commodities, eventually sparking widespread rioting and looting in several of Zambia's major towns. State security forces quelled riots with excessive force, killing at least fifteen people and arresting hundreds.[14]

To placate the urban population, Kaunda renounced the implementation of the IMF agreement in the late 1980s, stating that he could no longer adhere to the implementation of an adjustment programme that required him to kill his own citizens.[15] This decision, which did little to improve the general economic malaise, revealed the susceptibility of the one-party state to popular resistance. By July 1990, opposition to UNIP's rule had begun to coalesce around the newly formed MMD, which soon forced Kaunda to terminate one-party rule.

Political Overview

The declaration of the one-party state in 1972 was preceded by a competitive political environment characterised by a groundswell of popular support for Kaunda and his nationalist organisation that first found expression in the quasi-multi-party elections held in 1962. This support grew in the 1964 election where UNIP secured 70 per cent of the total votes cast and fifty-one of the sixty-five seats in parliament.[16] The main opposition African National Congress (ANC), led by Harry Mwaanga Nkumbula, obtained only nine seats.

Enthusiastic support for UNIP was short-lived. Nascent frustration with the perceived lack of progress after independence appeared first in the December 1968 elections. Although UNIP increased its support across the country in quantitative terms, the elections were, in real terms, a shock to the ruling party, which lost all its seats in Barotseland, and a comparative success for the ANC, which won twenty-four seats, compared to UNIP's eighty-one. The real extent of UNIP's hegemony was further tested by the emergence of the United Progressive Party (UPP) in August 1971. Its leader, Simon Mwansa Kapwepwe, Zambia's former vice-president (1967–1970), drew on urban post-colonial grievances, especially on the Copperbelt, and the feeling among Bemba-speaking communities in Northern and Luapula provinces that the expected benefits of independence had not trickled down to them in proportion to the sacrifices they had made during the nationalist struggle.[17] This increasingly unfavourable

---

13 Larmer, *Rethinking African Politics*, p. 242.
14 *Ibid.*, p. 243.
15 Baylies and Szeftel, 'The Fall and Rise', p. 80.
16 David C. Mulford, 'Northern Rhodesia: Some Observations on the 1964 Elections', *Africa Report*, 9, 2 (1964), p. 13.
17 Miles Larmer, '"A Little Bit Like a Volcano": The United Progressive Party and Resistance to One-Party Rule in Zambia, 1964–1980', *International Journal of African Historical Studies*, 39, 1 (2006), pp. 49–83. Also see Sishuwa Sishuwa, '"A

political landscape, alongside a looming electoral alliance between Kapwepwe's party and the ANC, accelerated UNIP's institution of the one-party state in 1972.

Having successfully undermined these political challenges, Kaunda and UNIP went on to claim their 'victory' in the 1973 general election, which was a 'yes' or 'no' referendum about the president. At 40 per cent, the national turnout was the lowest recorded since independence and just under half of the 82.5 per cent in the 1968 general election.[18] Such a large decline in electoral participation suggested that followers of the proscribed opposition ANC and UPP had stayed away. In 1977, Kapwepwe and Nkumbula joined UNIP, making clear their intent to challenge Kaunda for leadership of the party at its forthcoming convention. But both were thwarted by a bureaucratic sleight of hand when, a few weeks before the party congress, UNIP amended its constitution to require that presidential hopefuls had to have been card-carrying UNIP members for five years.[19]

Kapwepwe and Nkumbula contested their disqualification in court, but their lawsuit was dismissed three months before Kaunda was re-elected unopposed.[20] Kaunda dealt with less serious political challengers more straightforwardly. For example, he frequently dismissed those who flouted the UNIP Leadership Code, effectively a mechanism of political control enforced by senior leaders on their juniors. He also attempted to undermine internal opposition to his rule by sending those he suspected of having wider political ambitions into the diplomatic service and parastatal companies, as well as by constantly reshuffling his Cabinet.[21] It was within this context of a political system designed to prevent the emergence of individual political leaders or 'big men' that Sata tried to become just such a figure.

With political change blocked by these rule changes, opposition to Kaunda, and to UNIP's formal hegemony during the second decade of one-party rule, was diverted into other institutions. First was an unsuccessful military takeover in October 1980. Instigated by members of Zambia's intellectual and business elite, the coup attempt exposed growing frustration with the one-party state and the

---

White Man Will Never Be a Zambian": Racialised Nationalism, the Rule of Law, and Competing Visions of Independent Zambia in the Case of Justice James Skinner, 1964–1969', *Journal of Southern African Studies*, 45, 3 (2019), pp. 503–23.

18   Carolyn Baylies and Morris Szeftel, 'Elections in the one-party state', in Cherry J. Gertzel, Carolyn Baylies, and Morris Szeftel (eds), *The Dynamics of the One-Party State in Zambia*, Manchester: Manchester University Press, 1984, p. 29. Voter turnout was to improve in subsequent years. For instance, it increased to 67 per cent in 1978 before declining to 65.6 per cent in 1983 and 59 per cent five years later.

19   Miles Larmer, 'Zambia's Mineworkers and Political Change, 1964–1991', PhD thesis, University of Sheffield, 2004, p. 154.

20   Larmer, *Rethinking African Politics*, p. 124.

21   Interview with Neo Simutanyi, Lusaka, 13 January 2014.

rapidly declining economic environment.[22] More effective opposition to UNIP and Kaunda was expressed through the trade union movement, represented by the Zambia Congress of Trade Unions (ZCTU) and the Mineworkers Union of Zambia. As Nordlund[23] and Larmer[24] have observed, the confrontational relationship between labour and the government throughout the 1980s merged with the more general discontent in the country over price controls and the removal of food subsidies, which sparked major riots in the urban centres.[25]

Foreign political developments and internal factors in Zambia proved decisive in the collapse of the one-party state. The release from prison of South Africa's anti-apartheid leader Nelson Mandela on 11 February 1990 and his visit to Zambia two weeks later, combined with Namibia's declaration of independence the following month, heralded the end of the liberation wars, long used by Kaunda as a justification for the preservation of single-party rule.[26] Yet at its National Convention in March, UNIP upheld the principle of the one-party system, dismissing calls for political reform. Ruling out a return to multi-party politics, which he claimed would take the country back to 'Stone Age politics', Kaunda asserted that the one-party state 'was a free choice and creation of the people of Zambia, not a military or an ideological imposition'.[27]

What followed in June 1990 was an explosion of unprecedented popular anger, expressed first in the form of the deadliest urban riots seen in Zambia's post-colonial history, and then another unsuccessful military seizure of power, which was widely endorsed on the streets of Lusaka. In contrast to the 1986 unrest that focused largely on the escalating prices of essential commodities, the 1990 riots were explicitly political in character.[28] These, alongside the formation of the MMD in July 1990, ultimately forced Kaunda and UNIP to repeal the one-party state legislation in December 1990. For the multi-party elections scheduled for October 1991, the MMD's candidate was the former ZCTU president, Frederick Chiluba. The reservoir of anger from labour joined popular discontent to deliver him an overwhelming majority.

---

22 Miles Larmer, 'Chronicle of a Coup Foretold: Valentine Musakanya and the 1980 Coup Attempt in Zambia', *Journal of African History*, 51, 3 (2010), pp. 391–409.
23 Per Nordlund, *Organising the Political Agora: Domination and Democratisation in Zambia and Zimbabwe*, Uppsala: Uppsala University, 1996.
24 Larmer, 'Zambia's Mineworkers'.
25 It is worth noting that Zambia went back to the IMF after 1988 and that this was one of the key elements that delegitimised the one-party state.
26 Hugh MacMillan, *The Lusaka Years: The ANC in Exile in Zambia, 1963 to 1994*, Johannesburg: Jacana Media, 2013, p. 260.
27 Charles Kachikoti, 'System not imposed: multi-party state rejected', *Times of Zambia*, 15 March 1990, p. 1.
28 Nordlund, *Organising the Political Agora*, p. 101.

Situating Sata, 1964–1983

Following Zambia's achievement of formal independence in 1964, Sata remained in Kitwe on the Copperbelt, where he attempted to make profitable use of the industrial relations training that he had received at Patrice Lumumba University in the Soviet Union. In early 1966, he established an industrial consultancy firm that went on to offer a wide range of services to mining companies and trade unions over the next four years. These included advice on how to implement the ongoing restructuring process of indigenising the country's workforce and on determining the appropriate wages of African mineworkers taking up jobs held previously by Europeans.[29] While working on the Copperbelt, Sata met and cultivated a close relationship with a white South-African-born businessman named Oliver Irwin who was a senior partner at the Zambian branch of Coopers & Lybrand, an international consultancy firm of chartered accountants headquartered in the United Kingdom. As shown in the next section of this chapter, in later years Irwin played a significant role in the development of Sata's political career.

With Irwin's help, Sata left Zambia for the UK in 1970 hoping to secure gainful employment and to study law at the University of London's School of Economics and Political Science.[30] These plans, however, fell through and he ended up taking a series of low-paying menial jobs. Sata recalled:

> When I went to England, it was not easy to live there. I was surviving on a small rent from Zambia. I worked for about three months in a laundry in Beckenham Hill in Bromley. I then went to work for Vauxhall [Car Assembly Plant] in Luton, for about six months, then I managed to get a job with British Rail, first as a porter at Beckenham Hill … [before I was] transferred to Victoria as a shunter. From there, I was promoted to be a conductor on the same trains and later on trained as a train driver.[31]

During his time abroad, he neither established contact with fellow Africans working or studying in the UK nor participated in any engagements of a political nature, despite the presence of a wide network of political figures exiled from southern Africa.[32] As such, the influence of being away or in 'exile' had minimal effect on his later political life. As Sata himself was to suggest several decades later, the only relevant lesson that he appears to have gained from his London

---

29   Interview with Michael Sata, Lusaka, 13 January 2013.
30   Interview with Joan Irwin, Johannesburg, 6 May 2014.
31   Aislinn Laing, 'Humiliating work as Victoria station porter helped Michael Sata become Zambia's president', *The Telegraph*, 23 January 2012. I am also grateful to Aislinn for sharing with me the full transcript of the interview that she had with Michael Sata on 22 January 2012.
32   Interview with Michael Sata, Lusaka, 13 January 2013.

years was the reinforcement of his outsider status, which he played to in his populist rhetoric:

> I swept London Bridge, I swept Victoria and I enjoyed it. If I went to England and I was treated like a gentleman, I would not have had any resolution to look after this country. But every hour I spent on manual work, every hour I was humiliated in England or degraded has helped me because that's the same way other people feel in the townships here. People are still walking long distances and are working long hours.[33]

Sata did, however, keep in touch with Bemba-speaking political actors in Zambia when required. For instance, in August 1971, he appeared at the South African Embassy in London as a representative of the opposition UPP, seeking a recommendation for

> a reliable printer who could be trusted to print their [the UPP's] material without there being any danger of it leaking out to pro-Kaunda elements.[34]

This material was for a forthcoming parliamentary by-election in Mufulira West on the Copperbelt featuring UPP leader Kapwepwe and Alexander Kamalondo, the candidate of the governing UNIP. It was indeed not feasible to print the material inside Zambia for fear of discovery because it involved many counterfeit UNIP membership cards. According to a then senior UPP strategist, the fake cards were required so that UPP supporters could enter the polling stations controlled by ruling party loyalists:

> [At the time] it was almost impossible to campaign during elections and so when there was a by-election and Kapwepwe stood in Mufulira, we knew that UNIP would be demanding UNIP cards before one could enter the voting booth. After Sata's unproductive visit to the South African Embassy in London, we [subsequently] printed UNIP cards in Lubumbashi [Democratic Republic of Congo] and handed them over to our members. We did our campaign through tracking individuals in the voters' registers. And that was why Dunstan Kamana, the then outspoken *Times of Zambia* Managing Editor, wrote in the editorial: 'Who campaigned for Kapwepwe? It was UNIP! And who voted for Kapwepwe? It was UNIP'.[35]

Kapwepwe went on to win the Mufulira West seat, despite not visiting the constituency during the campaign for fear of violence, polling 2,120 votes against Kamalondo's 1,814.[36] This strategy of electoral mobilisation bears a striking

---

33   Laing, 'Humiliating work', *The Telegraph*, 23 January 2012.
34   Larmer, *Rethinking African Politics*, p. 198.
35   Email correspondence with Kanyanta Manga Henry Sosala, 22 January 2016. Sosala went on to become Chitimukulu, the supreme traditional leader of the Bemba-speaking people, in the early 2000s.
36   Larmer, *Rethinking African Politics*, p. 79.

resemblance to one that Sata was to employ nearly forty years later as leader of the opposition Patriotic Front (PF). Faced with an incumbent who could afford to outspend the opposition, Sata urged Zambians to accept the electoral gifts that his political competitor offered them but to vote for the Patriotic Front (PF) when inside the polling booth.[37]

On his return to Zambia in 1973, Sata noted astutely that the economic and political centre of the country was shifting from the Copperbelt to the capital.[38] After spending a few months in Kitwe, he decided to migrate to Lusaka. Although Sata took a more convoluted route than most, he is representative of thousands of other ordinary Zambians and several political, trade union, and civil society actors who relocated from the Copperbelt to Lusaka in the 1970s in pursuit of better opportunities as the country's protracted economic recession deepened. In Lusaka, Sata extended his business consultancy to advertising, real estate, and construction. With the support of Irwin, who had relocated to Lusaka much earlier, he established a company that specialised in constructing low-cost housing units for the city's rapidly increasing urban population. By late 1975, Sata claimed that 789 houses had been built and sold in the capital city alone.[39]

Around this time, he began to appear frequently in the public media, sharply criticising the state takeover of private enterprises and the ever-narrower space for independent economic activity. He also raised an array of local grievances affecting many urbanites, such as inadequate public transport and housing facilities. A leading Zambian political scientist who was a student at the University of Zambia (UNZA) in the late 1970s recalled that:

> Sata struck me as an eccentric fellow who spoke his mind, exuding a rare brand of pragmatism. He was quite outspoken against certain aspects of the one-party state and was able to draw attention to himself. In the environment of one-party subservience, Sata appeared on national television several times, openly criticising the government. I knew Sata from those [television] programmes because I saw someone [who was] courageous enough to say things that were a taboo at that particular time. He spoke against the Leadership Code, which proscribed public leaders from running businesses and limited them to owning only one car and farm. Sata criticised that [policy], saying 'we can't be a nation of poor people'.[40]

---

37 Sishuwa Sishuwa, 'Defying the Incumbency Theory: Explaining Sata's victory in the 2011 Zambian elections', *Democracy in Africa*, 1 December 2011, <http://democracyinafrica.org/defying-the-incumbency-theory> (9 March 2016).
38 Interview with Michael Sata, Lusaka, 13 January 2013.
39 Ibid.; Michael Sata, curriculum vitae, April 2011.
40 Interview with Neo Simutanyi, Lusaka, 13 January 2014. See also Neo Simutanyi, 'The Zambia we want', *The Post*, 4 September 2006, p. 26.

In line with the general policy at the time, the government nationalised his firm in 1975, driven in part by Sata's increasing criticism of the policies of the one-party state. With his business ambitions frustrated, he attempted to run in the primary elections for the Kabwata parliamentary seat in 1978.[41] However, the UNIP Central Committee rejected his candidacy on the grounds that he had not been a member of the party for the minimum three years. Responding to the decision, Sata sued the party Secretary General, arguing that he had been a card-carrying member of UNIP since the early 1960s. Rodger Chongwe, Sata's legal representative in the case, recollected that his client was further accused of being a drunkard and a virulent critic of the government whose actions were seen as 'inimical to the interests of the State'.[42]

In a remarkable move that underlines a higher degree of judicial independence in the one-party state than is usually acknowledged in the literature, the courts overturned the decision of the Central Committee in late 1980.[43] Although it came two years after his initial attempt to seek elective public office was foiled, this ruling paved the way for Sata to become a ward councillor for Bauleni, one of Lusaka's urban informal settlements, in January 1981.[44] He was to rise fairly rapidly thereafter, starting with his bid to become the MP for Kabwata constituency in the 1983 elections.

Deeper Pockets:
Sata, Business Elites, and the 1983 Parliamentary Elections

In 1982, the government repealed the law that provided for primary polls, one of the two stages of elections to the National Assembly.[45] The move represented UNIP's attempt to increase political participation and address the low voter turnouts experienced in the 1970s. Although prospective candidates still had to apply to the party's Central Committee, the abolition of the primary stage paved the way for more contestants to appear on the ballot than the previously permitted three. It also set the stage for greater voter choice and more open electoral contests, starting with the 1983 parliamentary elections.

UNIP's commitment to opening the political process was not merely a smokescreen. Of the 874 candidates who had applied for adoption throughout the country in 1983, the Central Committee rejected only forty-six.[46] A total

---

41   Interview with Michael Sata, Lusaka, 13 January 2013.
42   Interview with Rodger Chongwe, Lusaka, 28 November 2015.
43   *Ibid.*
44   Interview with Michael Sata, Lusaka, 13 January 2013.
45   Bornwell C. Chikulo, 'The Impact of Elections in Zambia's One Party Second Republic', *Africa Today*, 35, 2 (1988), p. 38.
46   Daniel Posner, *Institutions and Ethnic Politics in Africa*, Cambridge: Cambridge University Press, 2005, p. 174.

of 823 candidates thus stood for parliamentary office, in contrast to 317 in 1973 and 344 in 1978.[47] The larger pool of candidates in 1983 represents an opening up of the political space, which in turn made election to the National Assembly more competitive. In Lusaka, the average number of contestants in each of the province's eight constituencies rose to six – a national record – demonstrating an explosion of interest in parliamentary political engagement.[48]

In this more competitive environment, parliamentary hopefuls faced the problem of how to distinguish themselves from the rest. Membership of UNIP was not enough, as all candidates belonged to the ruling party. Another problem was that UNIP maintained control over the policy messages on which parliamentary contenders could mobilise the electorate. In each constituency, for example, candidates appeared in community halls at the same time and under the supervision of local party leaders. They were given fifteen to twenty minutes each to impress voters on assigned topics that ranged from one-party participatory democracy, the significance of the colours on the national flag, and humanism (the official state ideology), to the state of the economy, party organisation, local government, and social security.[49] Occasional deviations from these topics were tolerated in instances where the contestants wished to amplify them with personal experiences or anecdotes. Campaigning on any sectional appeals or subjects not sanctioned by the party was expressly prohibited. Any candidate who broke these restrictions faced disqualification from the race and possible suspension from UNIP, whose electoral rules stated that:

> the election campaign ... should focus on those issues which concern you and the nation and not on personalities. It must be based on the desire to bring together all our communities instead of dividing them; it must be used to integrate rather than fragment, to build the nation instead of dividing the people.[50]

As in previous elections, UNIP upheld its policy of not funding the campaigns of aspiring MPs. The responsibility for financing was left to the individual nominees themselves, which advantaged those with personal wealth, allowing them to mobilise voters beyond the formally administered campaigns. The regulations narrowed the subjects on which parliamentary candidates could differentiate themselves and achieve electoral success. What strategies, then, did they employ to mobilise political support in this constrained context of the newly competitive single-party elections? The case of Kabwata constituency in

---

47 Ibid.
48 Times Reporter, 'Results of parliamentary elections', *Times of Zambia*, 1 November 1983, p. 7.
49 Interview with Derrick Chitala, Lusaka, 22 October 2015.
50 United National Independence Party, *The UNIP Manual of Rules and Regulations Governing the 1983 General Elections* (Lusaka: Zambia Information Service, 1983), p. 13.

Lusaka, where eleven parliamentary contenders including Sata stood, is a useful study in answering this question.

Created in 1968, Kabwata constituency covered four of the five most densely populated planned suburbs in the city of Lusaka at the time: Kabwata, Chilenje, Libala, and Kamwala. Although a significant number of unemployed and poor residents lived in the area, most of Kabwata constituency's populations were middle class and public service workers.[51] Going into the election, four candidates stood out as frontrunners. These included the incumbent MP Maxwell Sibongo – a prominent local businessman who was also Governor of Lusaka Rural – and Mary Kaluluma Mwango, who had held the seat from its inception in 1968 until 1978. The other two were Derrick Chitala, a recent graduate from UNZA, and Sata.

During the formal campaigns, which were conducted in English, the official language, the incumbent, Sibongo, tried to win electoral support by highlighting his close relationship with President Kaunda.[52] This strategy however proved detrimental to his re-election prospects because it fed into widespread accusations that he was an establishment candidate more preoccupied with sub-national level concerns than the grievances of his constituents. William Banda, the UNIP Lusaka District Youth Chairman who supervised the Kabwata election campaigns, recalled that voters regularly heckled Sibongo's speeches for 'lack of development'.[53] Several senior Kabwata residents who attended the campaigns disclosed in interviews that the incumbent had failed to deliver any tangible benefits to his constituency.

Mwango campaigned on a promise to build on her record in the first decade of the constituency's existence, buttressing this message with a reference to her personal standing and reputation.[54] As the only female in a crowded field of male candidates, she also tried to canvass electoral support based on her gender. Numerous respondents recalled that Mwango argued that a female candidate better understood the immediate concerns of Kabwata residents and was better placed to implement UNIP policies at the constituency level. However, as with Sibongo, the absence of visible achievements from her time as MP of Kabwata undermined her campaign.

Chitala was said to have mesmerised his audience consistently with his clear understanding and articulation of the theories and politics of UNIP humanism. He also drew attention to his education credentials, pointing out a strong link between an MP's education level and their capacity to represent constituents effectively. In doing so, he was seeking to distinguish himself from the other ten candidates, none of whom had a university degree. Banda

---

51   Interview with Michael Sata, Lusaka, 13 January 2013.
52   Ibid.
53   Interview with William Banda, Lusaka, 23 October 2015.
54   Ibid.; Interview with Derrick Chitala, Lusaka, 22 October 2015.

recalled that Chitala's command of the English language made him a standout candidate during formal campaigns:

> Rallies were held in Chilenje, Kabwata and Evelyn Hone College Community Halls ... The best candidate was Chitala. He explained the finer details of the party policy and spoke very well about the local issues that affected Kabwata. Sata [by contrast] was not conversant with many of the subjects that candidates were asked to discuss in community halls. He struggled throughout [the formal campaigns] to impose himself on the people.[55]

Chitala recollects that inadequate financial resources adversely affected his campaign:

> I had very little money [with which] to engage in informal or covert campaigns, especially in the evenings when we tried to establish more intimate interactions with voters in order to understand their concerns. UNIP did not provide finances. Everyone had to raise his own resources. Sata [by contrast] had bags of money. His white friends supported him. At one time, I carried several of my supporters to a beer hall in Chilenje so that I could buy beer for them, but when we arrived, I was told that Sata had bought all the beer ... The people we found said 'keep your money, or, if you want, join us and drink for free. Sata has paid for everyone who wishes to drink but does not have money.' I told my supporters that 'let us go and find a different beer hall', but they said 'why should we go elsewhere when we have free beer here?' They sat down and started drinking the beer that Sata had bought.[56]

Chitala's personal qualities and educational stature also ended up working against him. In a classic populist strategy, Sata attacked Chitala as part of the manipulative elite and presented himself as emblematic of the ordinary people. Martha Zulu, Sata's campaign manager in 1983, recalled how her team exploited Chitala's 'high up there' posture:

> People from UNZA were called *apamwamba, bo punzila* [the relatively established and prosperous educated elites who live in high-class suburbs and hardly mingle with ordinary people], Derrick [Chitala] was high up there. He did at times look down on the people on the ground, especially the marketers. He was very arrogant and that alienated him from many people. But it [that image] allowed us to use it against him.[57]

Sata emerged to become the only candidate who managed to mount a large-scale campaign operation. In the absence of any legitimate way to raise large amounts of money without attracting state scrutiny, Sata turned to the business elites to finance his campaign. The most prominent was Oliver Irwin, a white

---

55   Interview with William Banda, Lusaka, 23 October 2015.
56   Interview with Derrick Chitala, Lusaka, 22 October 2015.
57   Interview with Martha Zulu, Lusaka, 26 October 2015.

businessman who, as has previously been noted, was a senior partner at the Zambian branch of Coopers & Lybrand, an international consultancy firm of chartered accountants. Irwin arrived in Zambia in the late 1950s at the height of the copper boom, having been headhunted to open a local office.[58] In addition to being involved in farming and aviation, the chartered accountant soon discovered the more lucrative business opportunity of 'helping' white expatriates seeking to move their money from Zambia in the early years after independence.[59]

At the time of independence, Kaunda, worried about capital flight from the local economy, encouraged white residents to take up Zambian citizenship as a demonstration of their commitment to the country.[60] When these appeals fell on deaf ears, the government introduced a law that prevented expatriates from sending more than half of their salaries outside the country. According to Irwin's wife at the time, several white expatriates 'offered huge amounts of money' to the Coopers & Lybrand senior partner after he promised to facilitate money transfers overseas. Taking advantage of their desperation, Irwin 'kept the money' instead:

> After independence, the [Zambian] state set up a special intelligent unit called SITET [State Investigations Team for Economy and Trade], headed by Fred Alan, to investigate people trying to externalise money. Many whites after independence were unsure of their place in the new Zambia and wanted to export foreign currency to a much safer place such as Europe. Irwin offered to legitimately find ways to externalise their money for them using Coopers. The clients were required to sign a form to show that they had committed a crime ... They offered him huge amounts of money, but Oliver Irwin later claimed that the ledger was stolen in London in a taxi. The truth was that he kept the money.[61]

When his would-be customers complained, he politely reminded them that they were transgressing Zambia's currency restrictions and threatened to inform the authorities himself of this fact.[62]

The injection of additional funds into his business helped to make Irwin, who had taken Zambian citizenship in 1966, one of the wealthiest businessmen in the country by the early 1980s. In a context where the state was taking control of a greater slice of the economy, many businessmen sought political protection or influence. Irwin set his sights on ex-businessman-turned-politician Sata, as well as three other candidates standing in different constituencies, to whom he made substantial donations.[63] According to Irwin's widow, other politicians

---

58   Interview with Joan Irwin, Johannesburg, 6 May 2014.
59   Ibid.
60   Interview with Kenneth Kaunda, Lusaka, 19 October 2015.
61   Interview with Joan Irwin, Johannesburg, 6 May 2014.
62   Ibid.
63   Ibid.

who were sponsored by her husband and who frequented their home included future President Rupiah Banda, who lost Lusaka's Munali parliamentary seat in the 1983 elections, Chieftainess Nkomeshya, who won the Chongwe seat in the same year, and Alexander Chikwanda, who later went on to become Zambia's Minister of Finance. By financing their campaigns, Irwin sought to create a lobby group in government that would help secure and develop his business interests.

Proving 'under-the-table payment' for political activities is one of the hardest things to do. Although Sata admitted receiving support from 'my friend Irwin', he declined to state the amount or to explain how he got Irwin to offer him financial assistance.[64] Two key witnesses recalled in separate interviews that Irwin gave Sata about US$20,000 for his 1983 parliamentary election campaigns. One of these is Stelios Sardanis, a close family friend who was staying with the Irwins at the time. He revealed that:

> Sata used to come home quite frequently in the run-up to the elections and almost on each occasion, I saw him leaving with lots of money. I would put the amount at approximately US$20,000 though the precise figure should be more than this because he collected money on several occasions.[65]

The other witness is Irwin's wife, who offered general insights on how Sata got her husband to give him campaign funds:

> Irwin has played a huge role in the rise of many politicians and businessmen in Zambia. Prominent politicians and businessmen like Rupiah Banda, Alexander Chikwanda, Bruce Munyama, Enoch Kavindele and Emmanuel Kasonde all secured funding from him. He liked people who were below him so that he could control them or those above him so that he could use them, and they in turn also used him. He called them his lackeys. He used them to negotiate on his behalf, for instance, with the Bank of Zambia officials on business deals that needed the approval of the Central Bank. He never got his hands dirty. Sata offered to help him secure his businesses and since by that time [the time of the 1983 Kabwata by-election] their relationship was already established, my husband ... gave him about US$20,000.[66]

Martha Zulu, Sata's campaign manager in the 1983 election, confirmed that:

> Irwin did play a major role in financing Mr Sata. There were others who were supporting him especially in the white farming community because they knew him as a person who would deliver. But the main support came from Irwin ...[67]

The large amounts of money that Sata extracted from Irwin had some strategic efficacy, as it enabled him to circumvent the limits of the campaign process

---

64   Interview with Michael Sata, Lusaka, 13 January 2013.
65   Interview with Stelios Sardanis, Lusaka, 26 September 2014.
66   Interview with Joan Irwin, Johannesburg, 6 May 2014.
67   Interview with Martha Zulu, Lusaka, 26 October 2015.

and brought valuable funds to his campaign coffers – giving him a degree of autonomy. Zulu recalled:

> During the campaigns, he hired several cars, but we also used our personal vehicles and Mr. Sata bought us fuel. We used to go door-to-door in the evenings, starting from Kabwata, Chilenje and then Libala and Kamwala. We would talk to women. We also gave voters *chitenges*, t-shirts. Some were given mealie-meal [cornmeal from which Zambians derive their staple food]. But the thing that he did most was to buy people beer and they really appreciated him for that.[68]

When Sibongo, the incumbent, complained that he might lose the elections because businessmen were bankrolling his opponents, Sata theatrically appeared at Sibongo's prominent retail store in Chilenje suburb with a group of his supporters:

> He [Sata] bought everything that was in the shop from mealie meal to cooking oil and told his supporters to get whatever they wanted for free. He said 'I don't want Mr Sibongo to lose on account that he did not have money. I have now given him money, so let him go and campaign.'[69]

Chitala, one of Sata's rivals in the election, corroborated Zulu's testimony of this incident.[70]

As Sibongo feared, Sata's lavish campaign overwhelmed his opponents, none of whom had access to the kind of resources he could marshal. His campaign strategy made a significant impression on the voters. By buying beer for voters, he portrayed himself as a provider of tangible benefits at a time when the economic environment had constrained the capacity of political elites, including his opponents, to meet the patronage expectations of their supporters. The consumption of beer occupies an important place in Zambian political history. An earlier and well-established literature on the subject demonstrates that beer halls and alcohol consumption facilitated the expression and mobilisation of nationalist sentiment during decolonisation on the Copperbelt.[71] Later, at the 1969 and 1988 UNIP National Conventions, President Kaunda threatened to resign from his position if Zambians 'd[id] not cut down their excessive consumption of alcohol', stating that he did not want to preside over 'a nation of drunkards'.[72]

In the 1970s, Zambia's increasingly precarious economic situation made beer unaffordable for many urbanites. The scarcity of goods that characterised the

---

68 Ibid.
69 Ibid.
70 Interview with Derrick Chitala, Lusaka, 22 October 2015.
71 See Charles Ambler, 'Alcohol, Racial Segregation and Popular Politics in Northern Rhodesia', *Journal of African History*, 31, 2 (1990); Jonathan Crush and Charles Ambler (eds), *Liquor and Labour in Southern Africa*, Athens, OH: Ohio University Press and Pietermaritzburg: University of Natal Press, 1992, pp. 339–66.
72 Interview with Sikota Wina, Lusaka, 29 November 2015.

1980s did not extend to beer, as Zambian Breweries and indeed the traditional producers continued to function, but consumers' capacity to spend was limited. So Sata's capacity to buy beer during the electoral process was well received by voters. His extraction of large amounts of money from business elites was not simply a strategy of purchasing political support but also had significant symbolic implications. It represented a major statement that he knew where the resources needed to develop the constituency were and that he could secure them even from outside public office.

Sata went on to win the Kabwata seat by an overwhelming margin, securing the endorsement of 12,671 voters, with Sibongo a distant second with 3,635 votes. Such a convincing performance placed great pressure on Sata to address some of the key concerns of Kabwata residents if he was to avoid Sibongo's fate at the next polls.

Table 1 Results of the Kabwata parliamentary election, 1983.

Candidate	Total votes	Percentage of total votes
Michael Sata	12,671	46
Maxwell Sibongo	3,635	13
Siloni Paul Jere	1,963	7
Derrick Chitala	1,890	7
Phillip Kalinda	1,847	7
Silva Funkunta	1,635	6
Mary Mwango	1,268	5
Israel Chipungu	1,226	4
Nelson Phiri	656	2
John Pandani	408	1
Cheyani Mbewe	390	1
Total	27,589	

Source: 'Parliamentary Results', *Times of Zambia*, 1 November 1983, p. 7.

Meanwhile, Sata's relationship with Irwin flourished beyond the 1980s and lasted for several decades. Carl Irwin, one of Oliver Irwin's two surviving children, revealed that, when Sata formed the PF, it was his father who paid for the opposition leader's nomination fee for the 2001 election and helped him with related finances that were needed to set up the party.[73] When Oliver Irwin died in 2012, Sata, who was then President of Zambia, was among the pallbearers

---

73   Interview with Carl Irwin, Lusaka, 14 May 2015.

Photograph 3   President Michael Sata, as one of the pallbearers, carrying the casket (draped in the flag of Zambia) of Oliver Irwin on 23 February 2012.

at his burial. Addressing mourners, the President revealed that 'This man we are burying today made me who I am'.[74]

Looking After One's Own: Sata's Novel Solution to the Housing Shortage and the 1988 Election in Kabwata

The defeat of sixty-six of the 125 incumbent MPs in the 1983 election, including several in Lusaka, provided a lesson to Sata about what awaited him at the next election should he fail to deliver. As one incumbent MP who lost his parliamentary seat to a challenger was to reflect years later,

> Being an MP in the one-party state was a poisoned chalice. We were elected on a party platform but lacked the resources with which to address the salient socio-economic issues. This is why so many MPs lost. It is because we (MPs) struggled to meet people's expectations.[75]

Two years after his election as MP, Sata was appointed by President Kaunda as Governor of Lusaka Urban. Until this elevation, Sata's ability to deliver for his constituency was limited. In effectively making him the administrative head of the capital city council, Kaunda expressed optimism that Sata, whom he described as 'talkative', 'would be talking about the development of Lusaka [because the

---

74   Zambia National Broadcasting Corporation Television Main News, 23 February 2012.
75   Interview with Rupiah Banda, Lusaka, 12 February 2013.

city] could not afford to have a governor running it on an *ad hoc* basis'.⁷⁶ Kaunda's strategy of silencing 'talkative' or critical MPs involved giving them positions of influence such as District Governor or the relatively junior post of Minister of State. At the time of Sata's appointment, Lusaka Urban covered five of the eight constituencies in the province including Kabwata and was considerably larger than it had been twenty years earlier. The removal of colonial urban residence restrictions after independence encouraged large numbers of Zambians to move to the city.

According to the official census, the population of Lusaka doubled from 262,425 in 1969 to 535,830 in 1980, and this was caused in part by the decline of the Copperbelt.⁷⁷ This in-migration had major consequences for the provision of social services. An acute shortage of housing developed across Lusaka. The capacity of the state to address the housing problem was severely hampered by the crippling economic crisis, but that did not stop UNIP from making housing a priority in its 1984 policy document, encouraging councils to build homes for people in lower income brackets with a view to full home ownership.⁷⁸

Sata became Governor of Lusaka Urban a year after this plan's release. Until then, he had been constrained by the lack of funds, as the party rather than MPs had served as the primary vehicle through which patronage resources, including the Constituency Development Fund, were channelled to local authorities. Sata had regularly decried the state of suburbs in his constituency and urged authorities to improve living conditions there.⁷⁹ His appeals had consistently been ignored, but his new position now gave him the authority to effect the change that he had long campaigned for.

Claiming that he was acting in line with President Kaunda's call for the planned development of the capital and UNIP's policy on housing, Sata secured a US$2 million loan from the World Bank in conjunction with the National Provident Fund and the Lusaka Urban District Council (LUDC) for the construction of 10,000 low-cost housing units in Lusaka.⁸⁰ He proceeded to identify land for the exercise in Chilenje, one of the largest neighbourhoods in his constituency. The then LUDC Director of Buildings, Lovemore Mudenda, recalled that squatters were occupying the assigned land:

---

76 Times Reporter, 'KK bombshell: Mulemba, Mundia dropped', *Times of Zambia*, 25 April 1985, p. 1.

77 Central Statistical Office, *1980 Population and Housing Census of Zambia*, Lusaka, 1985, p. 3.

78 UNIP, *The National Policies for the Decade 1985–1995: Aims and Objectives of the Third Phase of the Party Programme*, Lusaka: Office of the Secretary-General, 1984, p. 32.

79 Mail Reporter, 'Sessional Committees Nominated', *Zambia Daily Mail*, 7 December 1983, p. 1.

80 Mail Reporter, 'K280 million plan on: Lusaka Urban district Council to build 10,000 housing units – Sata', *Zambia Daily Mail*, 23 September 1985, p. 1.

Initially, several round-thatched houses built during the colonial era occupied the land in question. Mr. Sata directed the Council to compensate the affected families. So that is how the occupants were given money to relocate to the villages. The cost of demolition and payment for relocation was K500 plus transport to one's place of choice. Towards the end of 1985, the construction of the Kajema flats [named after Kajema Constructions, the company that constructed the houses, owned by Greek and Zambian businessmen] commenced ... Sata called it home empowerment. When other councillors and MPs complained that the initiative should extend to their areas, he said 'this is just the beginning'. Since he was our boss, there was nothing else we could do.[81]

Not coincidentally, the construction of the Kajema flats was concluded a few months before the 1988 general elections. Far from the initial target, only 300 housing units were completed. Most of them were allocated to security personnel from the Zambia Army and Zambia Air Force, with the remainder going to civil servants such as nurses and teachers.[82] The beneficiaries of these houses rented them from the council at subsidised rates of K16 per month for a three-bedroomed house and K9 for a two-bedroomed one.[83] The distribution of the housing units was completed only in August 1988, eight weeks before the presidential and general elections. For the Kabwata seat, Maxwell Sibongo, whom Sata had defeated in 1983, was the only challenger this time round. Sata felt he had nothing to fear:

> What could Mr Sibongo say? He had his time, but what did he do for Kabwata? So, I told [the] people [that] 'this man had his time and he did nothing'. And I did not have to campaign because the people could see what I had done ...[84]

At the polls in October, Sata secured an even more decisive victory, winning 71 per cent of the total votes cast. As was the case throughout the country, several incumbents in Lusaka's urban constituencies lost their seats to challengers, demonstrating the competitiveness of the one-party state elections. In Munali constituency, for instance, incumbent Simon Kapata was trounced by Rupiah Banda, whom he had defeated in 1983.[85]

Table 2 Results of the Kabwata parliamentary election, 1988.

Candidate	Total votes	Percentage of total votes
Michael Sata	18,287	71.5
Maxwell Sibongo	7,277	28.5

Source: *Times* Reporter, 'Parliamentary Results', *Times of Zambia*, 1 November 1988, p. 7.

81 Interview with Lovemore Mudenda, Lusaka, 27 November 2015.
82 Interview with Michael Sata, Lusaka, 13 January 2013; interview with Lovemore Mudenda, Lusaka, 27 November 2015.
83 Ibid.
84 Interview with Michael Sata, Lusaka, 13 January 2013.
85 *Mail* Reporter, '6 Ministers Rejected', *Zambia Daily Mail*, 29 October 1988, p. 1.

Sata's decisive re-election had important implications. By building a modest number of houses, he had delivered tangible evidence of his achievements in office, consolidating his appeal among Lusaka's urbanites. It was no coincidence that the Kajema housing units were confined to his constituency alone and finished immediately before the elections. Even though Sibongo retained a residue of support, the outcome of the elections suggests that Sata had won over voters who had previously supported his opponents. The dramatic drop in the number of candidates who took part in the election also indicates that few fancied their chances against Sata's formidable electoral machine.

In showing that he could deliver housing, an important and emotive concern for urban residents, Sata found a way to make patronage work for him in a system in which it was not a key currency. The literature on single-party parliamentary elections elsewhere in Africa argues that MPs who were expected to distribute patronage benefits to their constituents typically ended up pocketing the public funds set aside for state projects.[86] Sata's patronage is unusual in this case in that he actually delivered. While this may have been because Sata thought that delivering social services was a sure way of improving people's lives and securing his re-election, it is possible, too, that he sought to build a credibility that other political leaders had already secured from the nationalist struggle. Having played a peripheral role in the anti-colonial struggle, Sata had lacked the appeal of nationalist figures such as Kaunda and Kapwepwe, who were seen as having delivered political independence. Throughout the 1970s and 1980s, UNIP figures who had taken part in the anti-colonial struggle made constant reference to their nationalist credentials, both as a strategy of mobilising political support and as cover in the face of growing complaints, particularly from disaffected urbanites, who, in the words of one respondent, argued that 'we cannot eat freedom'.[87]

By the 1980s, it was evident that political independence had not brought prosperity or even economic gains to most of the population.[88] The gulf between post-independence expectations and the lived realities for most people in the country had perhaps never been higher. Political elites increasingly began to bear the brunt of criticism from Zambians, especially in the urban areas, where the consumption of information was high. This was a dynamic situation that Sata recognised in the 1980s. By building houses when urban demand for housing

---

86 See Goran Hyden and Colin Leys, 'Elections and Politics in Single-Party Systems: The Case of Kenya and Tanzania', *British Journal of Political Science*, 2, 4 (1972), pp. 389–420; Joel D. Barkan and John J. Okumu, '"Semi-Competitive" Elections, Clientelism, and Political Recruitment in a No-Party State: The Kenyan Experience', in G. Hermet, R. Rose and A. Rouquié (eds), *Elections Without Choice*, London: Palgrave Macmillan, 1978, pp. 88–107.
87 Interview with Neo Simutanyi, Lusaka, 13 January 2014.
88 James Ferguson, *Expectations of Modernity: Myths and Meanings of Urban Life on the Zambian Copperbelt*, California: University of California Press, 1999, p. 12.

was high and state capacity to meet it was low, he was delivering the long-awaited fruits of freedom and at the same time creating his own source of legitimacy. It was a strategy that earned Sata the nickname a 'Man of Action', and that proved successful at the October 1988 polls.

Not Going Down with the Sinking Ship: Sata and the Transition to Multiparty Democracy, 1988–1991

Following his re-election as Kabwata MP in the 1988 elections, Sata continued to rise within the UNIP ranks. On 2 November 1988, President Kaunda removed Sata from his position as Governor of Lusaka Urban and appointed him Minister of State for Decentralisation in the first post-election reshuffle.[89] Although Sata's transfer appeared like a promotion, it was really a tried and tested strategy by Kaunda to undermine or prevent the emergence of potential challengers within UNIP. The prospects for decentralisation in the one-party state were slim, so the position – equivalent to a deputy ministerial portfolio, as it was not a Cabinet post – was somewhat ceremonial. Around the same time, it became apparent that UNIP was not going to be a long-term vehicle for Sata's political ambitions. There were clear signs of this. A foiled coup against Kaunda in 1988 showed mounting discontent with the one-party state, which increasingly suppressed the political opposition that was growing amidst a deteriorating economic situation. Yet Sata continued to back UNIP and Kaunda.

When several reform-orientated MPs called for the democratisation of the UNIP leadership at the party's March 1990 National Convention, Sata opposed such changes. Those who witnessed his performance recalled that his opposition to multi-party party democracy was so vociferous that it appeared as a point of principle:

> He [Sata] opposed the proposal to have secret ballot at [the] UNIP Convention. But he reserved his strongest opposition to the proposal that there should be term limits for UNIP and state presidency. He took the UNIP line that 'If the people want KK [Kenneth Kaunda] to serve them for an indefinite period – who am I to refuse?' It was the chorus position under a choirmaster with a whip in hand![90]

Another witness recollected that at the convention:

> Sata was one of those who shouted the loudest in support of Kaunda and the preservation of the status quo. He described those of us who were calling for political reform as confused, and stuck to the official line that removing Kaunda would spell doom for UNIP and for the country.[91]

---

89   Times Reporter, 'Cabinet reduced', *Times of Zambia*, 3 November 1988, p. 1.
90   Interview with Akashambatwa Mbikusita-Lewanika, Lusaka, 10 January 2014.
91   Interview with Vernon Mwaanga, Lusaka, 10 January 2014. Mwaanga even presented a paper at the March 1990 UNIP Convention calling for internal democracy and

Sata's position was disingenuous at best, as subsequent events were to reveal. In the aftermath of the June 1990 aborted coup and deadly riots over food prices, Kaunda announced that a referendum would be held in October to recommend whether Zambia should continue as a one-party state or revert to a multi-party democracy.[92] On 20 July 1990, the MMD was formed as a pressure group to campaign for the reintroduction of democracy in the forthcoming plebiscite. The subsequent public response to the planned referendum was so overwhelmingly negative that President Kaunda cancelled it in September 'to forestall an imminent split in the nation'.[93] He promised to amend the Republican Constitution to pave the way for multi-party politics and announced that multi-party elections would be held in October the following year, cutting short his five-year term.[94]

It was around this time of rapidly changing political circumstances that Sata began secret negotiations with leading figures in the MMD. Kaunda discovered Sata's activities and, furious, sacked him from his ministerial position in November 1990 for 'getting in touch with the other side'.[95] This effectively forced Sata out into the open. After Kaunda formally repealed the Constitution, to reintroduce multi-party politics in late December, the MMD transformed itself into a political party on 4 January 1991.

On 26 January 1991, Sata resigned from UNIP to join the MMD at a mass rally in Lusaka. The meeting gave him the opportunity to publicly display his worth to the newly formed opposition party by bringing about 5,000 supporters with him, who he said were 'workers in parastatals, the civil service and ordinary Kabwata residents who have decided to go with me'. After handing over his UNIP membership card, Sata proceeded to address the MMD leaders:

> The people of Kabwata have given me the mandate to speak for them without fear or favour and let me tell you (addressing Mr. Frederick Chiluba), I am not seeking a post in the MMD. My role will be that of party organisation, that's all.[96]

---

political reform. For details, see Akashambatwa Mbikusita-Lewanika and Derrick Chitala (eds), *The Hour Has Come! Proceedings of the National Conference on Multi-party Option*, Lusaka: Zambia Research Foundation, 1990, p. 80.

92 Matilda Mwenda, 'Kaunda names October 17 referendum day', *Times of Zambia*, 26 June 1990, p. 1.
93 Godfrey Malama, 'KK Scraps Referendum', *Times of Zambia*, 25 September 1990, p. 1.
94 Ibid.
95 Interview with Kenneth Kaunda, Lusaka, 29 April 2011. Also see *Times* Reporter, 'Kaunda sacks Sata in major reshuffle', *Times of Zambia*, 2 November 1990, p. 1.
96 Parliamentary Correspondent, 'Sata quits for MMD', *Times of Zambia*, 27 January 1991, p. 7. Sata's defection to the MMD is representative of several UNIP MPs who switched their political allegiance from the nationalist organisation to join the pro-democracy movement in the early 1990s. However, unlike Sata, who choreographed his move to the new party in a way that secured his political career, the others quietly joined the MMD much earlier and without much drama.

This was the politics of delivery at its best, and it was not accidental. Ten days before he quit UNIP, Sata had written to the MMD leadership, explaining how he would like to join the party. As the correspondence between MMD leaders shows, he had long planned his political move to achieve maximum impact:

MMD
Movement for Multiparty Democracy
P. O. Box 30561
Lusaka

16 January 1991

Mr A. N. L. Wina,
Chairman
Movement for Multiparty Democracy,
LUSAKA

Dear Sir,

I have received the attached letter from Hon. Michael C. Sata, Member of Parliament for Kabwata Constituency, which I think merits consideration.

Mr Sata is of the view that we are not doing enough ground work at the lower level and that there seems to be an attitude on the part of our officials that unless there is a national rally, they seem rather reluctant to organise small meetings w[h]ere local leaders can address the members of the public.

Mr Sata has suggested that a public meeting be held to be organised by the MMD Provincial leadership at Kabwata on Saturday, 26 January 1991 at which he would like to announce his formal resignation from UNIP.

I support this idea and I support the idea of holding several of these meetings in several other places to enable the District Officials to get the MMD message across the masses.

Since the other aspects concern organisation matters, I am sure that my colleague F. J. T. [Frederick Jacob Titus] Chiluba will deal with them in a satisfactory manner.

Yours faithfully,
(Signed)
Vernon J. Mwaanga
Chairman
Publicity and Public Relations Committee
Cc: All NIC [National Interim Committee] Members[97]

---

97 'MMD Correspondences', Personal File of Arthur Wina, 1991. I am grateful to Inonge Wina for granting me access to this important source.

Sata's professed aversion to a party position, and his declaration that he sought merely to support the movement and remove Kaunda from power was a strategic move to win the trust of the MMD leadership. It allowed him to show his commitment to the opposition party by presenting himself as a humble political figure prepared to take on any role. Of particular significance was the timing of Sata's letter and defection. Earlier in January, the MMD had announced that the party would hold its National Convention towards the end of February to elect substantive office holders who would replace the interim leaders. Seizing the opportunity, Sata recognised that he would have to resign weeks before the MMD convention if he was to get a chance to contest a party post.

A few weeks later, at the MMD convention in February, Sata's greater political ambitions came to the fore. In the race for the MMD presidency, featuring four contenders including Arthur Wina, the interim chairperson, Sata successfully campaigned for the Bemba-speaking Chiluba.[98] In a vote of thanks for Chiluba's acceptance speech, Sata advised the losing candidates to 'bury the hatchet' and support the party's new leader, warning that 'factions in any form would split the MMD' and undermine its electoral prospects.[99] He also 'made an earnest appeal to Mr Chiluba to listen to the people and [, if elected,] deliver the goods instead of dwelling on slogans'.[100] Contrary to Sata's earlier assurances, he challenged Mwami Maunga, a founding member of the MMD, for the position of party chairperson for local government and housing. Now a shrewd campaigner, Sata defeated his only rival after he polled 873 votes (representing 84.3 per cent of the total votes cast) against Maunga's 162 (15.7 per cent).[101]

At the landmark October 1991 multi-party elections, Sata went on to defend his Kabwata parliamentary seat on the MMD ticket, while Chiluba and the MMD won a resounding victory against Kaunda's UNIP. On 2 November 1991, precisely a year after Kaunda had dismissed Sata from his ministerial post, the new President Chiluba appointed him as Minister of Local Government and Housing. Under the MMD, Sata would carry on where he left off in UNIP – his political career only temporarily interrupted by Zambia's seemingly momentous political transition.

---

98   The other two contenders for the MMD leadership were Edward Shamwana, a former High Court judge who was also involved in the organisation of the 1980 coup attempt against Kaunda, and Humphrey Mulemba, who served in various positions under Kaunda's Cabinet.
99   Times Reporter, 'I will strive for equality – Chiluba', *Times of Zambia*, 2 March 1991, p. 1.
100 *Ibid.*
101 Times Reporter, 'Results of the MMD Convention', *Times of Zambia*, 6 March 1991, p. 7.

3

Constructing a Power Base in a Dominant Ruling Party

THE CLOSING decade of the twentieth century in Zambian politics was dominated by the Movement for Multiparty Democracy (MMD) and President Chiluba, who rose to power in November 1991 after defeating incumbent President Kaunda and his United National Independence Party (UNIP) – the nationalist movement that had ruled Zambia since independence in 1964. Chiluba secured 76 per cent of the presidential vote in 1991 and about 69 per cent five years later.[1] Against its 1991 total of 125 of the 150 seats in parliament, the MMD increased its parliamentary representation to 131 seats in 1996.[2] Over the course of his decade-long rule, Chiluba embarked on a drive to liberalise the economy and consolidate the democratic space that had permitted his party to gain power.

When the MMD ascended to power, it inherited an economy on the verge of collapse. Widespread shortages of essential commodities, skyrocketing inflation, swelling debt, a highly volatile local currency and a bloated civil service – long used by Kaunda as a patronage political machine – all required an urgent economic recovery programme.[3] With copper exports, on which Zambia's gross national product overly depends, at an all-time low due to the declining price of the commodity on the international market, the MMD had little choice but to turn to multilateral institutions such as the International Monetary Fund (IMF) and World Bank for help. However, donors, who had suspended all financial assistance to Zambia just before the 1991 elections,

---

1   Elections Supplement, *Times of Zambia*, 25 November 1996. Also see: Electoral Commission of Zambia, 'Past election results', <https://www.elections.org.zm> (3 November 2023).
2   *Times* Reporter, 'MMD scoops 131 seats', *Times of Zambia*, 24 November 1996, p. 1.
3   Per Nordlund, *Organising the Political Agora: Domination and Democratisation in Zambia and Zimbabwe*, Uppsala: University of Uppsala, 1996, pp. 104–05.

demanded the implementation of a package of economic structural adjustment reforms as a precondition for the resumption of aid.[4]

Starting early in 1992, Chiluba's government embarked on a decade-long radical economic liberalisation programme partly in response to donor prescriptions, but also as a way of fulfilling the MMD's own pre-election campaign promises.[5] The reformist drive resulted in the privatisation of about 250 state-owned industries, the removal of trade barriers, the liberalisation of financial markets and agricultural marketing, and the reduction of state support of education and health.[6] By the end of Chiluba's first term in office, most of these reforms had been fully implemented. For instance, foreign exchange and price controls had been abolished, all tariffs for trade and imports had been removed, state support for agriculture had been substantially reduced, and user fees for education and health introduced.[7]

The MMD's commitment to privatisation waned considerably after the 1996 elections, particularly when it came to the country's strategic copper mining industry. However, the fact that much of Zambia's international development assistance from the mid-1990s onwards had become tied to the sale of the mines left the government little choice.[8] In March 2000, the mining conglomerate, Zambia Consolidated Copper Mines, was sold to Anglo-American Corporation, after differences were resolved about whether it should be unbundled or sold as a single unit, ending the most rapid economic liberalisation process in contemporary Africa.

Chiluba's government had, by the turn of the century, managed to fulfil its promise to move the country from state capitalism towards free market enterprise. However, the net effect of its rapid economic liberalisation policies was a general contraction of the economy, increased poverty levels, and a marked decline in living standards. Privatisation, for example, led to job cuts, severe unemployment, and widespread urban discontent, while the removal of subsidies for agriculture paved the way for the destruction of small-scale farming,

---

4   Lise Rakner, 'Do Interest Groups Matter in Economic Policy-Making? Reflections from a Zambian Case Study', *CMI Working Paper 1994:4*, Bergen: Chr. Michelsen Institute, 1994, p. 4.
5   Indeed, most of the MMD leaders, especially parts of the business elite, were in favour of many of these structural reforms.
6   Miles Larmer, 'Zambia Since 1990: Paradoxes of Democratic Transition', in Abdul Mustapha and Lindsay Whitfield (eds), *Turning Points in African Democracy*, New York: James Currey, 2009, pp. 114–33.
7   Ibid.
8   Lise Rakner, *Political and Economic Liberalisation in Zambia, 1991–2001*, Uppsala: Nordic Africa Institute, 2003, p. 77.

especially in more remote rural areas.⁹ By the end of the MMD's second term, economic reform in Zambia was widely regarded as a failure.

This chapter analyses Michael Sata's attempt to construct a power base within the ruling MMD against this broader political and economic backdrop between 1991 and 2001. To understand Sata's political activities, we need to understand the broader historical context of this decade, which was heavily conditioned by the internal politics of the MMD and President Frederick Chiluba's expected retirement in 2001. Thus, following this introduction to the chapter, the next section provides an overview of the political economy of this period, and the role of succession within it. The final section narrows the discussion to focus on Sata's attempt to construct a power base, used here to mean a group of people or constituency on which a particular political party or leader relies for support. These may be geographical, ethnic, class, religious, or policy in character. An individual of great influence in a power structure, such as the leader of a country, can also be classified as a base but only in relation to the wider groupings in which their authority functions.

In this chapter, I argue that between 1991 and 2001, Sata set out to build constituencies of support for the MMD (in the short term) and a power base for himself (in the longer term) by exploiting ethnic identities in Bemba-speaking rural constituencies to mobilise electoral support, employing a populist strategy in urban areas to cultivate political influence, and developing close ties of solidarity with President Chiluba in order to increase his political advantage and obstruct the presidential ambitions of his potential competitors within the MMD. Although the first two points have been noted by other researchers, this has been in relation to Sata's time in opposition politics after 2001 rather than while he was in the MMD, where he developed both the ethnic and the populist strategies.¹⁰ As the next chapter demonstrates, urban and ethnic constituencies were the same bases of support that Sata successfully mobilised after quitting the MMD and forming his own political party in 2001, and that propelled his rise to power ten years later.

---

9   For instance, employment figures in the formal sector fell from 544,200 in 1991 to 429,406 by the end of Chiluba's rule. In the mining sector, the employment rate shrank to 36,780 in 2000 from 64,800 in 1991. Central Statistical Office, 'Formal Employment Trends in Zambia, 1991–2010', *Labour Force Survey Report*, 2010. See also Larmer, *Zambia since 1990*, p. 120.

10   See, for instance, Miles Larmer and Alastair Fraser, 'Of Cabbages and King Cobra: Populist Politics and Zambia's 2006 Election', *African Affairs*, 106, 425 (2007), pp. 611–37; and Nic Cheeseman and Marja Hinfelaar 'Parties, Platforms and Political Mobilization: The Zambian Presidential Election of 2008', *African Affairs*, 109, 434 (2010), pp. 51–76.

Zambian Politics, 1991–2001

After winning the 1991 election, the MMD attempted to liberalise the media and consolidate democracy over its decade-long rule, as per its campaign promises. Although the Zambian media remains one of the most limited and constrained on the continent, several independent newspapers and community radio stations, such as *The Post* and *Radio Phoenix*, emerged to contest and criticise sharply the excesses of government and to expose the corruption of Chiluba and his officials. These were later to provide much-needed platforms of dissent against Chiluba's attempt to extend his rule beyond the constitutionally prescribed two five-year terms. Apart from the declaration of two states of emergencies in 1993 and 1997 and the arrests that followed of several opposition figures, the occasional detention of independent journalists, mainly from *The Post*, and the widespread accusations of intolerance within the ruling party, Chiluba and the MMD generally managed to entrench civil liberties and consolidate the multi-party political system. The establishment and existence of several political parties and civil society organisations, and the existence of an independent and credible judiciary, serve to reinforce this point. However, democracy on a national scale was not reflected within the ruling party.

With Kaunda out of the way, it did not take long before cracks began to appear within the MMD broad political alliance that had defeated him. The first split occurred in August 1992 when two Cabinet ministers and founding MMD leaders, Akashambatwa Mbikusita-Lewanika and Baldwin Nkumbula, resigned from the government over Chiluba's alleged corruption. Mbikusita-Lewanika, the MMD chairperson for the finance and economic committee, and Nkumbula later quit the ruling party altogether and called for leadership change.[11] The second split took place in April 1993, when Chiluba sacked several Cabinet ministers including two – Arthur Wina (Education) and Humphrey Mulemba (Mines) – who had unsuccessfully challenged him for the party presidency at the inaugural convention in March 1991.[12] The dismissed ministers quit their MMD positions, and some of them regrouped, with those who had left earlier, to form the National Party (NP). The ruling party's fractiousness continued later in June when Rodger Chongwe, until then the Minister of Legal Affairs, quit the MMD in protest against Chiluba's leadership and established his own party, the Liberal Progressive Front. By November 1993, when the MMD held its mid-term convention, over fifteen MMD senior leaders and ministers had resigned or

---

11 Akashambatwa Mbikusita-Lewanika, *Hour for Reunion: Movement for Multiparty Democracy: Conception, Dissension and Reconciliation*, Mongu: African Lineki Courier, 2003, p. 261.

12 Ketson Kandafula, 'Chiluba drops 4', *Zambia Daily Mail*, 16 April 1993, p. 1.

been dismissed, and Chiluba had almost finished transforming the MMD from a broad coalition to a personalised patrimonial machine.[13]

Further evidence of factionalism in the MMD came in June 1995 ahead of the party's second National Convention, where budding successors sought to secure important positions that they thought would give them greater advantage, influence, and control. This time, the party's Deputy National Secretary, Derrick (now Mbita) Chitala, together with Dean Mung'omba, its Deputy Treasurer and Minister in the Office of the President, were expelled from the MMD for expressing their presidential ambitions and their opposition to the government's neo-liberal economic agenda.[14] Mung'omba and Chitala went on to form their own political party, the Zambia Democratic Congress (ZDC). The ruling party's implosion continued in early 1996 when Guy Scott, a founder member and the MMD's Chairperson for Agriculture and Cooperatives, who was also Chiluba's first Minister of Agriculture, quit the ruling party to establish his own political platform, the National Lima Party.[15]

These power struggles within the MMD coincided with the devastating effects of its radical economic liberalisation programme and the return of former president Kaunda to politics in early 1995, which gave UNIP a new lease of life. The MMD's defeat to NP and UNIP candidates in seven of the fourteen parliamentary by-elections held between August and October 1995, including in constituencies previously thought to be its strongholds, suggested voters' disenchantment with the ruling party's performance.[16] As the 1996 elections drew closer, and as trade unions' criticism of the government's economic performance intensified, it appeared that Kaunda and the breakaway parties would succeed in presenting a credible challenge to the MMD's grip on power.

Chiluba's government responded by attempting to strip Kaunda of his Zambian nationality and have him deported to Malawi, from where his parents originated. When this plan failed, the government introduced a constitutional clause that required a presidential candidate to have both parents born in Zambia, effectively excluding Kaunda and prompting UNIP to boycott the polls.[17] Pitted against less-established, poorly funded, and weak opponents, Chiluba easily retained the presidency. In the wake of his re-election to his second and,

---

13 Dan Piaget, 'The Internal Politics of the MMD, Zambia', MSc Dissertation, African Studies, University of Oxford, 2009, p. 32; Miles Larmer, *Rethinking African Politics: A History of Opposition in Zambia*, Surrey: Ashgate Publishing, 2011, p. 258.
14 Gero Erdmann and N. Simutanyi, 'Factionalism in an African Party System: The Case of Zambia', Unpublished paper, 2006, p. 10.
15 Interview with Guy Scott, Lusaka, 8 April 2011.
16 Rakner, *Political and Economic Liberalisation*, p. 108.
17 Times Reporter, 'Kaunda barred', *Times of Zambia*, 18 October 1996, p. 1; Times Reporter, 'It is a discriminatory Constitution: UNIP backs out', *Times of Zambia*, 24 October 1996, p. 1.

according to the constitution, final term, succession once again took centre stage in the internal politics of the MMD. By January 2000, a quartet of senior MMD leaders – Godfrey Miyanda (Vice-President), Sata (National Secretary), Ben Mwila (National Treasurer), and Christon Tembo (National Trustee) – had shown their intentions to succeed Chiluba.

Amidst growing speculation that he was planning to extend his rule beyond the prescribed constitutional term limits, Chiluba moved to ban any discussion and campaigning on presidential succession, arguing that the party may not survive a divisive leadership contest and promising to handpick his successor instead. Calling the move undemocratic and insisting that the party constitution did not give Chiluba such powers, Mwila defied the ban and publicly announced his intentions to contest the presidency of the MMD at the convention, commencing his campaign in May.[18] Sata called for his expulsion from the party, a proposal that was effected in July 2000, two months before Mwila formed his Zambia Republican Party (ZRP).[19]

As the next presidential and general elections approached, Chiluba announced in February 2001 that he would consider seeking a third term if the MMD, whose constitution restricted him to two consecutive five-year terms, endorsed him at its convention slated for April 2001, and later succeeded in amending the Republican Constitution.[20] The president's plot won the support of Sata, who became its most vociferous proponent, in the expectation that Chiluba would nominate him as his successor if his attempt to extend his rule failed. However, Chiluba's plans met the disapproval of Miyanda and Tembo, who not only urged him to step down but also galvanised internal and public opposition to the proposed constitutional amendments. At a tumultuous convention, twenty-two members of parliament (MPs) opposed to Chiluba's third term, including the two dissenting presidential hopefuls, were expelled from the party.

With their ambitions disrupted, and like many others before them, Miyanda and Tembo proceeded to form their own political parties a few months before the presidential elections.[21] Chiluba succeeded in having the MMD constitution amended and securing another term as party president, but his plans hit a snag at the national level when he failed to raise the two-thirds majority support in

---

18   Amos Malupenga, 'Mwila announces his candidacy', *The Post*, 26 May 2000, pp. 1 and 4.
19   Amos Malupenga, 'Sata vows to break Mwila', *The Post*, 1 June 2000, pp. 1 and 4.
20   Amos Malupenga, 'I will go for a third term, says Chiluba', *The Post*, 12 February 2001, pp. 1 and 4.
21   Miyanda founded the Heritage Party (HP) while Tembo went to lead the Forum for Democracy and Development (FDD).

parliament that was required to change the Zambian constitution.[22] Defeated, he named his one-time vice-president Levy Mwanawasa, who had retired from politics, as his successor in August 2001. Claiming that 'even the Pope does not pick his successor',[23] Sata quit the MMD in protest against Chiluba's choice and, like other presidential hopefuls before him, formed his own political party.

Imagining the National Presidency

Sata's attempts at building a power base within the MMD during Chiluba's ten years can be divided into two phases: 1991–1995 and 1996–2001. The first phase spans Sata's consolidation of his image as a 'Man of Action' and his rise as the 'Bemba leader' and requires discussion of the populist and ethnic strategies that he employed to mobilise support for the MMD while also building a power base for himself. The second phase focuses on Sata's reign as MMD National Secretary, which gave him a prime position to consolidate his power base within the ruling party and to advance his presidential ambitions while obstructing those of his potential competitors.

Consolidating the Image of a 'Man of Action'

Until December 1995, when the MMD held its second National Convention at which several Cabinet ministers tried to secure influential positions in the ruling party, the campaign to succeed President Chiluba, which started in earnest as early as 1992, was conducted using government positions and resources. The fact that Chiluba had been elected with a clear majority not only confirmed his popularity but also dissuaded those with presidential ambitions from challenging him for the party's topmost political job. Instead, and while waiting for him to complete his presidential mandate, budding successors chose to use their portfolios in government to enhance the MMD's urban support in the short term and build power bases for themselves in the longer term. To this end, the effective running of one's ministry or constituency became important evidence of work, which, in addition to rendering credibility to one's political voice, demonstrated performance or delivery on a public scale.

Below, I illustrate this interplay between individual agency and structure using Sata's experiences at the Ministries of Local Government and Housing (1991–1993) and Labour and Social Security (1993–1994), the first two of the four Cabinet

22 The literature on presidential term limits in Chiluba's Zambia has conferred significance to civil society's role in blocking Chiluba's plans to secure an unconstitutional third term. However, and as I demonstrate later in this chapter, far more significant to the collapse of Chiluba's bid was the opposition to his attempts within the MMD.
23 Webster Malido, 'I will retire after being President, says Sata', *The Post*, 26 October 2001, pp. 1 and 4.

positions to which Chiluba appointed Sata between 1991 and 2001.[24] I have chosen to focus on these two ministries to analyse Sata's politics during this period because they represented the urban poor and the workers – constituencies that were central to the MMD's 1991 electoral victory and, as we shall see in the next chapter, to Sata's later political career. How the MMD in power addressed the concerns of these main supporters of the movement for political change was as important to its future electoral prospects as to the political careers of the individual ministers responsible for such bases. By identifying and analysing some of Sata's actions at both stations, I demonstrate how he attempted to placate these constituencies in the name of fulfilling the MMD's campaign promises, while building an urban support base for himself at the same time.

Sata, Housing Shortages, and the Urban Poor

The provision of affordable housing and improved sanitation, particularly for urban residents in the densely populated suburbs of Lusaka and the Copperbelt, had been one of the key campaign promises made by Chiluba and the MMD prior to the 1991 elections. Severe economic decline in the last years of Kaunda's rule had seriously inhibited the government's ability to provide adequate social services along the lines of the social democratic welfarist policy promoted by UNIP. This had adverse effects on urban housing development.[25] Public resources for the building of new low-income residential housing were in short supply, in some cases unavailable, leading the state to concentrate its efforts on areas of greater need such as disaster management. In addition, high inflation weakened the country's currency, leading to high-interest rates for loans, and a reduction in the value of savings and purchasing power, which in turn raised living and, especially, construction costs.

Beyond the effects of inflation on the provision of housing, a highly bureaucratic and ineffective land allocation system contributed to the difficulties the country faced in meeting the demand for affordable housing. Thus, a critical shortage of cheap but decent accommodation, and the growth of a disenfranchised class of urbanites who were dissatisfied with coping with the hardships of a poorly performing economy, including a patronage system that favoured those who were closely associated with UNIP, became a rallying point for mobilisation of discontent.[26] Chiluba and his

---

24 As well as heading the Ministry of Health (1994–1996), Sata was also Minister without Portfolio (1996–2001) during Chiluba's tenure. For Sata's actions in the Ministry of Health, see Melle Leenstra, 'Beyond the Façade: Instrumentalisation of the Zambian Health Sector', Doctoral Thesis, Leiden University, 2012, pp. 158–79.

25 See for instance, Carole Rakodi, 'Housing in Lusaka: Policies and Progress', in Geoffrey J. Williams (ed.), *Lusaka and Its Environs: A Geographical Study of a Planned Capital City in Tropical Africa*, Lusaka: Zambian Geographical Association, 1986, pp. 189–207.

26 Sam Phiri, 'MMD Manifest bring class issue to the fore', *Times of Zambia*, 2 March 1991, p. 6.

team, riding on this wave of disaffection, and criticising the Kaunda government's policies as haphazard, were able to forge links and foster solidarity between disenchanted workers and the urban poor. However, the paucity of delivery on the MMD's campaign promise of improved housing and services for poor urbanites became clear in the years immediately following Kaunda's defeat.

Having criticised the Kaunda government's approach to housing as chaotic, the MMD's lack of any plan on housing – at least until 1996 when a national housing policy intending to commit 15 per cent of the national annual budget to housing development was drawn up – laid their shallow campaign promise bare. For almost its entire first term in office, the MMD government had allocated no financial resources to the Ministry of Local Government for the construction of new housing.[27] The Ministry of Local Government and Housing also happened to be Sata's first ministerial station in Chiluba's administration. His spell in the UNIP government as governor and MP in Lusaka had placed Sata in a position to understand the centrality of housing to the concerns of urban residents in low-income areas. He had also understood the threat that the government's inaction and delays in addressing housing posed to the MMD's support base much earlier than many of his ruling party colleagues. Indeed, Sata's election as the MMD Chairperson for Local Government and Housing at the party's February 1991 National Convention was based on his launching a successful campaign that highlighted his experience in addressing urban housing challenges.[28]

Sata's stance on housing became clear early on when the Minister of Finance, Emmanuel Kasonde, presented the MMD government's first national budget on 31 January 1992, allocating a total of K1,135,789,607 to the Ministry of Local Government and Housing.[29] This figure included grants for disbursement to all civic local authorities in the country, the construction of roads, and the improvement of utilities such as water supply, sewerage, and access. No funds were provided for housing development, which prompted criticism from UNIP and several Lusaka residents who cited the move as evidence of Chiluba's and the MMD's lack of commitment to the concerns of the middle class and urban poor.[30]

---

27 The consequence of this sustained neglect of housing development was an increased demand for housing by urbanites. For an overview of the housing situation during the transition in Lusaka, see Ann Schlyter, 'Housing Policy in Zambia: Retrospect and Prospect', *Habitat International*, 22, 3 (1998), pp. 259–71. For a study that focuses on the Copperbelt, see Emmanuel Mutale, *The Management of Urban Development in Zambia*, Surrey: Ashgate, 2004. For a more comprehensive national picture, see Paul Makasa, *Sustainable Urban Areas: 1996 Zambia National Housing Policy*, Amsterdam: IOS Press, 2010.
28 Interview with Michael Sata, Lusaka, 13 January 2013.
29 *Times* Reporter, 'Budget Speech', *Times of Zambia*, 1 February 1992, p. 4.
30 Interview with Michael Sata, Lusaka, 13 January 2013.

Trying to quell the growing discontent and frustration over housing, Kasonde appealed for patience, arguing that the government had inherited dry coffers and the priority at that time was to resuscitate the ailing economy. Noting the unpopularity of Kasonde's decision, Sata, who had developed a reputation as a 'Man of Action' during his time in UNIP (see the previous chapter), quickly distanced himself from the Minister of Finance's position. Labelling Kasonde as a rich businessman, a technocrat who understood neither urban politics nor the problem of the urban poor, and someone who had become an active member of the MMD only in 1990, just prior to their electoral victory, Sata was able to cast himself as a man of the people.[31]

In March 1992, two months after the budget presentation, and true to his name as a 'Man of Action', Sata directed the Lusaka City Council, which fell under the jurisdiction of his ministry, to build 132 blocks of flats in Chilenje Township in his Kabwata constituency. The contract was given to Merzaf, a private construction company owned by George Mermigas, a Greek businessman and close associate of Sata who had helped finance his campaign for parliamentary office. Told that the civic authority was unable to raise the K761 million demanded by the contractor, Sata directed the Permanent Secretary of the Ministry of Local Government and Housing 'to allocate some of the grants intended for payments to various local authorities throughout Zambia towards this project'.[32]

Ignoring criticisms from within and outside the MMD that the need for open and competitive bidding procedures had been overlooked, that ministerial funds meant for council operations throughout the country had been diverted, and that the 'housing empowerment scheme' had been localised to Sata's constituency alone, construction took off in March 1992 and continued until Chiluba moved Sata to the Ministry of Labour in August 1993. Sata's successor at local government, Rodger Chongwe, refused to commit any more funds to the initiative, arguing that it was initiated corruptly, not sanctioned by Cabinet, and amounted to nothing less than an attempt by his predecessor to secure his re-election to parliament – as demonstrated by his failure to replicate it elsewhere.[33] The result of these criticisms was that the project stalled and it was not until some years later that the Lusaka City Council, in an attempt to recoup some of the lost money, rescued it by completing the partly finished houses before selling them off.[34] By the time Sata left the Ministry of Local

---

31   Interview with Dipak Patel, Lusaka, 18 January 2013.
32   Staff Reporter, 'Sata deal under probe', *Weekly Post*, 17 April 1992, p. 1; Bright Mwape, 'Cobra's bite in Merzaf exposed: Sata diverted money meant for various councils to this project', *The Post*, 7 October 1994, p. 1; *Times* Reporter, 'Sata under probe', *Times of Zambia*, 7 May 1992, p. 1.
33   Interview with Rodger Chongwe, Lusaka, 13 January 2013.
34   Interview with Wynter Kabimba, Lusaka, 16 January 2013.

Government and Housing, however, about fifty houses had been constructed,[35] with important implications for his political profile.

First, as he had done under UNIP, Sata demonstrated his capacity to satisfy urbanites' grievances, where others had failed, in this case Kasonde and the government. Building houses at a time when housing demand was high and not being met was a populist move targeted at the middle class for later use as a success story about what he could achieve on a small scale or at constituency level, and, by implication, what he could do for the rest of the city and indeed the whole country, if allowed to tackle the problem.[36] Second, Sata had presented clear evidence of his ability to act and thus enhanced his consciously cultivated image as a 'Man of Action' who gets things done. That the project collapsed soon after he had left the Ministry of Local Government and Housing only served to reinforce this perception.

Sata's rent-seeking behaviour also meant that he succeeded, as he had done under the one-party state era, in committing government resources to what was effectively a personal project on the pretext that he was helping consolidate the ruling party's support among the urban poor and the workers. Responding to criticism from a fellow MMD MP, Stanford Hlazo, that his project had paralysed councils' operations countrywide throughout 1992, Sata justified his actions on grounds that:

> [the] expenditure was in line with the MMD manifesto which states under the housing section that cheaper but good housing must be availed to people. Merzaf is a venture I feel nice to be associated with [because] it is in the direction of the MMD planned development. Just what kind of development does Hlazo hope to champion if he can condemn what the MMD is doing?[37]

The development also enabled Sata to begin cultivating a close relationship with President Chiluba, securing his position in the party and furthering his political advantages. When vice-president Levy Mwanawasa pleaded with Chiluba to dismiss the 'Man of Action' for breaching tender regulations, Sata claimed that local government and housing was one of UNIP's remaining power bases and that his efforts at Merzaf would both undermine that support and shift it to the MMD. Presenting himself as the personification of experience, notwithstanding the fact that he had not occupied senior posts in Kaunda's government, Sata attributed Mwanawasa's concerns to MMD leaders' inexperience in government as well as their failures in managing the expectations

---

35   Ibid.
36   Interview with Neo Simutanyi, Lusaka, 13 April 2014.
37   Richard Chiyabi, 'Sata refutes project funding misuse', *Zambia Daily Mail*, 15 November 1993, p. 5.

of transition.[38] Although this explanation satisfied Chiluba, who openly praised the Minister of Local Government and Housing as 'a good grassroots organiser',[39] it infuriated Mwanawasa, who accused the President of condoning corruption and promoting neopatrimonialism. When Mwanawasa quit his Cabinet post in July 1994, he cited frustration with Chiluba's failure to punish Sata, on the Merzaf saga and other subsequent indiscretions, as the main reasons for his resignation:

> I find it extremely unfair that it should be alright for an ordinary citizen to be prosecuted in a court of law when Sata is not prosecuted just because he is a cabinet minister. I am of the view that Sata is untouchable, and I should instead resign my position [as Republican vice-president] and leave him with those who think he is indispensable.[40]

By then, Sata had long moved on to a different ministry. 'Sata does the right things the wrong way',[41] concluded a prominent local journalist in a hard-hitting exposition of the duplicitous, self-serving career of Sata, but an exposition that arguably had no impact at all on that career. That comment could sum up his entire political life.

Labour Under a Delusion: Sata, Trade Unions, and Economic Restructuring

Organised labour, expressed in the form of the Zambia Congress of Trade Unions (ZCTU) and the Mineworkers Union of Zambia (MUZ), had been the MMD's main constituency of support prior to the 1991 elections.[42] Aside from campaigning for a return to multi-party politics, the trade unions contributed financial and material resources to the creation of the MMD. Several of the MMD's key personnel, such as Frederick Chiluba (former ZCTU Chairman-General), Newstead Zimba (former ZCTU Secretary), and Chitalu Sampa (former ZCTU Treasurer), arose from the leadership ranks of the labour movement. In the subsequent national election campaign, the two unions laid their organisational infrastructure throughout the country at the disposal of the MMD, culminating in the defeat of Kaunda's UNIP.[43] This pre-election role, combined with the fact that the new President, Chiluba, and two Cabinet ministers, Zimba and Sampa, came from its ranks, raised hopes within the

---

38 Amos Malupenga, *Levy Patrick Mwanawasa: An Incentive for Posterity*, Grahamstown: NISC, 2008), pp. 65–67.
39 Jowie Mwiinga, 'A snake in the grass', *Weekly Post*, 22 February 1994, p. 7.
40 Malupenga, *Levy Patrick Mwanawasa*, p. 280. Also see *Times* Reporter, 'Veep resigns from Cabinet', *Times of Zambia*, 4 July 1994, p. 1.
41 Jowie Mwiinga, 'A snake in the grass', *Weekly Post*, 22 February 1994, p. 7.
42 See Miles Larmer, *Mineworkers in Zambia: Labour and Political Change in Post-Colonial Africa*, London: I.B. Tauris, 2007; and Nordlund, *Organising the Political Agora*.
43 Ibid.

labour movement that the 1991 electoral victory would bring about improved welfare for its members. The unions also expected a closer alliance with the new government that would see them become more actively involved and consulted in matters of state.

Labour's optimism was, however, short-lived. Once in power, the MMD embarked on a rapid implementation of policies of economic liberalisation and the privatisation of state parastatals, generally enacting severe austerity measures on public spending. The speed with which companies were closing, scaling down operations or laying off workers ushered in an unparalleled era of retrenchments and a steep deterioration in living standards.[44] These conditions prompted the labour unions to adopt a more critical stance with respect to the government's economic trajectory as early as November 1992, when ZCTU president Fackson Shamenda 'wondered who was benefiting from the structural adjustment programme since workers were thrown onto the streets everyday while those still in employment were struggling hard to survive'.[45] Shamenda advocated a more gradual implementation of austerity measures and demanded that ZCTU be consulted regularly on labour issues since it bore the brunt of explaining to its members how a government that owed its existence to the trade unions could pursue anti-worker policies. These grievances, however, attracted no favourable response from the first Minister of Labour, Ludwig Sondashi, whose performance, the ZCTU chief charged, 'left much to be desired'.[46] To the great disappointment of the trade union leadership, 'not even President Chiluba, Newstead Zimba and Chitalu Sampa, who came from us [i.e. the ZCTU] came out to defend the workers' cause'.[47]

In August 1993, Sata replaced Sondashi as Minister of Labour. At the time Sata assumed his duties, the major concerns of the trade unions remained those of the pace of economic liberalisation, the lack of dialogue between labour and the government, and the growing perception that Chiluba and his colleagues were insensitive to their core constituency. During his short spell as Minister of Labour (he was moved to another ministry in January 1994), the 'Man of Action' attempted to repair ZCTU's strained relationship with a government that it still saw as its own. At the heart of the trade unions' complaints was the failure of the government (and particularly the Minister of Labour) to convene quarterly meetings with representatives of workers and employers, as stipulated in the industrial relations regulations.[48] Recognising that only one such meeting had

44 Larmer, *Rethinking African Politics*, p. 258.
45 *Times* Reporter, 'Unionists tick off SAPs', *Times of Zambia*, 18 November 1992, p. 1.
46 *Times* Reporter, 'ZCTU overlooked, says Shamenda', *Times of Zambia*, 19 October 1992, p. 1.
47 Interview with Alec Chirwa, Lusaka, 21 March 2014.
48 Rakner, *Political and Economic Liberalisation*, p. 95; Interview with Alec Chirwa, 21 March 2014; Interview with Fackson Shamenda, Lusaka, 24 March 2014.

taken place before, Sata convened a tripartite labour council meeting with trade unions and the Zambia Federation of Employers within weeks of taking office.[49] It was a move that distanced him from his predecessor's dismal record.

Most importantly, he began to engage the unions beyond the tripartite structures by holding regular and informal meetings with the organisational leadership. Sata justified these talks on the need to 'understand the problems that workers were facing at the time and explain to them why we (the government) were implementing structural adjustment'.[50] Shamenda notes that, unlike his predecessor, Sata 'met ZCTU almost monthly. He would regularly call us to his office to present our concerns to him.'[51] Unions thus saw Sata as the medium through which they could relay their grievances to Cabinet and reach a president who had turned his back on a key constituency. Alec Chirwa, then ZCTU General Secretary, confirmed both Sata and Shamenda's accounts and highlighted how the Minister of Labour attempted to be the bridge between unions and the government, and present himself differently from the collective:

> Sondashi marginalised us. He found no time to talk to us. But not Sata. He was with us [ZCTU], more understanding and was not keen to the implementation of SAPs [Structural Adjustment Programmes]. In private meetings, Sata would say 'I do not support SAPs, but I am bound by collective responsibility ... I have no control. I am just a Minister of Labour. Majority of members in Cabinet are in support [of economic restructuring], so what can I do?' He told us that he was going along because he was persuaded by the principle of collective responsibility ... [and] that if he was in control, he would have done things differently.[52]

Sata further attempted to address labour's concerns on the speedy implementation of the economic reforms in several other ways. He challenged union members to be as strong and united as he and the labour movement were during the anti-colonial struggle, despite having played a minimal role in the nationalist movement.[53] This position, which Sata conveyed to ZCTU leaders in private meetings but never stated publicly, undermined Chiluba's active encouragement of different unions within the same industry, which union leaders saw as an attempt to fragment and weaken the ZCTU.[54]

Moreover, Sata encouraged the unions to present their grievances on the negative impact of structural adjustment policies directly to the International

---

49 Interview with Alec Chirwa, 21 March 2014.
50 Interview with Michael Sata, Lusaka, 13 January 2013.
51 Interview with Fackson Shamenda, Lusaka, 24 March 2014.
52 Interview with Alec Chirwa, 21 March 2014.
53 Telephone interview with Austin Muneku, 17 July 2015.
54 Interview with Alec Chirwa, 21 March 2014; Interview with Fackson Shamenda, 24 March 2014.

Financial Institutions (IFIs).[55] ZCTU followed this up in December 1993 when they travelled to the World Bank and IMF to plead for more gradual implementation of the economic reforms. Rakner wrote that in the aftermath of this trip, the Minister of Labour took President Chiluba's side by publicly castigating the unions for unilaterally approaching the IFIs to make their case on the harshness of austerity measures in the country.[56] If this was a valid claim, it would indicate that Sata was giving contradictory messages to different constituencies with competing interests. (As yet there is no evidence to substantiate Rakner's account, as the newspaper source that she cited does not report such a story.)[57]

Sata's overtures to the unions during this period cemented their support for the MMD in the short term and, in the long term, helped consolidate his own position within the power structure in several ways. To start with, courting the unions on a regular basis represented Sata's attempt at addressing their longstanding concerns about being neglected in formal decision-making processes, and, in this way, at neutralising their militancy so that they would not rise against the MMD. It was also a populist strategy designed to distance himself from Chiluba and his former ZCTU colleagues' perceived betrayal of labour while demonstrating his own faithfulness to a strategic constituency with an extensive national presence and structure that was already part of the MMD power base. In public, Sata was the Minister of Labour who executed and defended government policy on liberalisation and privatisation. In private, he was an outspoken critic of the same government policy and an ally of union leaders.

Constant interaction with workers' representatives was also a way of enhancing his political standing and relationship with them, casting himself as a defender of their interests whom they should remember and present to their membership as such. By claiming that he 'would have done things differently', the 'Man of Action' rationalised that the unions, which were beginning to question their support for the ruling party, should not leave the MMD but should back him to take over from President Chiluba once he stepped down so that he could solve workers' problems and restore the strength of the labour movement. In the wake of Sata's exit in early 1994, it took only a few months before ZCTU leaders protested against his successor, Newstead Zimba, and appealed to President Chiluba to bring back the 'Man of Action', highlighting the positive relationship

---

55 Interview with Alec Chirwa, 21 March 2014.
56 Rakner, *Political and Economic Liberalisation*, p. 95.
57 Rakner cites a 16 December 1993 *Times of Zambia* newspaper for her account. However, my fieldwork research found no record of it in the *Times of Zambia*, *Zambia Daily Mail*, or *The Post* in December 1993. When contacted, Rakner conceded that 'It is entirely possible that I – at some point – have made a mistake – either when I worked on the PhD ms into the book, or when I actually took the notes/photocopied'. Personal correspondence with the author, 10 August 2015.

he had managed to cultivate with unions during his brief time at the Ministry of Labour.[58] In later years, after he had established the opposition Patriotic Front (PF), the unionists with whom Sata worked while in the MMD joined his party and helped his campaign, especially among formal sector workers. Shamenda went on to become a PF MP on the industrial Copperbelt and, after Sata won power in 2011, the Minister of Labour.

Having established a support base in urban areas, Sata realised the need to embark on a similar campaign in the rural areas. Building a power base outside the capital was strategically important because it would allow him to identify the grievances of voters in rural settings and devise strategies of mobilisation that could secure their support. It would also enable him to broaden his appeal beyond the urban constituencies. This is exactly what he attempted to do, starting late in 1993.

Becoming the Bemba Leader

The first and second sets of parliamentary by-elections after the landmark 1991 polls took place in November 1993 and April 1994, respectively. Both pitted the MMD against the NP, a breakaway opposition made up of several former MMD MPs from Northern, Copperbelt, Western, Southern, and North-Western provinces. The NP was founded by Chilufya Kapwepwe, an MP for Lunte constituency in the Northern Province, and two former ministers, Akashambatwa Mbikusita-Lewanika and Baldwin Nkumbula, who quit their Cabinet positions in August 1993 in protest against Chiluba's failure to stem corruption.[59] The trio were joined later by Emmanuel Kasonde (former Minister of Finance), Humphrey Mulemba (Mines), and Arthur Wina (Education), who, in the wake of their dismissals from government, all resigned from the MMD. Other MMD MPs who defected to the new party included Inonge Mbikusita-Lewanika, John Mulwila, and Katongo Maine.[60] Led by Inonge Mbikusita-Lewanika (President) and Kasonde (vice-president), the major strength of the NP lay in the fact that it brought together Bembas (Kasonde, Kapwepwe, and Maine), Tongas (Nkumbula) and Lozis (Wina and the two Mbikusita-Lewanikas), representing a multi-ethnic coalition of three of the country's most dominant groups.

Held about two years after the MMD rose to power, the by-elections were important for several reasons. For the MMD, they represented a litmus test of whether the party still commanded a majority following across the country as it

---

58 Times Reporter, 'ZCTU blasts State', *Times of Zambia*, 8 August 1996, p. 2; Interview with Newstead Zimba, Lusaka, 13 April 2014.

59 Akashambatwa Mbikusita-Lewanika, *Hour for Reunion: Movement for Multi-Party Democracy: Conception, Dissension and Reconciliation*, Mongu: African Lineki Courier, 2003, p. 14.

60 Staff Reporter, 'Resignations plunge MMD into crisis', *Weekly Post*, 13–19 August 1993, pp. 1, 4, 8.

had in 1991. Having been put in office by an electorate that was arguably more eager to get rid of Kaunda than it was committed to the MMD, the elections presented the ruling party with a chance to find out what its actual constituencies of support were, beyond the general appeal of democracy. The MMD further envisioned that defeating the MPs who had left the party would signal voters' endorsement of its performance in power and their disapproval of the defectors' exit.

In the absence of an alternative policy framework, the challenge for the NP was two-fold. The first was to become effectively what it claimed to be: a national party, with parliamentary representation in most provinces, including the politically important Northern Province, where most of the vacant seats were. The second was for the ex-MMD MPs to show that they had won the seats on the MMD ticket based on their individual popularity rather than on the platform on which they had stood. Recapturing the seats, especially in areas seen as MMD strongholds, would demonstrate that the electorate had moved with them. It would also represent voters' endorsement of their decision to leave the ruling party. If they were able to retain their seats, it would also indicate a significant reconfiguration of political power.

Given that the rival contenders in each of the affected constituencies belonged to the same ethnic group, the nature of campaigning, especially the strategies and messages of the competing candidates and the political platforms on which they were standing, assumed great significance in influencing the outcome. Below, I examine these campaign strategies and messages, focusing on two constituencies: Malole and Chinsali. In relation to this, I demonstrate the ways in which Sata attempted to mobilise support for the MMD candidates while boosting his own political reputation as 'the Bemba leader' out to protect the region from opposition encroachment.

The selection of Malole and Chinsali in this analysis is explained by the fact that both constituencies are in the Northern Province, home to the Bemba-speaking people and to Sata himself. In addition, in both constituencies, the opposing candidates sought to position themselves as the Bemba leader that Sata wanted to become. Furthermore, Sata, who at the time of both by-elections was an MMD MP in the capital, Lusaka, campaigned actively in both constituencies. He was the MMD campaign manager for the November by-election in Malole and played a central role in the outcome. Although the ruling party chose someone else to lead its campaign in the Chinsali by-election, Sata still found his way to the area to campaign for the MMD candidate. As in Malole, his campaign message was to contribute significantly to the electoral result.

The Malole By-election, 11 November 1993

The Malole seat fell vacant after the incumbent, former Minister of Finance Emmanuel Kasonde, quit the MMD to join the NP, on whose ticket he now sought to return to parliament. Until his resignation in 1993, Kasonde was the

Northern Province MMD founding chairperson and seen widely as the Bemba leader and political guardian of the region. He was also credited for the party's excellent showing in the area during the 1991 elections, when Chiluba won 77 per cent of the presidential vote and the MMD secured all but one of the province's twenty-one parliamentary seats.[61] Having polled 12,036 votes against his opponents' combined total of 461 in the 1991 polls, Kasonde expressed confidence in retaining his seat, declaring before the polls that voters 'are hundred percent solidly behind me'.[62] At the time of the Malole by-election, Kasonde was the NP vice-president.

Standing in Kasonde's path was the ruling party's Dismus Kalingeme. Kalingeme was a little-known local businessman whose nomination made the outcome of the by-election appear to be a foregone conclusion.[63] The MMD appointed Sata, its then local government and housing chairperson, as its lead campaigner in Malole. Once the campaigns got underway, Kasonde mobilised electoral support on a platform of continuity with development. He exploited his positive record as an MP, highlighted by one prominent local journalist as his greatest asset: 'Kasonde has probably done more than any other politician over the years to develop Malole and lives right in the middle of his constituency.'[64]

Citing the electrification of the area, improved water, and sanitation, the construction of more health and education facilities, and the upgraded road infrastructure as some of his accomplishments, the National Party vice-president pledged to build on that performance and urged the electorate to give him another chance, though on a different platform. He also addressed himself to wider concerns and, notwithstanding his own role in it, accused Chiluba's government of tolerating corruption and democratic backslides, and disrespecting civil liberties, in a manner that was reminiscent of the UNIP era.[65] Of particular importance was the fact that Kasonde confined his campaign message to developmental subjects in a way that suggested a desire to protect his reputation as a 'man of integrity' and that displayed a confidence arising from the knowledge that Northern Province was his power base.

If Kasonde was concerned with protecting his reputation, Sata was determined to dismantle it. Exploiting reports in the state-run media that the electorate in Malole were opposed to Kasonde's departure from the MMD,

---

61 Electoral Commission of Zambia, 'Past Election Results', <https://www.elections.org.zm> (3 November 2023).

62 Ibid.; Antony Kunda, 'Kasonde to contest seat on the NP ticket', *Weekly Post*, 13–19 August 1993.

63 Interview with Sikota Wina, Lusaka, 12 April 2014.

64 Jowie Mwiinga, 'Profile: Emmanuel Kasonde', *Weekly Post*, 21 December 1993, p. 7.

65 Gideon Simwinga, 'By-elections lacked proper information', *National Mirror*, 29 November–5 December 1993, pp. 5–7; Times Reporter, 'Spotlight: Tribalism mars Zambian politics Malole campaigns', *Times of Zambia*, 8 November, 1993, p. 11.

Sata embarked on an ethnic mobilisation campaign strategy against the NP candidate. He accused Kasonde of being a 'sell-out' who had let the Bembas down by forming an alliance with Tonga and Lozi politicians. Warning Bembas that they risked becoming second-class citizens under an NP leadership headed by a Lozi, Sata presented Kasonde as betraying the Bemba-speaking people and urged voters to reject his candidature and secure 'our province' from Tonga–Lozi encroachment:

> Your son, Kasonde, has betrayed you. He has teamed up with Lozi tribalists ... he will sell you to Lozis and Tongas. You (i.e. Bembas) will become second-class citizens in the new party.[66]

Dramatising Kasonde's 'conversion' by constantly referring to him throughout the campaigns as an 'Emmanuel Liswaniso' – a typical Lozi name – who, by associating with the NP, had forfeited his ethnic identity, the MMD chief campaigner depicted Kalingeme as a bona fide and genuine Bemba. He urged the electorate to reject Kasonde, arguing that voting for the former Finance Minister amounted to endorsing his betrayal of the Bemba-speaking group.[67] This was despite Sata's own complicated ethnic background. Although he was Bemba-speaking, Sata belonged to the Bisa, one of the smaller ethnic groups that is integrated among the dominant Bemba group in Northern Province.

When the Malole by-election results were announced, Kasonde was shocked as much by the result as by the scale of his defeat. Kalingeme, a political amateur, polled 1,765 votes against Kasonde's 664.[68] A senior MMD leader hailed the result as 'the end of Kasonde's political career. We have killed him.'[69] Local election monitors and political analysts identified the ruling party's use of the 'ethnic card' as responsible for Kasonde's loss:

> There was an element of rejection of NP by the Bemba-speaking voters as a reaction to charges that NP was a Lozi–Tonga party trying to use Mr Kasonde for a foothold in the area and to cloak itself in a semblance of a nationally based organ.[70]

For Sata however, the Malole result was significant in four ways. First, it represented the triumph both of his ethnically tinged campaign message and, more importantly, his attempt at building a power base outside the capital.

---

66 Post Reporter, 'Emerging patterns of Tribalism', *The Post*, 23 July 1999, p. 8; Staff Reporter, 'Malole campaigns turn tribal', *National Mirror*, 6 November 1993, p. 1.
67 Interview with Sikota Wina, Lusaka, 12 April 2014; Daniel N. Posner, *Institutions and Ethnic Politics in Africa*, Cambridge: Cambridge University Press, 2005, p. 188.
68 Hastings Nyasulu and Richard Chiyabi, 'Kasonde falls', *Zambia Daily Mail*, 13 November 1993, p. 1.
69 Ibid.
70 Ketson Kandafula, 'Vital lessons to note after by-elections', *Zambia Daily Mail*, 18 November 1993, p. 6.

Second, it meant that he had succeeded in presenting the MMD as the party for the Bemba-speaking people and prevented the NP, which he claimed was a Lozi–Tonga alliance, from establishing a foothold among the Bembas, at least for the time being, in the Northern Province. Third, he had not only desecrated the credibility of Kasonde in Malole but had effectively ended his political influence in the area. The former Minister of Finance 'might have been Bemba when he was still a member of the MMD – he was in fact a relative of the Bemba Paramount Chief – but his defection to the NP marked him as an outsider'.[71] Lastly, Sata had succeeded in positioning himself as the new Bemba leader of the Northern Province, and had put himself in a strong position in the race to succeed Chiluba.

The Chinsali By-election, 7 April 1994

Held five months after Malole, the Chinsali by-election resulted from Katongo Maine's defection from the MMD to the NP, on whose ticket she now sought to return to parliament. Her opponents were the MMD's little-known Charles Museba, and Chilufya Kapwepwe, a founding leader of the NP, who, instead of re-contesting her Lunte constituency seat (also in the Northern Province) chose to stand as an independent in protest against the party's decision to overlook her application for nomination. A brief discussion should be given of these pre-election divisions in the NP over which candidate to float in Chinsali, as the divisions were to affect the campaigns of both Maine and Chilufya Kapwepwe significantly.

In seeking to be the NP's flag bearer in Chinsali, Maine justified her application on grounds that she was the immediate past incumbent, had easily won the seat in 1991, and was resident in the area. Her bid won the support of party leaders such as Kasonde and Mulemba, who argued that the NP would stand a better chance of establishing a presence in the Northern Province if she was given an opportunity to defend her seat.[72] This optimism, however, was not shared by other senior party leaders such as Akashambatwa Mbikusita-Lewanika, who not only underplayed the importance of the incumbency advantage by citing Kasonde's loss in Malole, but also urged the party to adopt Chilufya Kapwepwe owing to her strong family ties in the area. Her father, Simon Mwansa Kapwepwe, had been a prominent political figure in Zambian politics, and was, like her, born in Chinsali. He was also one of Zambia's foremost nationalists and a founder member of UNIP. He had served as Zambia's vice-president from 1967 until 1969, when he fell out with President Kaunda and quit his Cabinet post over concerns that the 'people of the northern part of Zambia, the Bemba-speaking people', had not been sufficiently rewarded for their role in the nationalist struggle. They 'have suffered physically ... demotions and suspensions because of my being Vice-President'.[73]

---

71 Posner, *Institutions*, p. 188.
72 Interview with Katongo Maine, Chinsali, 17 December 2013.
73 Miles Larmer, 'Simon Kapwepwe: Zambia's greatest intellectual politician?', *Bulletin and Record*, November 2011, pp. 43–44.

Simon Mwansa Kapwepwe subsequently resigned from UNIP and formed the earlier noted United Progressive Party (UPP) in August 1971, which rose to seriously challenge the ruling party's political hegemony before it was banned in February 1972 over alleged violence.[74] Alongside several of his UPP colleagues, Kapwepwe was imprisoned for several months until December, when Kaunda declared Zambia a one-party state. He died in January 1980 after suffering a stroke, aged 57. Of great consequence is that although Kapwepwe's critics see him as a Bemba nationalist whose political ideas and practice rested on ethnic identity and mobilisation, in the Northern Province he was a popular hero seen as 'the Bemba leader' of the time. It was this cherished historical legacy that his daughter hoped to tap into for her campaign, almost thirteen years after his death. Thus, when the NP chose to float Maine on the party's ticket, Chilufya Kapwepwe decided to run as an independent candidate, viewing herself as the clear favourite:

> I stood in Chinsali because I felt it would be a much easier seat to win than Lunte. The MMD had a lot of resources and we saw how Kasonde lost in Malole.[75]

Once the campaigns got underway, Chilufya Kapwepwe focused her message on the need to improve both agriculture and added-value agricultural products to diversify the economy and reduce its reliance on copper. She further pledged to work with community women's groups and establish village industries such as pottery and basket weaving to ease the high levels of poverty in the area.[76] As Kasonde had done in Malole, Kapwepwe's daughter addressed herself to wider concerns, criticising the MMD's intolerance and its clampdown on civil liberties and the rising levels of corruption in government.

The NP candidate, Katongo Maine, on the other hand, anchored her re-election bid on the need for continuity to prevent the disruption of the development projects she had initiated. Maine cited the construction of a Norwegian-funded multi-purpose youth centre, numerous women's empowerment schemes, and the procurement of a community ambulance as evidence of her positive record, upon which she was seeking a fresh mandate.[77] Maine's re-election efforts, however, were undermined by the ongoing divisions within the NP that put a stress on the party's human and material resources. In Chinsali, this infighting

---

74 Alongside ethnic considerations, Kapwepwe also raised classic populist issues that won him support in urban areas, especially on the influential Copperbelt. For a comprehensive and excellent analysis of how Kapwepwe's UPP rose to challenge Kaunda's political hegemony, see Miles Larmer, '"A Little Bit Like a Volcano": The United Progressive Party and Resistance to One-Party Rule in Zambia, 1964–1980', *International Journal of African Historical Studies*, 39, 1 (2006), pp. 49–83.
75 Interview with Chilufya Kapwepwe, Chinsali, 12 December 2013.
76 Ibid.
77 Interview with Katongo Maine, Chinsali, 17 December 2013.

expressed itself in the emergence of two competing factions. One group was led by Kasonde, Mulemba, and Inonge Mbikusita-Lewanika, who supported Maine as the party's candidate; the other group comprised Akashambatwa Mbikusita-Lewanika and Nkumbula, who campaigned for the independent candidate, Chilufya Kapwepwe.[78]

Brought back from the diplomatic service, the MMD contestant Charles Museba initially struggled to strike a positive chord with the electorate, not least because of the widespread perception that he had been away from Chinsali for too long to understand their grievances.[79] That he was competing against not only the incumbent but a formidable independent candidate with an illustrious name made Museba's and the ruling party's task even harder. While it was easy to downplay Maine's achievements by linking them to her previous membership to the MMD, campaigning against Kapwepwe's daughter proved to be particularly problematic for Museba. Not even the deployment of considerable public resources for partisan use seemed to curtail the growing momentum of Chilufya Kapwepwe's campaign. As the MMD campaign manager in Chinsali recalled, it was only after Sata joined and breathed a new lease of life into the party's campaign that its electoral prospects changed.[80]

As he had done for Emmanuel Kasonde in Malole, Sata took his 'you are betraying Bembas' theme to Chinsali. First, he presented Maine as a traitor who was seeking re-election on a political platform that stood for the exclusive promotion of non-Bemba interests, and urged voters to decline her attempts to convert them to a collaborative role.[81] But Sata reserved his harshest criticism for Chilufya Kapwepwe, the independent candidate. Engaging in what Chilufya Kapwepwe referred to as 'a very nasty campaign', but one that resonated with local audiences, Sata claimed that Simon Mwansa Kapwepwe's daughter was the NP's proxy candidate and another flag carrier of Lozi and Tonga ethnic interests.[82]

At the time of the by-election, Chilufya Kapwepwe was in a romantic relationship with Akashambatwa Mbikusita-Lewanika, a Lozi. Although their relationship had begun 'as far back as 1983',[83] it was largely unknown in Bemba-speaking areas, including Northern Province. Seeking to socially discredit Chilufya Kapwepwe as an electoral opponent in the short term and as a rival for Bemba leadership in the longer term, Sata, who himself was dating Christine Kaseba, a Bemba speaker, dragged the duo's love affair into the political domain and turned it into a campaign subject. Sata accused Chilufya Kapwepwe of

78 Ibid.
79 Interview with Katele Kalumba, Lusaka, 22 April 2014.
80 Ibid.
81 Interview with Katongo Maine, Chinsali, 17 December 2013.
82 Interview with Chilufya Kapwepwe, Chinsali, 12 December 2013.
83 Interview with Akashambatwa Mbikusita-Lewanika, Lusaka, 12 April 2014.

betraying her father and the Bembas more generally, arguing quite crudely that she had traded her kin for a sexual affair. As Sikota Wina, then MMD National Chairman for Elections and himself Lozi, recalled, Sata 'told the people [i.e. electorate] in Chinsali that "had the father been here, he would have been very sad to be let down by her for going out with a Lozi man",[84] a telling suggestion that Chilufya Kapwepwe's relationship with Akashambatwa Mbikusita-Lewanika would not have won the approval of her father, and demeaned what he stood for.

To communicate this campaign message effectively, Sata relied on the Bemba language and its rich traditional sayings and proverbs. Drawing on provocative sexual metaphors, as attested by both opposition and MMD campaigners in Chinsali, Sata constantly referred to Mbikusita-Lewanika and Chilufya Kapwepwe as 'umwinshi' and 'ibende', respectively.[85] In the Bemba language, *umwinshi* denotes a pounding stick that goes into a mortar (*ibende*) when people grind maize or cassava. The sexual connotations of this message were clear. As one senior MMD leader who was also the party's official campaign manager in the by-election recalled, the resultant message was

> effective and loaded. The crowd received it well because prior to that, the people wanted to hear the answer to the question of why Chilufya was walking away from the MMD. After Sata explained, they said 'ah, now we understand'. The things he said energised the audience and they started laughing. You could see they were enjoying it and found his message entertaining and even convincing.[86]

Highlighting his adeptness at understanding local context, and supported by an affective engagement with the place, Sata carefully constructed a sexual narrative that presented Chilufya Kapwepwe as a victim of a Lozi sexual predator who did not love her but was merely using their affair to gain political mileage by aligning himself with the daughter of a prominent Bemba. By openly appearing in Chinsali 'to support her for political and personal reasons',[87] rather than Maine, Mbikusita-Lewanika was seen as confirming his opportunism, as well as the accusation that Chilufya Kapwepwe was the NP's unofficial candidate. Akashambatwa Mbikusita-Lewanika was also seen as betraying his party in the same way that Chilufya Kapwepwe was perceived as betraying her father's legacy. By appealing to the electorate to reject both Maine and the independent

---

84   Interview with Sikota Wina, Lusaka, 16 December 2013.
85   Interview with Katele Kalumba, Lusaka, 22 April 2014; Interview with Akashambatwa Mbikusita-Lewanika, Lusaka, 12 April 2014. 385Interview with Sikota Wina, Lusaka, 16 December 2013; Interview with Chilufya Kapwepwe, Chinsali, 12 December 2013; Interview with Akashambatwa Mbikusita-Lewanika, Lusaka, 12 April 2014; Interview with Katele Kalumba, Lusaka, 22 April 2014.
86   Interview with Katele Kalumba, Lusaka, 22 April 2014.
87   Interview with Akashambatwa Mbikusita-Lewanika, Lusaka, 12 April 2014.

candidate, Sata was urging them to help preserve Kapwepwe's legacy in defence of Bemba interests. He was also calling on them to recognise the MMD as the genuine platform for the expression of Bemba interests and, most importantly, acknowledge him as 'the new Kapwepwe'.

In a rebuttal that made a strong reference to broader Zambian national concerns, and not just Bemba ones, Chilufya Kapwepwe criticised Sata's 'dirty campaign' and argued that he was the one misrepresenting her father's legacy. She further argued that her relationship with a non-Bemba was a clear testimony of her nationalist credentials, saying:

> I am a Zambian first and my father fought for this country not as a Bemba but a Zambian. I can have a relationship with anyone I want.[88]

Chilufya Kapwepwe's argument for a 'Zambian first' nationalism revealed her detachment from a politics that was locally constituted, and she was defeated crushingly at the polls. The MMD candidate polled 1,802 votes, three times more than her aggregate of 471 votes. Maine received just 259 votes.[89] While Maine, the NP candidate, blamed the intra-party wrangles for her defeat, Chilufya Kapwepwe blamed Sata's smear campaign, as did Mbikusita-Lewanika.[90] For Sata, however, the outcome of the Chinsali by-election strengthened his post-Malole position as the new leader of the 'Bemba nation'. Sata had not only succeeded in keeping the opposition at bay, but also effectively secured the complete control of the Northern Province. Having cultivated the support of urbanites (1992–1993) and established a power base in rural areas (1993–1994), what remained for Sata was simply for him to consolidate his position by seeking parliamentary representation in Bembaland and securing an influential position in the MMD. This is exactly what he did next, starting in 1995.

Controlling the MMD as National Secretary

At the MMD's second National Convention in December 1995, senior members of Chiluba's Cabinet secured top leadership positions that would give them greater influence in the party. Amongst these were Vice-President Godfrey Miyanda, who was elected as MMD vice-president, Minister of Health Michael Sata, who became the party's National Secretary, Minister of Defence Ben Mwila, elected as party Treasurer, and the Minister of Foreign Affairs, Christon Tembo, who became the party Trustee. Over the course of the next five years, with President Chiluba constitutionally barred from extending his stay in office at the end of his

---

88 Interview with Chilufya Kapwepwe, Chinsali, 12 December 2013.
89 Vernacious Mwansa, 'MMD sends opposition parties reeling: it's all MMD', *Zambia Daily Mail*, 9 April, 1994, p. 1.
90 Interview with Katongo Maine, Chinsali, 17 December 2013; Interview with Chilufya Kapwepwe, Chinsali, 12 December 2013; Interview with Akashambatwa Mbikusita-Lewanika, Lusaka, 12 April 2014.

second term in 2001, the quartet, fancying their chances, attempted to position themselves as his successor.

Former Republican and MMD Vice-President Levy Mwanawasa, following his unsuccessful challenge for the party presidency against Chiluba, announced he would retire from active politics after the convention and not defend his parliamentary seat in the November 1996 elections.[91] With former Minister of Finance Kasonde out of the way, having left the MMD for the opposition NP, Mwanawasa's exit meant that Miyanda, Mwila, and Tembo (who succeeded Miyanda as Zambia's vice-president in December 1997) became Sata's main challengers for the ruling party's topmost job. Below, I demonstrate how Sata, as the MMD National Secretary, attempted to obstruct the presidential ambitions of his three competitors within the ruling party in a manner that furthered his own ambitions.

Stopping Vice-President Miyanda from Establishing a Power Base

Miyanda was born in Mufulira on the Zambian Copperbelt on 1 December 1944.[92] After a career in the military (1964–1977), a leading role in the botched 1980 attempted coup against President Kaunda, and a brief stint as leader of the short-lived opposition National Democratic Alliance, he joined the MMD in January 1991 – the same time as Sata. A month later, during the party's convention, he was elected as its first National Secretary, and took the decision not to run for parliamentary office in the subsequent general election. In government, Chiluba nominated Miyanda to parliament and appointed him to the position of Minister without Portfolio, a role that was created essentially to administer party activities using government resources. In a move that highlighted Miyanda's close relationship to the President, he was elevated to the position of vice-president of Zambia when Mwanawasa quit his Cabinet post in July 1994. Miyanda's dual role as the party's 'enforcer-in-chief' and Chiluba's deputy, combined with his revered public reputation as 'Mr Clean', as well as his popular appeal amongst 'born-again' Christians, gave him an early advantage in the succession race.[93]

However, in the run-up to the MMD convention in late 1995, Miyanda came under increasing public criticism from Sata, who frequently cast him as an administrator who had run down the party and disconnected it from its grassroots support base. Characterising the MMD as 'sick', in need of 'treatment', and weakened to a point where it was not ready for the 1996 elections, Sata advocated 'a stronger leadership and more efficient research unit which would

---

91 Anthony Mukwita, 'Chiluba retains the MMD presidency', *The Post*, 22 December 1995, p. 1. Also see Malupenga, *Levy Patrick Mwanawasa*, pp. 131–32.
92 Interview with Godfrey Miyanda, Lusaka, 3 December 2013.
93 Jowie Mwiinga, 'Profile: Godfrey Miyanda: the most sober man in the MMD Cabinet', *The Post*, 17 May 1994, p. 7.

supply party cadres [supporters] with information on party programmes and activities'.⁹⁴ As the date of the convention drew nearer, Miyanda announced that he would not be defending his position as National Secretary, opting instead to contest as vice-president, a position that had been held by Mwanawasa, who had decided to challenge Chiluba for the leadership of the party. Miyanda viewed the position of vice-president of the party as 'more senior than the National Secretary'.⁹⁵ With Miyanda out of the way, Sata announced his candidature for MMD National Secretary a week before the convention got underway.⁹⁶

At the intra-party polls, Miyanda's votes easily overtook those of his competitors, Tembo and Luminzu Shimaponda, the Minister of Lands. The final poll was 901 votes for Miyanda against the duo's combined total of 337.⁹⁷ Highlighting the prime position that Miyanda occupied in the succession contest after the convention, the state-run *Zambia Daily Mail* hailed the new MMD vice-president:

> Miyanda's victory came as no surprise to many political pundits who felt that his main rival, Shimaponda, may have overrated himself ... [He] is highly regarded not only in MMD circles but by opposition leaders as well, has exhibited rare fortitude in difficult circumstances and rightly earned the title of 'defender of MMD', which he used in his campaign manifesto. He is imbued with the qualities of Mr Clean. The MMD needs such a man desperately at a time when the party is striving to improve its battered public image.⁹⁸

As for Sata, he easily defeated his competitors for the position of National Secretary, having run against the much-fancied Vernon Mwaanga, Frederick Hapunda, and Newstead Zimba. The former MMD Chairperson for Local Government and Housing polled 616 votes, ahead of Mwaanga (470), Hapunda (136), and Zimba (16).⁹⁹

In June 1996, amidst Sata's complaints that he lacked sufficient funds to run the MMD effectively ahead of the presidential and general elections, Chiluba re-established the position of Minister without Portfolio, which had been shelved since 1994 when Miyanda was appointed vice-president, and moved Sata from the Ministry of Health to fill the new position. This meant that Sata now occupied both posts that had been held previously by Miyanda, and now had enormous funds at his disposal for party mobilisation and other activities.

---

94 Milimo Moyo, 'The MMD is weak and not ready for 1996, says Sata', *The Post*, 18 December 1995, p. 6.
95 Interview with Godfrey Miyanda, Lusaka, 3 December 2013.
96 Moyo, 'The MMD is weak', p. 6.
97 John Phiri, 'Big guns tumble: Miyanda, Sata romp home as Mwaanga, Zimba, Chipimo fail', *Sunday Times*, 24 December 1995, p. 1.
98 Comment, 'MMD's new team', *Sunday Times*, 24 December 1995, p. 6.
99 Phiri, 'Big guns tumble', p. 1.

Miyanda, meanwhile, informed President Chiluba of his intention to stand as an MP in Petauke. Petauke was not only an influential rural constituency in the Eastern Province, but it was also where Miyanda's parents hailed from, although he himself had grown up on the Copperbelt. The President expressed support for Miyanda's plans and urged him to visit the area to acquaint himself with local party structures, traditional leaders, and other key social groups or networks.[100] After a fact-finding trip to Petauke, Miyanda returned to Lusaka to relay to the President the positive reception that he received 'not just in Petauke but the whole province. I was readily accepted, and it was clear that I would easily win the seat.'[101] Chiluba, who was responsible for MMD parliamentary adoptions, assured his vice-president that he would be adopted to contest the seat that had been won overwhelmingly by a UNIP candidate in the 1991 elections. In October, Miyanda announced that he would contest the Petauke parliamentary seat in the 1996 polls.[102]

Earlier in August 1996, Sata had declared that he would seek parliamentary election in Mpika Central constituency in the forthcoming elections.[103] Mpika was not only Sata's hometown constituency but was also considered the gateway to the Northern Province. The Mpika seat was then held by Guy Scott who later chose not to stand again. (Scott, a close ally of Sata who became vice-president when Sata won the presidency of Zambia in 2011, revealed that he had 'only stood in Mpika in 1991 at the request of Sata, who promised to campaign for me and said he needed me to reserve the seat for him ahead of the 1996 election'.[104]) Sata's announcement was preceded by an extensive tour of the area long before Chiluba nominated the MMD's would-be parliamentary candidates. Sata, a Bemba-speaking Bisa (one of the ethnic groups in Mpika), claimed that he had left Kabwata constituency for Mpika Central because he wanted to unite 'all Zambians' in the area 'against (some) Bisa people spearheading a campaign that only their tribesmen (not Bembas) should contest the polls and control Mpika district'.[105]

When Sata learnt about Miyanda's plans to stand in a rural constituency in mid-October 1996, and a few days before Chiluba handed the National Secretary the list of MMD parliamentary candidates for public announcement, he approached the President in private and advised him against nominating

100   Interview with Godfrey Miyanda, Lusaka, 3 December 2013.
101   *Ibid.*
102   *Ibid.*
103   *Times* Reporter, 'I will stand in Mpika, says Sata', *Times of Zambia*, 15 August 1996, p. 1. Sata had left Mpika in 1955 for work on the Copperbelt. After Zambia's independence, he settled in Lusaka. Despite this long absence from his birthplace, Sata still regarded himself as a local person in tune with the daily concerns.
104   Interview with Guy Scott, Lusaka, 18 March 2012.
105   *Times* Reporter, 'I will stand in Mpika, says Sata', p. 1.

Miyanda for Petauke.¹⁰⁶ Motivated by the desire to stop a rival from building a regional power base and presenting himself as an advisor with vast political experience, Sata argued that Eastern Province was one of the opposition UNIP's remaining strongholds and fielding the vice-president there was too risky, adding especially that Miyanda had neither strong personal nor political ties in the area, having grown up on the Copperbelt. To avert the embarrassment of having a ruling party and State vice-president losing a parliamentary election to Kaunda's party, Sata recommended that Miyanda be adopted instead in Kabwata, his former constituency in Lusaka, where Sata would help in his campaign.¹⁰⁷ Before considering Chiluba's response, it is worth contextualising Sata's argument about the threat posed by UNIP to Miyanda's electoral chances in Eastern Province.

Of the twenty-five seats that UNIP won in 1991, nineteen came from the Eastern Province, which critics viewed as Kaunda's home area even though he was born and raised in Chinsali, Northern Province. After its defeat in 1991, and in the wake of Kaunda's subsequent retirement from politics, UNIP went into a sharp decline. In September 1994, Kaunda made a dramatic return to politics, announcing that he had come back to liberate Zambians from the MMD's austerity measures, and was elected UNIP President in February 1995. Invigorated by Kaunda's return, and having failed to register any victory since 1991, UNIP won three of the eight parliamentary by-elections held in October 1995, all of them in constituencies previously considered MMD strongholds.¹⁰⁸ Going into the 1996 polls, the former ruling party was the main opposition to the MMD. Given the momentum that UNIP gained with Kaunda's comeback and the party's parliamentary strength in Eastern Province, Sata's argument that Miyanda could not be guaranteed victory in Petauke was thus not without foundation.

Persuaded, Chiluba agreed to have Miyanda stand in Kabwata, but expressed the fear that the vice-president would reject this late change, especially as Chiluba had already consented to Miyanda's request to contest the Petauke seat. According to Chiluba's former Minister of Presidential Affairs and two other senior MMD leaders, Sikota Wina and Katele Kalumba, Sata then convinced Chiluba to send Miyanda to represent the country on the tenth anniversary of Samora Machel's death in Mozambique, a trip that the President had earlier indicated he planned to attend.¹⁰⁹ On 24 October, while the vice-president was

---

106   Interview with Michael Sata, Lusaka, 13 January 2013. Sata's testimony was corroborated by both Miyanda and Silwamba, the minister in charge of the presidency; Interview with Eric Silwamba, Lusaka, 19 March 2013; Interview with Godfrey Miyanda, Lusaka, 3 December 2013.
107   Ibid.
108   Rakner, *Political and Economic Liberalisation*, p. 108.
109   Interview with Eric Silwamba, Lusaka, 19 March 2013; Interview with Katele Kalumba, Lusaka, 22 April 2014; Interview with Sikota Wina, Lusaka, 16 December 2013.

out of the country, Sata released the names of the successful 'MMD candidates chosen by President Chiluba', with Miyanda standing in Kabwata.[110] A little-known Potiphar Mwanza Mumbi was named the ruling party's contestant for Petauke Central. Around the same time, UNIP announced that it would boycott the presidential and general elections in protest at the government's controversial constitutional amendments that disqualified Kaunda and his vice-president from seeking public office.[111] Kaunda further warned of civil disobedience if the changes were not repealed, prompting speculation that UNIP might reconsider and field parliamentary candidates, especially in its traditional constituencies such as Eastern Province.

Upon learning of the eleventh-hour alteration to his proposed parliamentary candidacy after his return from Maputo, Miyanda expressed his displeasure to Chiluba, who explained and upheld the decision.[112] Chiluba also told Miyanda that though UNIP had announced a national boycott, some of the party's candidates were likely to defy their national leadership and run for parliamentary office. In the subsequent national elections, both Miyanda and Sata went on to win their respective parliamentary seats, polling 76.67 per cent and 84.82 per cent against their opponents.[113] Sata's other two main challengers, Tembo and Mwila, chose to stand in urban constituencies: Tembo won the Chawama seat in Lusaka while Mwila secured Luanshya on the Copperbelt. UNIP did not field candidates in eighteen of the nineteen constituencies in the Eastern Province, including Petauke, where the MMD's Mumbi defeated two challengers from smaller parties in a landslide win.[114] Both the process and the outcome of these elections had important ramifications for Sata's and Miyanda's political futures.

The first is that, by blocking Miyanda from standing in Petauke Central constituency, Sata succeeded in preventing a potential challenger from building a rural power base that could have been used as a springboard for a presidential bid. National politicians who have rural constituencies generally attempt to mobilise electoral support by claiming control of the regions or provinces in which their seats fall or where they were born. As Nyangira argued in the case of Kenya, African political leaders generally seek political success by attempting to secure the backing of their ethnic group before translating that support into

---

110 Times Reporter, 'Miyanda to stand in Kabwata', *Times of Zambia*, 25 October 1996; Mukalya Nampito, Miyanda contest Kabwata', *The Post*, 25 October 1996, p. 5.
111 Times Reporter, 'UNIP backs out', *Times of Zambia*, 24 October 1996, p. 1.
112 Interview with Godfrey Miyanda, Lusaka, 3 December 2013.
113 Electoral Commission of Zambia, 'Past election results', <https://www.elections.org.zm> (3 November 2023). Sata defeated five other Bemba-speaking candidates to win the Mpika seat.
114 Ibid.

intra-elite acceptance.'¹⁵ Miyanda's preference for Eastern Province rather than Copperbelt suggests he was aware of the transient nature of urban support and the significance of having a rural base. It also indicates Miyanda's strategic aspiration to secure a reliable power base from which he could marshal regional backing and ultimately project himself as a potential presidential suitor to the nation. While Chiluba might have been genuinely concerned about the prospects of defeat for his deputy, Sata's strategic exclusion of Miyanda from the informal adoption process, and his subsequent placement of the vice-president in a constituency where he would not be able to marshal ethnic support, demonstrates that he considered 'Mr Clean' a long-term threat to his own presidential ambitions.¹¹⁶

The second consequence is that Sata's victory in Mpika cemented his support among the Bembas, the largest ethnic-language group in Northern Province, and thus enhanced his own bid to succeed Chiluba. Having spent thirteen years as an MP in the capital, where he already had a strong urban support base, Sata recognised the importance of understanding and tapping into rural grievances before launching a national campaign. His pre-election message that he was out to stop Bisa domination of Mpika, despite being Bisa himself, shows an early attempt to win the support of the Bemba and unite their numerically strong vote behind his leadership; this was a mobilisation strategy that, as we shall see in the next chapter, he honed and extended to other Bemba-speaking rural communities.

Another consequence was that Sata strengthened his position within the MMD power structure and consolidated his relationship with President Chiluba. A year after the elections, and in the wake of a failed military coup against his government in late October 1997, Chiluba dropped Miyanda as vice-president for unexplained reasons, in a move that highlighted the duo's souring relationship. He appointed Christon Tembo as Miyanda's successor in Cabinet.¹¹⁷ Also affected by the reshuffles was Ben Mwila, who was transferred from the powerful portfolio of Minister of Defence to the lowly Minister of Energy.¹¹⁸ The fall from grace of Miyanda and Mwila represented a major triumph for Sata, who retained his Minister without Portfolio post and remained the most senior Cabinet figure after the president and the new vice-president, Tembo. Having successfully prevented Miyanda from establishing a power base, all Sata needed

---

115 Nicholas Nyangira, 'Ethnicity, Class, and Politics in Kenya', in Michael G Schatzberg (ed.), *The Political Economy of Kenya*, New York: Praeger, 1987, p. 26.

116 Asked when he started having presidential ambitions, Sata responded: 'When Chiluba was President. We all knew that he would one day go, so we aspired to succeed him. When you are a politician and a minister in Cabinet, the next position you want is President.' Interview with Michael Sata, Lusaka, 13 January 2013.

117 Mukalya Nampito, 'New Vice-President Tembo says I feel great', *The Post*, 3 December 1997, p. 1.

118 *Ibid.*

to do to put himself in pole position in the succession race was to deal with his three opponents' positions in the party, since none of them held a rural, stable, or clearly marked power base. Sata, the National Secretary, also hoped to secure President Chiluba's backing for his presidential bid. This is exactly what he attempted to achieve next.

Reaping the Rewards? Sata, Internal MMD Opponents and Chiluba's Third-term Bid

Although events would not come to a head until early 2001, calls for a constitutional amendment to allow President Chiluba to seek a third term of office were heard first several years before. Almost as soon as he had secured a second five-year term in November 1996, some members of the MMD began to argue that Chiluba would need more than two terms to complete the national and developmental projects that he had initiated. Over the course of the next three years, this message intensified while Chiluba himself remained silent on the matter and banned any debate on succession, fuelling speculation that he was indeed interested in a third term. Criticism from local and international actors and growing consternation among foreign investors finally prompted Chiluba to publicly promise – first in January 1998[119] and then in October 1999[120] – that he would step down at the end of his second term as required by Zambia's constitution.

In early 2000, Ben Mwila, the MMD National Treasurer and Minister of Environment, urged Chiluba to follow these assurances by lifting the ban on succession and allowing those with intentions of running for the party presidency at the forthcoming convention to begin their campaigns. The President refused, citing the risk of intra-party divisions. In response, Mwila called for Chiluba's expulsion on grounds that he was exercising powers not given to him by the MMD constitution.[121] In defiance of Chiluba's directive, he declared his presidential candidature towards the end of May, claiming the support of his home area, most chiefs in the country, and the majority of ruling party members.[122] His announcement was met with strong opposition from Chiluba, who, insisting that he would choose his own successor, vowed to ensure that 'Zambia would never have a Ben Mwila as President'.[123] Until then, the MMD Treasurer was seen as one of Chiluba's close associates and an influential political figure in the ruling party who would win the succession race

---

119 Ndubi Mvula, 'I want to go – FJT [Chiluba]', *Sunday Mail*, 11 January 1998, p. 1.
120 *Post* reporter, 'Chiluba promises to step down', *The Post*, 26 October 1999, p. 1.
121 *Times* Reporter, 'Chiluba to deal with Ben Mwila', *Times of Zambia*, 29 March 2000, p. 1.
122 Amos Malupenga, 'Mwila announces his candidacy', *The Post*, 26 May 2000, pp. 1 and 4; Amos Malupenga, 'Chiefs want me for President, says B. Y', *The Post*, 29 May 2000, pp. 1 and 4.
123 Douglas Hampande, 'Chiluba vows to finish off Mwila', *The Post*, 1 June 2000, p. 1.

easily if Chiluba backed him. His falling out with the President, and his rivals' reaction to it, must be understood in the context of Mwila's close relationship with Chiluba since the MMD's early days.

Born in Kawambwa, Luapula Province, on 17 September 1943, Mwila had a short spell in the public service after independence, a successful career in business starting in 1970 and a brief stint in detention for alleged involvement in a failed 1988 coup attempt against President Kaunda, before joining the MMD in 1990.[124] He persuaded Chiluba – who was known to be his nephew and to have benefited greatly from Mwila's care during his formative years – to contest the MMD presidency, and helped finance Chiluba's successful campaign at the party's 1991 convention.[125] Mwila himself was elected MMD Treasurer. Seen as the MMD strongman of Luapula Province, Mwila spearheaded Chiluba's presidential campaigns in the area during the 1991 elections, introducing him to chiefs and other important local support networks. Establishing these networks was important as Chiluba had been born and raised on the Copperbelt Province. After winning a parliamentary seat in Luanshya on the Copperbelt, Mwila was named Minister of Defence in Chiluba's first Cabinet. He rose to become one of the President's close confidants during the MMD's first term, and entrenched his political position by retaining all his party, parliamentary, and Cabinet posts after the 1996 elections.

But cracks began to appear in Mwila's relationship with the President a year later. In December 1997, amidst accusations from Sata that the MMD Treasurer was eying the presidency and channelling party funds towards his campaign, Chiluba moved Mwila from the powerful portfolio of Minister of Defence to the lowly Minister of Energy, and later to Environment and Natural Resources. Feeling that Chiluba owed him a debt of gratitude for the help he had rendered to his successful presidential bid, Mwila became frustrated not just by his demotion and Chiluba's reluctance to anoint him as his successor, but also by what he saw as Chiluba's failure to put a stop to what he interpreted as Sata's attempts to promote his own presidential ambitions.[126] On defying the ban on the discussion of succession, Mwila prompted a reaction from Chiluba that raised fresh fears that he was still considering a third term in office. However, the falling out between Mwila and Chiluba enabled Sata to forge closer ties with the President and further his political advantage.

In the month after Mwila declared his presidential ambitions, Sata used his powers as MMD National Secretary to suspend him from the party on charges of insubordination against the President, the creation of parallel party structures and non-compliance with the ban on talking about succession.[127] Sata further

---

124   Interview with Ben Mwila Jnr, Kitwe, 28 March 2014.
125   Interview with Vernon Mwaanga, Lusaka, 10 January 2014.
126   Interview with Ben Mwila Jnr, Kitwe, 28 March 2014.
127   Times Reporter, 'B. Y. suspended', *Times of Zambia*, 23 June 2000, p. 1.

proposed to the MMD's National Executive Committee (NEC) that Mwila be expelled from the party. On 7 July 2000, the NEC, with Sata, Miyanda, and Tembo in attendance, ratified Sata's recommendation and Chiluba subsequently dropped Mwila from his Cabinet.[128] Amidst media criticism that he had orchestrated Mwila's expulsion, Sata claimed he was merely carrying out his duty as National Secretary and argued that he enjoyed a 'warm relationship' with the former MMD Treasurer: 'Ben Mwila is still my friend. We talk, joke, eat and drink tea together. I don't hold anything personal against him.'[129]

Although Mwila went on to form his own political party, his exit from the MMD had important consequences for Sata's presidential bid and the succession race. The first is that it eliminated one of Sata's most formidable opponents in the race to succeed Chiluba and thus consolidated the National Secretary's growing relationship with the President. Until his departure, Mwila had been seen as one of the strongest figures in the MMD and a wealthy businessman who, combined with his role as party Treasurer, had easily enough resources to finance his own campaign at the forthcoming convention. The fact that he came from Luapula and was Bemba-speaking meant that he could appeal to the same ethnic and regional bases as Sata. In Mwila's deteriorating relationship with Chiluba, Sata saw an opportunity to drive a wedge between the two leaders so that Mwila would not receive the President's backing. Later, he capitalised on the break in their relationship to have him expelled, eliminate his candidacy for the MMD presidency, and consign him to mounting his campaign for the Zambian presidency outside the advantages of the ruling party platform.

Related to the above point is that Mwila's exit narrowed the pool of candidates who saw themselves as potential successors within the MMD to Sata, Miyanda, and Tembo. The latter two supported Mwila's expulsion for the same reason as Sata: they saw him as a powerful political figure representing a major threat to their own presidential ambitions. His familial ties with Chiluba and his role in the President's rise to power had placed him in a strong position to take over the presidency. As Minister of Defence, Mwila had been virtually untouchable; even when he had been demoted to less influential ministries, he remained influential and, without reproach from the President, regularly refused to fund the party activities of Sata and Miyanda.[130] This entrenched position of influence and power had unsettled Mwila's rivals, including Tembo and Miyanda, who, when he finally fell out of Chiluba's favour, took advantage of the situation by ratifying Mwila's expulsion in the hope of securing their own positions and interests.

---

128 Times Reporter, 'B. Y. expelled', *Times of Zambia*, 8 July 2000, p. 1; Nicky Shabolyo, 'B. Y. loses ministerial post', *Zambia Daily Mail*, 11 July 2000, p. 1.
129 Sheikh Chifuwe, 'B. Y. is still my friend, says Sata', *The Post*, 13 July 2000, pp. 1 and 4.
130 Interview with Michael Sata, Lusaka, 13 January 2013; Interview with Godfrey Miyanda, Lusaka, 3 December 2013.

Unfortunately for Tembo and Miyanda, purging Mwila only served as a dress rehearsal for purging them.

The expulsion of Mwila also sent a signal that no one should express interest in succeeding Chiluba. In the wake of his exit from the MMD, calls for constitutional amendments to allow for a third term were reignited. Seventy-two District Administrators (DAs), representing each of Zambia's districts, joined ruling party supporters in clamouring for Chiluba's third term. The DAs were officially civil servants tasked with improving service delivery in rural areas but had really been appointed by Chiluba to promote his bid for a third term across the country using government resources.[131] Support for Chiluba's third term was based on the notion that the MMD – and, for some, the opposition too – lacked a suitable alternative candidate to take over and carry his vision forward. Towards the end of 2000, and working closely with DAs and some traditional leaders, MMD Deputy National Secretary Paul Tembo and Copperbelt MMD Provincial Secretary Regina Mwanza embarked on a national tour funded by Chiluba to build support for his plans within the party.[132] Revising his earlier public stance, the President endorsed the third-term debate and indicated that he would seek a third term of office 'if those calling for me to continue are in the majority'.[133]

Unsurprisingly, Paul Tembo and Mwanza reported in early February 2001 that it was the plea of the rank and file that the party constitution, which limited party presidential tenure to two consecutive five-year terms, be amended to enable Chiluba to seek a third term and lead the MMD into that year's national elections. In response, the party's National Secretary, Sata – who had emerged to become the most vociferous proponent of the campaign – promised to 'petition President Chiluba to stand for a third' term and set 24 March 2001 as the date on which the MMD's NEC would sit to consider the subject.[134] Meanwhile, evidence that support for Chiluba remaining in power was not shared widely within and outside the MMD began to emerge in February, rose considerably in March, and peaked in April.

Of the twenty-five ministers in Chiluba's Cabinet, fourteen rejected the planned changes to the constitutions of MMD and Zambia, and urged Chiluba

---

131 Rakner, *Political and Economic Liberalisation*, p. 113.
132 Interview with Regina Mwanza, Lusaka, 26 February 2013; interview with Enoch Kavindele, Lusaka, 29 April 2013.
133 Bivan Saluseki, 'Chiluba has endorsed third term debate, says Mwaanga', *The Post*, 8 February 2001, pp. 1 and 4; Amos Malupenga, 'I will go for a third term, says Chiluba', *The Post*, 12 February 2001, pp. 1 and 4.
134 Amos Malupenga, 'We will petition Chiluba to stand, says Sata', *The Post*, 7 February 2001, pp. 1 and 4.

to reaffirm his earlier promises that he would step down.[135] Joining the third-term dissenters outside the ruling party and government were trade unions, diplomats from the United States and Europe, and regional leaders.[136] But perhaps the most organised opposition to Chiluba's attempt to extend his rule beyond his prescribed constitutional term limits came from the Oasis Forum. Unparalleled in the country's history, the civic alliance represented 'an auspicious wedding of the legal authority of the lawyers, the moral authority of the Church, and the popular authority of the women's movement'.[137] Over the course of February, March, and April 2001, and working in close collaboration with those in the MMD opposed to Chiluba's bid, the Oasis Forum embarked on a series of public campaigns aimed at mobilising public opinion in support of the retention of term limits.[138] However, this barrage of local and international opposition did little to dissuade pro-third-term advocates within the MMD. Chiluba himself predicted a crushing defeat for those opposed to his plans.[139]

The long-awaited MMD NEC meeting at the end of March failed to produce a clear position on the issue and only highlighted growing factionalism within the party. No less than twenty-two of the forty-one NEC members rejected the third term.[140] After failing to reach consensus at this meeting, Sata announced that the MMD would hold an extraordinary convention on 27 April 2001 to decide the third-term debate and elect new office bearers. In the run-up to the conference, several senior Cabinet ministers opposed to the bid, including Miyanda and Vincent Malambo, the Minister of Legal Affairs, publicly announced their intentions to contest the MMD presidency and become the party's candidate in the coming general elections.[141]

By early April 2001, two competing factions had begun to emerge within the governing party. One group supported the third term and consisted of the

---

135 Amos Malupenga, 'I will go for a third term, says Chiluba', *The Post*, 12 February, 2001, pp. 1 and 4.
136 Joe Kaunda, 'ZCTU opposes third term bid', *The Post*, 12 March, 2001; Joe Kaunda, 'Diplomats oppose Chiluba's 3rd term', *The Post*, 27 April, 2001', pp. 1 and 6; Thabo Mbeki, 'Important steps to deepen democratic practice in Southern Africa', *ANC Today*, Vol. 1 (6), 11–17 May 2001.
137 Jeremy Gould, 'Subsidiary sovereignty and the constitution of political space in Zambia', in Jan-Bart Gewald, Marja Hinfelaar, and Giacomo Macola (eds), *One Zambia, Many Histories: Towards a History of Post-colonial Zambia*, Lusaka: Lembani Trust, 2009, p. 283.
138 *The Post*, 22 February 2001, pp. 1 and 4.
139 Staff reporters, 'I am determined to fight and win the battle against those opposed to my third term, says Chiluba', *The Post*, 5 April, 2001, pp. 1 and 4.
140 Interview with Sikota Wina, Lusaka, 28 February 2013; Interview with Vernon Mwaanga, Lusaka, 26 February 2013.
141 Brighton Phiri, 'I am standing for presidency – Miyanda', *The Post*, 26 April, 2001, pp. 1 and 4.

President and his supporters, such as Sata, who became its prime campaigner and regularly harassed dissenters, accusing them of disloyalty.[142] The opposing faction comprised several senior Cabinet ministers and was spearheaded by individuals who harboured their own presidential ambitions, such as Tembo and Miyanda, both of whom had held the position of the vice-president of the country. Tembo and Miyanda had hitherto tolerated the ban on the succession debate only because they were convinced Chiluba would not stand and might endorse their candidatures.[143] When Chiluba appeared determined to have a third term, they deserted him and began to mount internal opposition to his plans. Their aim, as was that of Chiluba's faction, was to claim the two-thirds majority support from party members that was needed to make changes to the MMD constitution.

Since their interests coalesced around Chiluba's exit, Tembo and Miyanda also joined hands with non-state actors, such as the Oasis Forum, in mobilising ruling party MPs to protect the national presidential term limits. Two weeks before the convention, fifty-nine MPs, including forty-three from the MMD led by Tembo and Miyanda, had signed a public declaration in opposition to Chiluba's plans.[144] Seeking opportunities for upward social mobility under a new leader and, as one MMD MP put it, to 'give chance to other ethnic groups besides Bembas to rule',[145] the legislators – the majority of whom came from non-Bemba speaking provinces – also pledged to veto any attempts to alter Zambia's constitution.

Chiluba, however, remained unmoved by the growing opposition to his bid. Supported by Sata, he expressed confidence in securing the needed amendments at the convention and vowed to 'fight on and win the battle against those opposed to my third term.'[146] Recognising that amending the Republican Constitution would require the support of a two-thirds majority of MPs in parliament, the President tasked MMD Parliamentary Chief Whip Vernon Mwaanga to work privately with the Speaker of the National Assembly, Amusa Mwanamwambwa, who was also a ruling party MP, to ascertain the extent of the opposition to his plans within the MMD. He also asked Mwaanga to establish the prospects for success of a constitutional amendment bill if taken to parliament and to try to

---

142 Interview with Godfrey Miyanda, Lusaka, 3 December 2013; Interview with Vincent Malambo, Lusaka, 19 April 2013.
143 Amos Malupenga, 'Chiluba told me he won't stand, says Miyanda', *The Post*, 23 March, 2001, p. 1; Sheikh Chifuwe, 'Chiluba promised me presidency – Nawakwi', *The Post*, 5 October 2001, p. 1; Interview with Edith Nawakwi, Lusaka, 26 February 2013.
144 Amos Malupenga, 'Chiluba loses third term bid', *The Post*, 12 April 2011, pp. 1–3.
145 Interview with Ackson Sejani, Lusaka, 26 February 2013.
146 Staff Reporters, 'I am determined to fight and win the battle against those opposed to my third term, says Chiluba', *The Post*, 5 April 2001, pp. 1 and 4.

win back the support of some of the dissenting MPs.[147] The pair were instructed to disclose their findings to him in due course.

Meanwhile, at Sata's instigation, Tembo and Miyanda, alongside twenty other ministers and MPs opposed to Chiluba's plans, were barred from attending the acrimonious MMD National Convention and were consequently prevented from either defending their positions or challenging Chiluba for the presidency.[148] Shortly thereafter, they were all expelled from the MMD for alleged anti-party activities before later unsuccessfully contesting their removal in the courts. Convention delegates voted to amend the party constitution and approved the re-election of Chiluba as president for a third term, which, according to MMD practice, meant that he would become the ruling party's presidential candidate in the forthcoming national elections.[149] With Chiluba having secured the top post, Sata defeated Vernon Mwaanga and retained his position as National Secretary on the next day of the convention.

With Chiluba's sights now firmly set on altering the Zambian constitution, even amidst criticism from donors that he should respect the supreme national law, Chiluba argued that 'upholding the Republican Constitution does not mean not changing it', and declared that 'victory [in amending it] is assured'.[150] A few days after the MMD convention, however, Mwanamwambwa and Mwaanga presented their report to the President: the groundswell of internal party opposition to the third term had risen to sixty-nine MPs, making it impossible for his bid to succeed.[151] To pass a constitutional amendment bill in parliament, Chiluba's faction needed the support of at least two-thirds of the legislators in the National Assembly. Of the total 158 MPs at the time, 131 belonged to the MMD, which meant that Chiluba needed the support of at least 106 MMD MPs to secure his wishes without any support from the opposition.

Dissuaded by the prospects of defeat, Chiluba capitulated, announcing on 5 May 2001 that he would not be 'standing for a third term. I will leave office at the end of my term.'[152] Until now, the literature on Zambian civil society and conventional wisdom in the country holds that it was the Oasis Forum that

---

147 Interview with Amusa Mwanamwambwa, Lusaka, 5 March 2013; Interview with Vernon Mwaanga, Lusaka, 26 February 2013.
148 Brighton Phiri and Amos Malupenga, 'Enough is enough, declares Tembo', *The Post*, 30 April 2001, pp. 1 and 4.
149 Amos Malupenga, 'MMD convention gives Chiluba third term', *The Post*, 30 April 2001, p. 1.
150 Amos Malupenga, 'Victory is assured, declares Chiluba', *The Post*, 3 May 2001, pp. 1 and 4.
151 Interview with Amusa Mwanamwambwa, Lusaka, 5 March 2013; Interview with Vernon Mwaanga, Lusaka, 26 February 2013.
152 Nicky Shabolyo, 'I won't stand – FJT', *Zambia Daily Mail*, 5 May 2001, p. 1.

was responsible for Chiluba's failure to secure an unconstitutional third term.[153] However, that narrative overstates the role of civil society and underplays the role that internal party dynamics played in this. As I have argued in greater detail elsewhere, the reluctance of the majority of MPs within Chiluba's own party to back his plans had more traction in persuading him to abandon the attempt to extend his rule.[154] Mwaanga, Mwanamwambwa, and former Minister of Presidential Affairs Eric Silwamba, who were known as Chiluba's loyalists and had supported his plans, stated that Chiluba was prepared to ignore pressure from civil society had there been cohesion and majority support within the ruling MMD coalition over the necessity of a third term.[155]

In the wake of his collapsed bid, Chiluba dissolved his Cabinet, before appointing Enoch Kavindele as new vice-president and maintaining Sata as Minister without Portfolio. He later announced that the MMD NEC would meet in August 2001 to elect the party's presidential candidate, and urged interested contestants to apply for consideration.[156] Sata was now poised for action, having helped remove his rivals from the MMD, namely Kasonde, Chilufya Kapwepwe, Mwanawasa, Mwila, and, more recently, Miyanda and Tembo. In supporting the third term, Sata had sought to demonstrate his loyalty to Chiluba against those whom he presented as disloyal. His strategy was to ride on Chiluba's presumed popularity to remain in positions of influence and, if the President's bid collapsed, secure his own endorsement before contesting the MMD presidency in the absence of his rivals. Ahead of the NEC meeting, however, Kasonde rejoined the ruling party, prompting speculation that he was being considered for nomination.

On 22 August 2001, Chiluba convened the much-anticipated NEC meeting with thirty-seven members in attendance and six candidates vying for the right to succeed him.[157] The nominees were Kavindele, Sata, Kasonde, Silwamba, and Minister of Defence Chitalu Sampa. The sixth contestant was Mwanawasa, the former vice-president, whom Chiluba personally added to the list.[158] Chiluba set the electoral rules by announcing that each NEC member could vote up to

---

153 See, for instance, Gould, 'Subsidiary sovereignty', in Gewald, *One Zambia*, pp. 275–93; Fr Joe Komakoma, 'Aluta continua!' *The Post*, 10 May 2001, p. 12.

154 See Sishuwa Sishuwa, 'Surviving on Borrowed Power: Rethinking the Role of Civil Society in Zambia's Third-term Debate', *Journal of Southern African Studies*, 46, 3 (2020), pp. 471–90.

155 Interview with Amusa Mwanamwambwa, Lusaka, 5 March 2013; Interview with Vernon Mwaanga, Lusaka, 26 February 2013; Interview with Silwamba, Lusaka, 19 March 2013.

156 Shelkie Chifuwe, 'There is no substitute yet for Chiluba-Sata', *The Post*, 1 August 2001, p. 1.

157 Interview with Michael Sata, Lusaka, 13 January 2013.

158 Malupenga, *Levy Patrick Mwanawasa*, p. 133.

three times during the first round and that the three lowest-placed candidates would be eliminated after that stage. Chiluba further explained that the top three would proceed to the second and final stage, where each NEC member would cast a vote. In the first round, Mwanawasa polled 30 votes and was followed by Kavindele (25), Silwamba (19), Sata (18), Kasonde (10) and Sampa (9). Mwanawasa also won the final round, after securing twenty-five votes against Kavindele's eleven and Silwamba's one vote.[159]

In separate interviews during my research, several MMD NEC members who attended the meeting revealed that Chiluba had approached them privately prior to the elections, campaigning for Mwanawasa.[160] Meanwhile, two of Sata's opponents, Kavindele and Silwamba, disclosed that they were asked to stand for election by Chiluba who, in addition to making it difficult for Sata to win, wanted to 'democratise' and legitimise his nomination of Mwanawasa with a competitive but stage-managed NEC election.[161] Chiluba's interest in blocking Sata remains unknown.[162] According to his loyalists, however, Chiluba, who was facing widespread accusations of corruption at the time, wanted a successor who would protect him from prosecution. As Kalumba, Mwaanga, and Silwamba all stated, Chiluba did not trust Sata enough to assign him that role.[163] Having carved a name for himself in the one-party state as a highly successful lawyer who had defended high-profile dissidents including Chiluba when he was arrested for advocating industrial strikes in 1981, Mwanawasa fitted the bill. Chiluba's choice of his erstwhile vice-president may have also been influenced by the fact that Mwanawasa came from a small ethnic group in Central Province, which would leave the MMD candidate totally dependent on Chiluba and his dominant Bemba-speaking group for electoral support.[164]

Disappointed by Chiluba, Sata quit his Cabinet position in September and dragged Mwanawasa's election to court, arguing that the MMD constitution did

---

159 I am grateful to Katele Kalumba for giving me access to his personal files. Also see Webster Malido, 'We will win, declares Mwanawasa', *The Post*, 24 August 2001, pp. 1 and 4.
160 Interview with Katele Kalumba, Lusaka, 22 April 2014; interview with Vernon Mwaanga, Lusaka, 26 February 2013; interview with Peter Machungwa, Lusaka, 11 April 2013.
161 Interview with Enoch Kavindele, Lusaka, 29 April 2013; Interview with Eric Silwamba, Lusaka, 19 March 2013.
162 Unfortunately, Chiluba died in June 2011, long before my research started.
163 Interview with Eric Silwamba, Lusaka, 19 March 2013; Interview with Vernon Mwaanga, Lusaka, 26 February 2013; Interview with Katele Kalumba, Lusaka, 22 April 2014.
164 So confident of support from the Bemba-speaking constituencies was Chiluba that during the campaigns for the 2001 elections, he encouraged Mwanawasa to stay at home, promising to 'deliver the presidency for me because he wanted to make sure that he was the boss', Malupenga, *Levy Patrick Mwanawasa*, p. 140.

not allow the NEC to choose the party's presidential candidate.[165] Having built a power base in the party, he further asked the courts to order the MMD to call for an extraordinary convention so that members could vote for a candidate of their choice.[166] In the same month, he formed a political party, the PF, as a fallback in case he did not succeed in overturning Mwanawasa's election. Edwin Lifwekelo, the PF's founding Secretary General, recalled that Sata established the party between 6 and 9 September while he still served as MMD National Secretary. Lifwekelo, who was one of Sata's loyalists in the MMD and quit the ruling party in the wake of Mwanawasa's election, revealed that Sata had placed him and his colleagues in charge of the new party until his court case against Mwanawasa was determined.[167]

On 24 September 2001, Sata resigned as MMD National Secretary. However, he distanced himself from the newly formed PF a few days after it was officially registered, claiming that he had 'no role whatsoever'[168] in it. Yet when the Lusaka High Court dismissed his case against Mwanawasa, he quit the MMD altogether in late October and took up the leadership of the PF, announcing plans to contest the forthcoming presidential elections.[169] When asked when he would retire from active politics, Sata argued that he would do so after serving as Zambia's President in State House: 'I am coming from grassroots politics to rule. I will retire from politics through State House.'[170]

A few days later, Sata launched his campaign for the Zambian presidency. As shown in the next chapter, the two main constituencies of support that Sata attempted to mobilise between 2001 and 2011 were the same ones he had spent time mobilising while he was in the MMD. What Sata did outside the MMD was simply to broaden his appeal in both rural and urban constituencies.

165   Nicky Shabolyo, 'Sata reigns', *Zambia Daily Mail*, 21 September 2001, p. 1.
166   Sheikh Chifuwe, Sata obtains High Court injunction: Mwanawasa's candidature in court', *The Post*, 8 October 2001, pp. 1 and 4.
167   Interview with Edwin Lifwekelo, Lusaka, 18 October 2012. According to its original certificate of registration held by the Registrar of Societies in Lusaka, the PF was formally registered on 2 October 2001, nearly a month after its formation and three weeks before Sata resigned from the MMD. The party's interim leadership comprised Joseph Chipili as National Chairman, Lifwekelo (Secretary), Quince Musesa (Trustee), Dan Mpandashula (Treasurer), and six Executive Committee Members: Mary Phiri, Nyathi Banda, Danny Mushingo, Chongo Kasula, Patrice Mwale, and Regina Sondashi. At the time of the PF's registration, Musesa, Mpandashula, and the six committee members were registered and full-time students at the University of Zambia. Also see Sheikh Chifuwe, 'I resigned to avoid being chased, reveals Sata', *The Post*, 5 October 2011, pp. 1 and 4.
168   Chifuwe, 5 October 2011, p. 4.
169   Amos Malupenga, 'Court throws out Sata's injunction', *The Post*, 11 October 2001, pp. 1 and 4; Staff Reporters, 'Sata quits MMD', *The Post*, 22 October 2001, p. 1.
170   Webster Malido, 'I will retire after being President, says Sata', *The Post*, 26 October 2001, pp. 1 and 4.

Figure 6 In response to public calls for him to retire from active politics in 2001, Sata, said 'the best way to do it [i.e., quit politics] was after serving five years in State House as Republican president'.

4

Building an Alternative Political Force

Between 2001 and 2011, the governing Movement for Multiparty Democracy (MMD), under the party and national presidencies of Levy Mwanawasa (2002–2008) and Rupiah Banda (2009–2011), and the opposition Patriotic Front (PF) led by Michael Sata dominated Zambian politics. Mwanawasa was sworn in as president on 2 January 2002 after a narrow win against Anderson Mazoka of the opposition United Party for National Development (UPND). He polled 28.69 per cent of the total vote, defeating Mazoka, who obtained 27.76 per cent, and nine other presidential candidates, including Sata who gained only 3 per cent.[1] Of the total 150 seats in parliament, the MMD won 69, followed by the UPND (49), United National Independence Party (UNIP) (13), Forum for Democracy and Development (FDD) (12), and Heritage Party (HP) (4). Like Ben Mwila's Zambia Republican Party (ZRP), Sata's PF obtained only one seat. This tally is striking since, five years later in the 2006 general elections, Sata only lost to Mwanawasa, who polled 42.98 per cent, by a 13.61 per cent margin. The PF captured forty-three seats in parliament and rose to become the largest parliamentary opposition, dislodging the UPND.

After President Mwanawasa died in office, a presidential by-election was held in October 2008, and despite having insufficient time and financial resources to mount a credible and effective campaign, Sata lost narrowly by 2 per cent to the MMD candidate, Banda, who gained 40 per cent of the total vote. In September 2011, during the country's general and presidential elections, Sata, making a

---

1   An important feature of the 2001 elections was that six of the eleven political parties that contested the presidency were led by former MMD figures who had either resigned or been expelled from the ruling party over the preceding decade in relation to the divisive succession question discussed in the previous chapter. These were Sata's PF, Miyanda's HP, Tembo's FDD, Mwila's ZRP, Mazoka's UPND, and Inonge Mbikusita-Lewanika's Agenda for Zambia, highlighting the consequences of a poorly managed succession process. Only UNIP, Social Democratic Party, National Citizens Coalition, and National Leadership for Development did not directly trace their origins from the MMD. For the election results, see Electoral Commission of Zambia, 'Past election results', <https://www.elections.org.zm> (3 November 2023).

fourth try for the presidency, secured the seat with 42.24 per cent of the total ballot, defeating the incumbent Banda, who got 35.63 per cent. In this election, Sata's PF did strikingly well, winning sixty seats in parliament, the most of any rival political party. Although parties do tend to be younger in Africa than in many other parts of the world, the PF's rise from 3 to 42 per cent of the popular vote over a ten-year-period is unusual. It is this remarkable rise of an opposition party and a leader's efforts to build it that I explore in this and the next chapter. The present chapter examines Sata's rise from 2001 to 2006. The subsequent period, 2006 to 2011, is covered in the following chapter.

I argue that the rise of Sata between 2001 and 2006 derived from his ability to garner support in urban constituencies, such as Lusaka and the Copperbelt, on a populist message, hand in hand with his success using an ethnic mobilisation strategy in Bemba-speaking rural areas. It is worth noting that both points have been made before, most notably by Larmer and Fraser,[2] Cheeseman and Hinfelaar,[3] and Cheeseman, Ford, and Simutanyi.[4] What this chapter does is to extend this scholarship and highlight underappreciated aspects, such as why and how Sata was able to enact the populist and ethnic strategies in a way that other leaders were not. By drawing on Sata's case, I show how opposition parties have been maintained in post-colonial Africa in a climate that inhibits the growth of alternative political forces. I also demonstrate that there are different processes of mobilisation that do not follow the taken-for-granted wisdom in Zambian scholarship, which has argued that, since the colonial era, winning political parties first arise in the urban areas of the Copperbelt and Lusaka.[5] Sata's PF indicates otherwise, showing electoral support emerging in the rural areas then moving towards an urban support base.

This chapter is organised into three sections. Following this introduction, the next section provides an outline of the main trends of the political economy of Zambian history between 2001 and 2011 to facilitate understanding of Sata's political activities. I have, however, chosen to examine Sata's politics over this decade in two chapters to demonstrate how he expanded his electoral strategy from an initial focus on ethno-regional and urban constituencies (2001–2006) to

2   Miles Larmer and Alastair Fraser, 'Of Cabbages and King Cobra: Populist Politics and Zambia's 2006 Election', *African Affairs*, 106, 425 (2007), pp. 611–37.
3   Nic Cheeseman and Marja Hinfelaar, 'Parties, Platforms and Political Mobilisation: The Zambian Presidential Election of 2008', *African Affairs*, 109, 434 (2010), pp. 51–76.
4   Nic Cheeseman, Robert Ford, and Neo Simutanyi, 'Is there a "Populist Threat" in Zambia?', in Christopher Adam, Paul Collier and Michael Gondwe (eds), *Zambia: Building Prosperity from Resource Wealth*, Oxford: Oxford University Press, 2014, pp. 339–65.
5   See, for instance, Alistair Fraser, '"Don't *Kubeba*!" Beyond Patronage Politics in the Zambian Elections of 2011', unpublished paper presented to the African History and Politics Seminar, University of Oxford, 25 February 2013.

consolidation and building of a wider national base in the subsequent five years. Both the 2001–2006 and 2006–2011 phases were characterised by relatively similar trends in the political economy of the country. Therefore, I provide an overview of the entire decade in this chapter and do not repeat this task in the next. The final section of this chapter focuses on Sata's attempts to build an alternative political force from 2001 to 2006. In both this and the next chapter, I try to show how Sata, in competition with the incumbent president during election campaigns, attempted to mobilise political support around the major themes that dominated the broader historical context of this decade. For this chapter, I look specifically at how anti-corruption measures and urban unrest in a time of economic decline, or a time of economic growth that did not translate into improved living conditions for the majority, formed the political context of Sata's rise in popularity.

Economic Trends in the 2000s

Much of the first term of Mwanawasa's presidency was characterised by a contracted and shrinking economy, inherited from the Chiluba era. Among the issues that Mwanawasa had to contend with was the mass unemployment that had resulted from redundancies caused by privatisation and the liquidation and closure of state enterprises. In addition, soaring inflation, high interest rates, and a crumbling mining sector were aggravated by Anglo-American Corporation's announcement in late January 2002 that it was pulling out of Zambia's key mining industry owing to the declining price of copper, the country's biggest export earner.[6]

The government's attempts to reverse the economic decline were severely undermined by a staggering external debt amounting to US$6.7 billion, which condemned Zambia to the classification of a Highly Indebted Poor Country (HIPC).[7] In February 2004, in an effort to qualify for debt relief as prescribed by the International Monetary Fund (IMF) and World Bank, the Minister of Finance announced severe austerity measures including a one-year wage freeze on civil servants' salaries, a 40 per cent increase on taxes, a halt in hiring public service labour, and reduced funding to social services.[8] While President Mwanawasa defended the implementation of the new structural adjustment policies as essential to economic recovery, the opposition, led by Sata's PF, cited them as evidence of a government that was unresponsive to suffering urbanites' concerns, and promised to deliver better working conditions (without explaining how).

---

6   Bivan Saluseki, 'Anglo-American to Depart from Zambia', *The Post*, 26 January 2002, p. 1.
7   Miles Larmer, 'Zambia since 1990: Paradoxes of Democratic Transition', in Abdul R. Mustapha and Lindsay Whitfield (eds), *Turning Points in African Democracy*, New York: James Curry, 2009, p. 125.
8   Interview with Leonard Hikaumba, President (2002–2014), Zambia Congress of Trade Unions, Lusaka, 12 April 2011.

Meanwhile, the government continued to scout for new mine investors on the Copperbelt until mid-2004, when European and Chinese investors were found. The London-based Vedanta Resources Plc, for instance, acquired a 51 per cent controlling stake in Konkola Copper Mine at a cost of US$25 million, while the Anglo-Swiss multinational Glencore made a substantial investment in Mopani Copper Mines.[9] The Chinese-owned NFC Africa Mining plc acquired Chambishi Copper Smelter at a cost of US$20 million.[10] Shortly afterwards, between 2005 and 2008, 'Zambia's copper mines and mineworkers again found themselves at the centre of national economic and political life. A dramatic rise in the international copper price made Zambia's mines profitable for the first time in 30 years.'[11]

Widespread concerns soon arose, however, that the new mine owners were not providing adequate wage packages and conditions of service. This was worsened by the new employers' decision to stop providing their employees with schools, hospitals, housing, subsidised food, free electricity, water, transport, and a host of other social amenities.[12] Responding to growing criticism, led by Sata, that the government was unresponsive to workers' concerns, Mwanawasa argued that the new mine owners should be given sufficient time to establish their operations and recoup their investment returns. The death of about forty-nine miners in a huge explosion at Chambishi mine in April 2005 highlighted the poor environmental and safety standards of Chinese-operated mines, and reinforced earlier opposition claims that the government was pro-business and anti-worker.[13]

Soaring unemployment in Mwanawasa's first term also affected the informal economy in which many attempted to eke out a living. In the urban centres, in particular Lusaka, the difficult economic situation was exacerbated by a large influx of migrants who had flocked to the cities following the MMD's rise to power in 1991 believing the change in power would result in greater economic opportunity. That these aspirations were met only partially was manifested visibly in the expansion of existing squatter settlements and the development of new ones. As shown by Gould, liberalisation policies also had a devastating effect on the livelihoods of rural folk, resulting in a wave of migration from the countryside to the towns.[14] Life in the urban centres of Lusaka and the Copperbelt was hard, and failed to meet the economic expectations of many of its new residents.

9   Sikota Wina, 'BGRIMM explosives', *The Post*, 26 April 2005, p. 23.
10 *Ibid.*
11 Miles Larmer, *Rethinking African Politics: A History of Opposition in Zambia*, Surrey; Ashgate Publishing, 2011, p. 260.
12 Interview with Rayford Mbulu, President (2005–2010), Mineworkers Union of Zambia, Kitwe, 23 March 2011.
13 Larry Moonze and Claudio Nombuso, 'Another Tragedy', *The Post*, 21 April 2005, pp. 1 and 4.
14 Jeremy Gould, *Left Behind: Rural Zambia in the Third Republic*, Lusaka: Lembani Trust, 2010, p. 97.

Chiluba had initially managed to deal with the expectations of this potential urban support base through patronage networks, alongside frequent wage increases and a housing scheme that saw public workers and pensioners purchasing government houses at extremely low prices. Later, stringent donor conditions prevented Chiluba from continuing with these enticements, and he resorted to election rigging as well as the exclusion of rival leaders from electoral contests, in an attempt to remain in power.[15] Mwanawasa on the other hand, though constrained too by the need to meet the International Financial Institutions' conditions, refused consistently to draw support by investing in populist clientelism. As I later demonstrate, the absence of effective trade union leadership to articulate workers' and the urban poor's grievances, as well as the government's aloof stance, provided fertile ground for opposition, especially populist mobilisation.

Zambia's economy improved markedly beginning late in 2005 when, after more than a year of uninterrupted implementation of austerity reforms, the country qualified for nearly 100 per cent debt relief. The resultant huge savings freed from debt repayments enabled the government to resume funding to key social sectors, such as education and health, and to invest in infrastructure, after Mwanawasa won a second term. Spurred by the rise in global copper prices, low inflation, a strong Kwacha (the national currency), an increase in domestic food production, and an anti-corruption drive that served as a plinth for attracting more foreign direct investment, Zambia witnessed sustained economic growth rates averaging 5–7 per cent between 2005 and 2008. The government could also finally begin recruiting public service workers and improving the conditions of its existing employees. To illustrate: after several years without wage increases, civil servants received a 25 per cent pay rise in 2006, 13 per cent the following year, and 15 per cent in 2008.[16]

By late 2008, when Banda became the new head of state after Mwanawasa's death, formal sector employment had officially risen to 544,339 from 415,894 five years earlier.[17] In the crucial mining sector, employment rose from 34,966 in 2001 to 65,311 in 2008.[18] The construction industry employed 14,075 Zambians by 2008, compared with its total of 2,406 jobs when Mwanawasa assumed office.[19] This positive economic movement continued until 2009 when, in the wake of the global financial crisis, copper prices dropped sharply, leading to the

---

15   Lise Rakner, *Political and Economic Liberalisation in Zambia, 1991–2001*, Stockholm: Nordic Africa Institute, 2003, p. 109.
16   Amos Malupenga, 'Govt. will look at MPs' demands after public service workers – VJ', *The Post*, 1 February 2008, p. 4.
17   Central Statistical Office, 'Formal Employment Trends in Zambia, 1991–2010', *Labour Force Survey Report*, Lusaka, 2012, p. 14.
18   Ibid.
19   Ibid.

loss of 19,065 jobs in the mining sector in 2009 alone.[20] While the price of copper later recovered, mining companies took advantage of the slide to successfully persuade Banda's administration to abolish the popular windfall tax introduced by Mwanawasa in early 2008 in an attempt to increase taxation of mining profits from 31.7 to 47 per cent.[21] However, not even this reduced flow of revenue from the mines disrupted the government's significant infrastructural investments in the form of roads, schools, and health posts throughout Banda's three-year tenure, which was characterised by continuity with most of Mwanawasa's fiscal policies and development programmes.

Political Trends

Though Mwanawasa had mainly been preoccupied with the revival of Zambia's economic fortunes during his first term, he also devoted considerable attention to fighting for legitimacy and building a power base for himself within the MMD and in the nation. Mwanawasa had been elected on a very weak mandate and the MMD had failed to secure a parliamentary majority. In addition, Chiluba's refusal to hand him the leadership of the party, as well as a petition put to the Supreme Court by the losing opposition to contest his election to office, all provided incentives for an urgent political realignment.[22] Beginning in early 2002, Mwanawasa set out to consolidate his power within the MMD, to widen his appeal beyond the areas where he received most votes, and to build a working coalition in parliament to enable his party to pass legislation.

In March 2002, the MMD's National Executive Committee (NEC), including several of Chiluba's key allies serving in Cabinet, elected Mwanawasa as acting party president.[23] The media suggested that Chiluba's move to concede party power could be attributed to his successor's alleged promise not to press corruption charges against Chiluba, as demanded by many Zambians. This claim, however, proved false when, in July 2002, Mwanawasa launched, as part of his 'New Deal' administration, an anti-corruption drive, and accused Chiluba of having plundered national resources.[24] He also lobbied parliament successfully to lift Chiluba's immunity from prosecution so that Chiluba could stand trial for alleged theft of more than $40 million of public funds.[25] Chiluba's prosecution lasted the duration of Mwanawasa's presidency. While it won the

---

20   Ibid.
21   Larmer, *Zambia since 1990*, p. 126.
22   Joe Kaunda and Reuben Phiri, 'FTJ refuses to leave MMD presidency', *The Post*, 25 February 2002, pp. 1 and 4.
23   Staff Reporters, 'Levy takes over MMD presidency', *The Post*, 24 March 2002, pp. 1 and 4.
24   Reuben Phiri and Amos Malupenga, 'Chiluba faces arrest', *The Post*, 17 July 2002, pp. 1 and 9.
25   Ibid.

President international respect and local support in non-Bemba speaking areas, it alienated him from some Bemba-speaking constituencies, especially after he dismissed Chiluba's loyalists from Cabinet in early 2003 and replaced them with several co-opted opposition members of parliament (MPs).

In a further exertion of power, Mwanawasa sacked his vice-president, Enoch Kavindele, in May 2003, over an accusation Kavindele had made against him about an oil procurement deal. The allegation was that Mwanawasa had breached tender procedures in the oil deal, which was mired in a lack of transparency and accountability. Nevers Mumba, a losing presidential candidate in the 2001 elections, replaced Kavindele.[26] This move, though, attracted the ire of the opposition who argued that Mumba's appointment to the position of vice-president violated the constitution, which prohibits the appointment to the National Assembly of a person who was a candidate in the preceding general election. In view of this, the opposition attempted an unsuccessful impeachment motion against Mwanawasa three months later. In addition, nearly four years after the presidential petition commenced, the Supreme Court ruled in Mwanawasa's favour in February 2005, despite having established that there had been several irregularities in his election to the presidency.[27] Mwanawasa's attempts to establish a grip on the MMD were completed in July 2005 when the party National Convention elected him president.[28]

Meanwhile, responding to popular demands by civil society organisations for constitutional and electoral reforms, Mwanawasa appointed a Constitution Review Commission (CRC) in April 2003 to rewrite Zambia's national law and propose the best mode of adopting a new constitution. The Commission completed its work in December 2005 and recommended that: a winning presidential candidate should secure a minimum of '50 per cent + 1' of the total vote; the vice-president should be elected alongside the president (as a running mate); Cabinet ministers should be appointed from outside parliament; and the new constitution should be processed through a referendum.[29] Initially,

---

26   Amos Malupenga, Joe Kaunda, and Brighton Phiri, 'I am humbled – Mumba', *The Post*, 29 May 2003, pp. 1, 4, 7 and 8. Brighton Phiri and Webster Malido, 'Mwanawasa justifies Mumba's appointment', *The Post*, 30 May 2003, pp. 1 and 3. Mumba was himself dismissed in October 2004 and was succeeded by Lupando Mwape, an MMD MP in the Northern Province. After Mwape lost his parliamentary seat in the 2006 elections to a PF candidate, Mwanawasa appointed Rupiah Banda, a UNIP loyalist, as his vice-president.
27   Brighton Phiri and Larry Moonze, 'Levy toast victory with champagne', *The Post*, 18 February 2005, pp. 1 and 4.
28   Amos Malupenga, Brighton Phiri, and Alfarson Sinalungu, 'Levy's victory is not genuine, says Kavindele', *The Post*, 16 July 2005, pp. 1 and 4.
29   Mung'omba Constitution Review Commission, *Report of the Mung'omba Constitution Review Commission*, Lusaka, 2005, p. 125.

Mwanawasa responded by claiming that such provisions were expensive and unsuitable for Zambia. Having been elected with a weak mandate, he was understandably reluctant, for instance, to invest in a provision that required him to win the presidency with more than half of the total vote cast. As the 2006 elections drew nearer, however, he backtracked and, pleading for more time, undertook to honour the wishes of the people soon after the 2006 elections.

After being elected with an improved mandate, in September 2007 Mwanawasa created a broad-based National Constitutional Conference (NCC) whose mandate was to examine, debate, and adopt the proposals to alter the constitution as contained in the draft constitution submitted by the CRC. With about 70 per cent of its 478 delegates consisting of politicians and government-appointed officials, civil society boycotted the NCC in protest at its composition, which the Oasis Forum argued was tilted towards the government.[30] As well as dispelling such concerns, Mwanawasa pledged to ensure that the 2011 elections were held under a new constitution. The NCC concluded its work in August 2010, two years after Mwanawasa's untimely death. Ignoring criticism from civil society that most of the progressive clauses were left out, Banda's administration took, in March 2011, a draft constitution bill to parliament for enactment into a new national law. The proposed legislation, however, failed to go through after the MMD's unsuccessful attempt to raise the support of at least two-thirds of the legislators in parliament, which was required for a constitutional change.[31] As a result, the constitutional review process that began in 2003 came crashing back down to the drawing board.

Banda, after taking over the presidency following Mwanawasa's death, started off as a weak compromise leader unable to undertake far-reaching Cabinet reshuffles without implications for his re-election chances. However, like Mwanawasa before him, he grew increasingly in confidence and set out to consolidate his authority within the governing coalition after he had settled into the presidency. He began by sacking from his Cabinet some of Mwanawasa's loyalists, such as the long-serving Minister of Finance, Ng'andu Magande, with whom he had competed for the leadership of the MMD and the right to succeed Mwanawasa. In January 2009, Banda became the interim MMD president and continued the alienation of Mwanawasa's close associates. The dramatic resignation, in July 2009, of the Minister of Defence, George Mpombo, a close Mwanawasa associate, highlighted the divisions within the MMD.[32]

---

30   Neo Simutanyi, 'The Politics of Constitutional Reform in Zambia: From Executive dominance to Public Participation', in Danwood M. Chirwa and Lia Nijzink (eds), *Accountable Governments in Africa: Perspectives from Public Law and Political Studies*, Tokyo: United Nations University, 2012, p. 38.
31   Bright Mukwasa and Ernest Chanda, 'MMD loses vote on Constitution', *The Post*, 20 March 2011, pp. 1 and 4.
32   Mutuna Chanda, George Chellah, and Patson Chilemba, 'MMD should allow Rupiah to be challenged – Mpombo', *The Post*, 7 July 2009, pp. 1 and 4.

Former president Chiluba, with whom Banda had begun to cultivate a close political relationship, was controversially acquitted of all corruption charges against him in mid-August 2009. The government's refusal to appeal against the court's judgement fed into the general perception that Banda had procured the acquittal on behalf of his ally and, unlike Mwanawasa, was tolerant of corruption.[33] As widely expected, Banda revised his earlier pledge to serve only the remainder of Mwanawasa's term (three years). In early 2010, he announced his intention to seek re-election and started to canvass support for his presidential candidature in the 2011 elections. Banda's turnaround prompted internecine factionalism in the ruling coalition and led to the expulsion of Magande and Mpombo, who had both expressed their intention to run for the MMD presidency at the party's forthcoming National Convention.[34]

In the final months of its reign, Banda's administration also faced constant criticism about democratic backslides, particularly the erosion of civil liberties. In January 2011, for instance, two local protestors advocating secession of the Western Province from the rest of Zambia, on the grounds that the central government had marginalised the area, were shot dead by state police.[35] About 117 others were arrested. As we shall see later, both the violent way the government supressed the political protests and the demand for devolution of power to local authorities became key electoral campaign issues in the region during the subsequent national presidential elections.

Meanwhile, another presidential hopeful, Minister of Works and Supply Mike Mulongoti, was dismissed from his Cabinet position in February 2011 and expelled from the ruling party a few weeks before the convention.[36] Having eliminated his opponents, Banda secured the MMD presidency unopposed in April 2011. However, five months later, when he came up against Sata in the Zambian presidential elections, he lost.

The Ethno-regional and Urban Opposition Leader

Sata's efforts at building an alternative political force during the first half of the MMD's final ten years in power can be divided into two sections: the Bemba leader and the urban leader. In the first section, I discuss the ethnic strategy that Sata employed to mobilise support in the Bemba-speaking provinces of Luapula and Northern. The second part examines his 'Man of Action' populist campaign, centred on economic grievances, which he launched in the urban constituencies of Lusaka and Copperbelt.

33 Chibaula Silwamba, 'Rupiah thanks Zambians for 'accepting' Chiluba's acquittal', *The Post*, 19 August 2009, pp. 1 and 4.
34 Patson Chilemba and Kombe Chimpinde, 'MMD ready for consequences of expelling Mpombo, Magande – VJ', *The Post*, 6 September 2010, p. 1.
35 Mwala Kalaluka, 'Cops shoot dead Mongu youth', *The Post*, 15 January 2011, pp. 1 and 4.
36 Kombe Chimpinde, Ernest Chanda, and Bright Mukwasa, 'It's a minor setback – Mulongoti', *Sunday Post*, 20 February 2011, pp. 1 and 4.

The Ethno-regional Bemba Leader

To understand how Sata tried to use Mwanawasa's anti-corruption campaign to further his own political ambitions in Bemba-speaking Luapula and Northern provinces, an analysis of his participation in the presidential elections of 2001 is required. Although it was not until early 2003 that events would come to a head, Sata's efforts to secure the MMD's main electoral bases, including the Bemba-speaking constituencies, date back to the formation of the PF in early September 2001. As discussed in the previous chapter, Sata formed his party, several weeks before he left the MMD, as a fallback when it became apparent to him that Chiluba was unlikely to anoint him as his successor. Until he openly joined the PF in late October, proxies, whom he had put in place while he sought to convince the courts to overturn Mwanawasa's election as MMD presidential candidate, ran the party. A long-time admirer of Zimbabwe's President Robert Mugabe, Sata had originally named his party MMD–PF (Movement for Multiparty Democracy–Patriotic Front) in recognition of Zimbabwe's governing ZANU–PF (Zimbabwe African National Union–Patriotic Front).[37] Much to his disappointment, the office of the Registrar of Societies, responsible for the registration of national political associations, refused to endorse the name on the grounds that it resembled the MMD too closely and was likely to confuse voters in the forthcoming presidential and general elections.[38]

After spending close to a month trying unsuccessfully to persuade the Registrar of Societies to register his party as MMD–PF, Sata reluctantly agreed to remove the MMD prefix and the PF was finally registered on 2 October 2001.[39] More than simply expressing his admiration for Mugabe, however, these efforts provide the earliest example of Sata's attempts to make the key constituencies of the ruling MMD party the backbone of the PF. This was particularly true for the Bemba-speaking and urban bases, which, as discussed in the previous chapter, he had mobilised successfully and persuaded to remain in the MMD over the course of the preceding decade. Sata had shrewdly anticipated that, if the courts dismissed his bid to overturn Mwanawasa's election, branding his political outfit as MMD–PF would go some way to enticing the MMD's core constituencies to his new party. As things turned out, his attempts both to overturn Mwanawasa's election and to maintain his links to the MMD failed.[40]

---

37 Interview with Guy Scott, Lusaka, 8 April 2011.
38 Ibid.
39 Ibid.
40 Amos Malupenga, 'Court Throws Out King Cobra's Injunction: Sata is destructive and out of touch', *The Post*, 11 October 2001, pp. 1 and 4.

Sata took up the leadership of the PF in late October, less than eight weeks before the December 2001 general elections. He began recruiting more members to his party. Notably he recruited Guy Scott, whom he had worked with in the MMD, and appointed him PF Spokesperson and Chairperson for Agriculture.[41] Lacking any distinct campaign message, Sata tried to win voters' support by highlighting his positive record as a 'Man of Action', which was an image he had cultivated when he worked under the presidencies of Kaunda and Chiluba. He also began a campaign to discredit Mwanawasa, describing him as 'Chiluba's dummy',[42] 'sick',[43] a 'cabbage'[44] and a non-Zambian 'Yao from Malawi'[45] who should not be entrusted with the national leadership. His efforts, however, struck no chord with most of the electorate. Out of the eleven presidential candidates who contested the polls, Sata finished seventh, as shown in Table 3. The 3 per cent of the national vote that he received came from the Bemba-speaking Luapula and Northern provinces. Although he had put up 104 candidates from his party to run for parliamentary office, only one, in his home area of Northern Province, succeeded.

Sata's poor electoral performance in 2001 resulted from three main factors. First, he lacked sufficient time to convert his individual organisational skills to the party level and marshal the necessary resources essential to mounting an effective campaign.[46] Nonetheless, even with his paltry 3 per cent of the total vote, Sata outperformed three other opposition leaders who had had more time than him to campaign. This outcome, given his party's limitations, highlighted Sata's potential to organise and, given enough time, to succeed.

---

41 Scott later rose to the positions of PF Secretary General and Vice-President.
42 Martin Kunolu, 'Mwanawasa is Chiluba's dummy – Sata', *The Post*, 24 December 2001, p. 4.
43 Sheikh Chifuwe, 'Mwanawasa's health has worsened – Sata', *The Post*, 22 December 2001, p. 5.
44 Joe Kaunda, 'I am steak, not cabbage, declares Mwanawasa', *The Post*, 22 December 2001, pp. 1 and 4. Sata's 'cabbage' remarks were in reference to the injuries Mwanawasa had suffered in 1992, while he was Zambia's Vice-President, following a near-fatal road traffic accident that was popularly alleged to have been an attempt to eliminate him.
45 Martin Kunolu, 'Mwanawasa is a Yao from Malawi, claims Sata', *The Post*, 16 November 2001, p. 4. Here, Sata was effectively drawing attention to the 1996 Constitutional amendment, introduced by Chiluba and discussed in the previous chapter, that prevented Kaunda from contesting the 1996 elections. By claiming that Mwanawasa was from Malawi, he was seeking to delegitimise his candidacy in the eyes of the voters by presenting him as a foreigner.
46 Interview with Michael Sata, Lusaka, 26 April 2011.

Table 3 Results of the presidential election, 2001.

Candidate	Party	Total votes	Percentage of presidential vote
Levy Mwanawasa	MMD	506,694	28.69
Anderson Mazoka	UPND	472,797	26.76
Christon Tembo	FDD	228,861	12.96
Tilyenji Kaunda	UNIP	175,898	9.96
Godfrey Miyanda	HP	140,678	7.96
Ben Mwila	ZRP	85,472	4.84
Michael Sata	PF	59,172	3.35
Nevers Mumba	NCC*	38,860	2.20
Gwendoline Konie	SDP	10,253	0.58
Inonge M. Lewanika	AZ	9,882	0.56
Yobert Shamapande	NLD	9,481	0.54
Total		1,738,048	98.4
Total voter turnout		1,766,356	67.81

* National Citizens' Coalition.
Source: Electoral Commission of Zambia.

A second factor that impacted Sata's electoral showing in 2001 was his closeness to Chiluba, which seriously damaged his reputation, especially in urban centres like Lusaka and the Copperbelt. Sata's key role in Chiluba's third term bid destroyed almost irreparably the support that he had once commanded from the public. Unlike the other opposition leaders, such as Tembo and Miyanda, whose campaigns benefited from the popular belief that they had defended the constitution from Chiluba's unsuccessful attempts to extend his rule, Sata had no coherent message to present to national voters and was widely regarded as a disruptive 'political clown',[47] a 'scatterbrain',[48] and a violent thug unworthy of electoral support.

Last, but not the least, the presence within the MMD of several prominent Bemba-speaking political figures from Luapula and Northern provinces such as President Chiluba (also leader of the ruling party), Minister of Defence Chitalu Sampa (National Chairman), Home Affairs Minister Peter Machungwa (Treasurer), and Minister of Finance Katele Kalumba (Chairperson for Health) made it difficult for Sata to persuade the Bembaphone electoral bases of

---

47   Sheikh Chifuwe, 'Sata is a clown, charges Kavindele', *The Post*, 14 November 2001, pp. 1 and 4.
48   Sheikh Chifuwe, 'Sata has a split mind, says Zukas', *The Post*, 22 December 2001, pp. 1 and 4.

the MMD to move with him to the PF.[49] In addition, as demonstrated in the previous chapter, the fact that Sata had earlier presented the governing MMD as the rightful political platform for these constituencies made his task even harder. To compound this, the lack of a political message that would sway not only Bemba political leaders, but also Bemba-speaking voters more broadly, undermined his campaign. However, when President Mwanawasa launched his anti-corruption drive in July 2002, he provided Sata with the narrative to mobilise this constituency and resurrect his declining political fortunes in the ensuing years.

The Ethno-regional Bemba Leader: Sata, Anti-corruption, and Ethno-regional Appeal

Calls to lift Chiluba's immunity from prosecution so that he could stand trial for his alleged plunder of national resources started soon after Mwanawasa's election.[50] Mwanawasa initially resisted these appeals, citing a lack of sufficient evidence on which to initiate a court case. However, increased criticism from the independent press, civil society, donors, and opposition parties that he was shielding his predecessor from legal action, along with his divisive feud with Chiluba for the leadership of the MMD, appear to have persuaded Mwanawasa to rethink his position. Going along with President Mwanawasa's recommendation, Parliament withdrew Chiluba's immunity in July 2002. Chiluba legally challenged the decision on procedural grounds, making an appeal to the Supreme Court. He lost the case in February 2003 and his trial commenced.

Charged alongside Chiluba were several top officials from his administration, such as former Minister of Finance Katele Kalumba, ex-Permanent Secretary Stella Chibanda and senior economist Bede Mphande. Others included former Zambia Security Intelligence Service Director General Xavier Chungu, Zambia's former Ambassador to the United States of America Atan Shansonga, and former Zambia National Commercial Bank Managing Director Samuel Musonda. The rest were Chiluba's ex-presidential aide Richard Sakala, two former managing directors of Access Financial Services Limited, Faustin Kabwe and Aaron Chungu, former Ministry of Health Permanent Secretary Kashiwa Bulaya, and former Secretary to the Treasury Boniface Nonde. All but one (Sakala) of the twelve accused persons were Bemba-speaking figures from Luapula and Northern provinces, home to Sata and the Bemba-speaking ethno-language group.

The prosecution of Chiluba and his co-accused divided the ruling party into two factions: those allied to the former president, and those who retained loyalty to Mwanawasa. The former group, comprising mainly prominent

---

49   Interview with Katele Kalumba, Lusaka, 11 March 2012.
50   Brighton Phiri and Speedwell Mupuchi, 'Probe Chiluba over $90m theft – Prof. Hansungule', *The Post*, 22 February 2002, pp. 1 and 4.

Bemba-speaking figures who held senior positions in the MMD, such as National Chairman Chitalu Sampa, Treasurer Peter Machungwa, International Relations Chairperson Valentine Kayope, and several lawmakers from Luapula and Northern provinces, protested against Chiluba's prosecution, contending that it was an ethno-regional campaign. Mwanawasa rejected the claims and challenged the Chiluba loyalists, whom he also accused of planning to 'form a [breakaway] party on a tribal basis', to quit the MMD:

> Chiluba did not put me in power but the electorate. If you can't fit in the new deal government, get out and don't waste time. I have no apologies to [make to] thieves ... Don't think that you are clever, just leave the party because you are stinking and dirty.[51]

Mwanawasa, seeking to build a power base for himself both within the MMD and across the country and to win support for his agenda on economic reform, embarked on a national campaign to mobilise support for his anti-corruption drive. He sharply criticised the excesses of the Chiluba era and vowed to ensure that

> all plunderers stand trial [and] fail in their way to elude justice. We are going to ensure that they suffer the same consequences they caused on you (the Zambian people) when they were running government. I am determined to fight corruption and financial indiscipline in government. I came into politics to fight corruption and revive the economy ... I have no apologies to [make to] thieves. I repeat, they are stinking; they are dirty ...[52]

Starting in early 2003, Mwanawasa also began purging dissenting MMD leaders from government and the ruling party, though some of them obtained court injunctions that stayed their expulsions until the 2006 elections. It is worth noting that, apart from the fragmentation of opposition parties and the use of state resources, Mwanawasa's narrow victory in 2001 was secured mainly on the electoral support that he obtained from the Bemba-speaking areas, where Chiluba and other Bemba MMD leaders overtly campaigned for him. It was therefore expected that senior Cabinet positions and the allocation of significant state resources would head to the Bemba. The pre-election deals reinforce this point. Prior to the December 2001 elections, and as a condition for his adoption as MMD's presidential candidate, Chiluba had drawn for Mwanawasa a list of prominent Bembas to be appointed to government after elections to maintain MMD support in the Bemba-speaking heartlands.

---

51 Webster Malido, 'You are stinking, dirty, Levy tells MMD rebels', *The Post*, 9 March 2003, pp. 1 and 5.

52 Webster Malido, 'I have no apologies to thieves – Levy', *The Post*, 13 April 2003, pp. 1 and 4; *ibid*.

Figure 7 In March 2003, President Mwanawasa criticised as 'stinking and dirty' ruling party Members of Parliament who questioned his anti-corruption campaign. This remark was seized upon and turned into a campaign message against him by Sata.

Chiluba specifically identified one of them, Emmanuel Kasonde, a prominent Bemba politician, for the position of vice-president.[53]

More inclined towards technocracy rather than populist or clientelist networks, Mwanawasa rewrote these pre-election bargains after ascending to power. Ensuring that no Bemba speaker occupied the top two positions in Cabinet, a first in Zambia's political history, he appointed Enoch Kavindele, a non-Bemba from North-Western Province, as vice-president. In addition to dropping Machungwa, Sampa, and Eric Silwamba (formerly Presidential Affairs Minister), who were three of Chiluba's closest allies and had campaigned heavily for him in Bemba-speaking areas, from his Cabinet, Mwanawasa also filled the public service – especially foreign missions, which had been packed with Bemba speakers under Chiluba – with technocratic staff from different ethnic groups, prompting the perception that Bemba speakers were being marginalised. This sentiment was exacerbated by the outcome of the 2001 presidential election, which confirmed arguments by Posner[54] and Scaritt[55] on the enduring salience of ethnicity to Zambia's political configuration, particularly if the top three positions of the most successful political parties are considered.

The MMD's victory in 2001 had hinged on winning the Bembaphone heartlands where Chiluba had ethno-regional appeal, as well as Central Province, where Mwanawasa hailed from. The UPND had won in Southern province, where its Tonga leader Mazoka came from, and in the Western and North-Western provinces, where Mazoka had built support around other ethnic 'big men' from those regions.[56] The FDD, whose leader Tembo hailed from Eastern Province, performed well in the east, though the party had also benefited from urban discontent in Lusaka arising from the third-term debacle. The fact that the UPND emerged from the elections as the largest parliamentary opposition, followed by the FDD, meant that, for the first time since independence, the dominant Bemba-speaking group had little representation at the top political level, as both the presidency and the top opposition positions went to non-Bemba speaking groups. In Mwanawasa, Mazoka, and Tembo, the Bemba-speaking group saw not only a threat to their historical dominance of the political space but a relocation of power to other ethno-language groups.

---

53   Interview with Katele Kalumba, Chiengi, 7 April 2011; Interview with Vernon Mwaanga, Lusaka, 18 April 2011.
54   Daniel Posner, *Institutions and Ethnic Politics in Africa*, Cambridge: Cambridge University Press, 2005.
55   James Scaritt, 'The Strategic Choices of Multi-ethnic Parties in Zambia's Dominant and Personality Party System', *Journal of Commonwealth and Comparative Politics*, 44, 2 (2006), pp. 234–46.
56   Sata had refused to join the UPND in 2001, claiming it 'was formed to fight Bemba'; Interview with Michael Sata, Lusaka, 26 April 2011.

It is within this broader political context, including Mwanawasa's failure to honour pre-election bargains, that the prosecution of Chiluba and his co-accused, the expulsion of influential Bemba-speaking politicians from the MMD, and the absence of a party led by a Bemba speaker among the country's main political parties after the 2001 elections, that Sata's rise must be understood. These factors combined to strengthen Bemba-speaking MMD leaders' claims of victimisation and stimulate a sense of exclusion among the electorate in the Bemba-speaking rural communities, illustrated by the complaints of several chiefs. Mwata Kazembe, the most prominent chief in Luapula Province, Chiluba's home area, led the complaints a few months into Chiluba's trial, saying he was 'offended by the arrest of Chiluba'.[57] Another traditional leader, Katuta Kampemba, said 'people in the region were very disappointed with Mwanawasa who was now harassing Chiluba after he [Chiluba] put him in office'.[58] Appealing to the President to drop the charges against Chiluba and his co-accused, Kampemba contended that 'it is normal for anyone to make a mistake by way of stealing'.[59] (Although Mwanawasa was later to seek to pacify the situation upon realising the danger that Sata posed, most Bemba votes had already left the MMD by then and were never to return.) For disaffected Bemba-speaking politicians, the implosion of the ruling party from within meant that there was need for another centre of power. For the voters, the absence of any political party or leader that could articulate their frustrations with and demands on the state in the aftermath of the 2001 polls meant that there was need for realignment.

Capitalising on the Bembas' sense of victimisation, Sata welcomed the disenchanted Bemba MMD members into the PF and began a conscious and sustained ethnic mobilisation as a counter-reaction to the kind of politics that Mwanawasa represented. While Mwanawasa used his anti-corruption drive to break away from his predecessor's stronghold and establish his own alignment of political support, Sata took and reversed Mwanawasa's seemingly innocuous remark that MMD Bemba-speaking MPs opposing his anti-corruption fight were 'stinking and dirty'. The statement was depicted cynically by the PF leader as a criticism of all Bemba-speaking people in general, which helped him to mobilise Bemba voters. He described the government's anti-corruption campaign that had resulted in the arrest and prosecution of Chiluba and his Bemba-speaking co-accused as a moral attack against the Bemba-speaking people, who in prejudiced popular stereotypes had been portrayed as thieves. This mobilisation activity in the rural hinterlands of Bemba-speaking constituencies launched the PF. From April 2003 up to the 2006 elections, Sata rallied the alienated MMD

---

57   Sheikh Chifuwe, 'I am offended by Chiluba's arrest – Mwata Kazembe', *The Post*, 30 June 2003, pp. 1 and 6.

58   Claudia Nombuso, 'Don't probe Chiluba, Luapula chiefs tell Levy', *The Post*, 30 July 2002, pp. 1 and 4.

59   Ibid.

> *Figure 8* PF campaign advertisement.

members, and embarked on a series of public rallies and community radio programmes in Bembaphone heartlands claiming that Mwanawasa was out to persecute Bembas.

Conducting his campaign exclusively in the Bemba language, and targeting mainly the rural areas, Sata's ethnic mobilisation strategy found fertile ground amongst a dominant ethno-regional group that was feeling increasingly relegated to the peripheries of political control. He claimed that Mwanawasa had 'insulted the people of Luapula and Northern provinces who gave him a resounding support in the 2001 elections by suggesting that they were not capable of holding certain positions in government'.[60] Sata also attempted to mobilise political capital using the arrest of Chiluba and his co-accused:

> Voting for MMD will be endorsing the arrests of Katele [and] Chiluba ... Mwanawasa has shown that he was very evil by arresting Chiluba who handpicked him to be MMD candidate. He has thanked you by arresting Chiluba, Katele Kalumba and Xavier Chungu. Why should it only be the people from Luapula to be plunderers? You people have been rejected in MMD and you should realise this ... Even if Mwanawasa found you fighting with a lion, he will assist the lion to finish you off. You need to chase this mafia.[61]

Campaign advertisements, like the one above, with the words 'Stinking, dirty and chaff MMD Members are welcome in PF. Levy [Mwanawasa]'s message is

---

60 Sheikh Chifuwe, 'Levy has shown that he was very evil by arresting Chiluba, says Sata', *The Post*, 22 June 2003, p. 3.

61 Sheikh Chifuwe, 'Voting for MMD will be endorsing arrests of Katele, Chiluba – Sata', *The Post*, 27 June 2003, pp. 1 and 4.

loud and clear. Get out!! There is plenty room in the Boat [the PF's symbol]', were placed in the print media, capturing the ethnic theme that formed the core part of Sata's electoral message.

Several senior Bemba-speaking MMD ministers and leaders, who were dismissed from Mwanawasa's government between 2003 and 2006, found Sata's electoral message appealing, and joined him on the campaign trail. Asked to exculpate himself from charges that he, together with MMD National Chairman Sampa and Treasurer Machungwa, was campaigning for Sata, MMD Northern Province chairperson, Daniel Kapapa, responded:

> I have been suspended because I am stinking and dirty. I categorically deny these charges levelled against me. I am a very honest and sincere member of MMD. What is there now is marginalisation, vindictiveness, victimisation and persecution. This axe [of suspension] falls on me purely because I am stinking, dirty and come from a province which stinks. Therefore, I don't expect anything good whatsoever if I exculpated myself. I know that this axe is still falling on many other stinking Bembas. So my appeal is that let me live in peace.[62]

Sampa, also from Northern Province and who, like his suspended colleagues, was eventually expelled from the party before defecting to Sata's PF, complained bitterly that Mwanawasa had turned against him and the Bemba-speaking people.[63] Another leading MMD MP from Luapula, Afrika Chungu, took his protests to parliament, reproving Mwanawasa sarcastically:

> We have a lot of rivers in Luapula. I wonder why we can be dirty and stinking. Where is the smell coming from? If we have committed a crime, please tell us. We are ready to make an empire.[64]

Machungwa, the expelled MMD Treasurer and one of the longest serving ruling party MPs from the Bembaphone region, recalled that:

> Mwanawasa was known to say statements like 'Bembas have dominated Zambia and they should never rule this country for the next 100 years. ... I am going to ... reduce them in government and other private institutions to 15%'. If you noticed, the number of [Bemba-speaking] PS [Permanent Secretaries] in government before Mwanawasa came was quite high, but when he came, he reduced them. In fact, to some degree, even admission to institutions like [University of Zambia] UNZA was affected. He withdrew

---

62   Amos Malupenga, '"I have been suspended because I am stinking and dirty" – Kapapa', *The Post*, 4 April 2003, pp. 1 and 6.
63   McDonald Chipenzi, 'Levy has turned against me – Sampa', *The Post*, 12 June 2006, p. 3.
64   Bivan Saluseki, 'We are not stinking and dirty, says Chungu', *The Post*, 1 September 2004, p. 3.

most Bembas from Zambian missions abroad. These were not written directives, but we knew his aim was to reduce our influence. He stated at one time that 'you Bembas are stinking'. ... In a war situation, the enemy of your enemy becomes your friend. Since Sata was fighting Mwanawasa when I was also doing the same, we became friends [and] joined him on the campaign trail to explain to the people in Luapula and Northern provinces that we are being alienated and forsaken.[65]

Machungwa's testimony might be slightly overstated, but it confirms the enduring political uses of ethnicity as a valuable strategic resource noted by Posner and Scaritt.[66] In addition, the widespread complaint that Mwanawasa's appointments were based on nepotism, or, as Sata claimed, 'the Mwanawasa family tree' (his relatives), reinforces the view on the significance of ethnicity in this context.[67]

Sata's ethno-regional-coloured campaign message and his argument for a Bemba-speaking president reached a climax in 2006 when he pledged that, if elected, he would drop all the corruption charges that Chiluba and his allies were facing in the courts:

> I won't arrest Chiluba, Xavier Chungu, Katele Kalumba, Faustin Kabwe, Kashiwa Bulaya, Samuel Musonda and Boniface Nonde. I will only ask them to explain how they used plundered money on Mwanawasa. You don't have selective persecution and all from Luapula and Northern provinces. The question of turning Northern and Luapula provinces [into] a region of criminals is not fair.[68]

The PF leader's position won him support from the Bemba-speaking accused. At a public press briefing called a few days before the 2006 general elections, a weeping Chiluba appealed to the Bemba-speaking heartlands:

> We have suffered enough! I urge you all on 28th September to vote for Michael Sata. Let us get into the boat before the floods swell. I am sure he will remove pettiness in politics, which Mr Mwanawasa has introduced in Zambia.[69]

Guy Scott, the PF vice-president, recalled that Sata's position on Chiluba was not shared by the party, revealing Sata's central and decisive role within the PF and confirming one of the features of a charismatic political party – loyalty to the leader.[70]

65 Interview with Peter Machungwa, Lusaka, 3 April 2011.
66 Posner, *Institutions and Ethnic Politics in Africa*; and Scaritt, 'The Strategic Choices of Multi-ethnic Parties in Zambia's Dominant and Personality Party System', *Journal of Commonwealth and Comparative Politics*, 44, 2 (2006), pp. 234–46.
67 *Times* Reporter, 'Levy hacks at "family tree"', *Times of Zambia*, 15 June 2004, p. 1.
68 George Chellah, 'Sata pledges to stop Chiluba's prosecution', *The Post*, 26 September 2006, pp. 1 and 4.
69 Speedwell Mupuchi, 'Chiluba urges Zambians to vote for Sata', *The Post*, 18 September 2006, pp. 1 and 4.
70 Interview with Guy Scott, Lusaka, 8 April 2011; Kurt Weyland, 'Clarifying a Contested Concept: Populism in the Study of Latin American Politics', *Comparative Politics*, 34, 1 (2001), pp. 1–22.

At the polls, both Sata and the PF received substantial significant electoral support throughout the Bembaphone region. Sata defeated Mwanawasa in thirteen of the fourteen constituencies in Luapula and secured 43 per cent of the total presidential vote in Northern Province.[71] Of the two provinces' combined total of thirty-five parliamentary seats, Sata's party won eighteen while the rest were shared between different political parties and independent candidates.[72] The fact that Sata did not raise any other campaign issues in Bemba-speaking communities outside his pledges to stop the prosecution of Chiluba and his co-accused shows the success of his ethno-regional strategy of electoral mobilisation. However, Mwanawasa's winning eleven of the twenty-one constituencies in Northern Province (to Sata's ten) demonstrates the strategy's limitations.[73]

Sata's overwhelming support in Luapula resulted from the fact that most of the Bemba-speaking figures accused of corruption (including Chiluba) came from Luapula, which explains why Sata spent so much time campaigning in the area. Mwanawasa's electoral success in Northern Province may have resulted from his appointments of Nevers Mumba (2003–2004) and, after Mumba's dismissal, Lupando Mwape (2004–2006) to the position of Zambia's vice-president. Both leaders were Bemba speakers from Northern Province and their appointment represented Mwanawasa's attempt to appease Bemba voters and stem Sata's ethnic campaign in the area.

To summarise this section, Sata's ability to secure Bemba-speaking MMD constituencies between 2001 and 2006 must be understood to result from a factional power struggle within the MMD emanating from Mwanawasa's political realignment, the prosecution of Chiluba, and his Bemba-speaking co-accused, and Sata's subsequent ability to prey on such issues to his political advantage. Arising from their opposition to Chiluba's prosecution, several important Bemba-speaking political figures, such as Sampa and Machungwa, who occupied senior positions in the MMD and had campaigned for Mwanawasa in the 2001 elections were, between 2003 and 2006, expelled from the ruling party before they joined Sata's PF. The implosion of the MMD led to its losing touch with some of its key bases in the Bemba heartlands, where an overriding sentiment of marginalisation arose, and which Sata harnessed, winning significant electoral support.

The Urban Leader

In this section, I analyse the role that the economy played in Sata's rise from 2001 to 2006. Focusing on the Lusaka and Copperbelt provinces, I show how growing urban discontent with the severe economic conditions proved fertile ground for Sata to mobilise electoral support with a populist narrative, and present himself

---

71   Electoral Commission of Zambia, 'Past election results', <https://www.elections.org.zm> (3 November 2023).

72   Ibid.

73   Ibid.

as a 'Man of Action' who could get things done. By aligning himself with the daily struggles of the workers and urban poor, Sata was able to distance himself from the economic policies of the governing MMD that had overseen a drastic and austere restructuring of the economy, leaving many destitute. I show that Sata's ability to articulate urbanites' unmet demands, and position himself and his party as viable alternatives, derived from his individual experiences and populist interventions developed over the entire span of his public career.

'The discursive construction of an enemy': Sata, Economic Recovery, and Urban Unrest

Laclau notes that 'there is no populism without discursive construction of an enemy'.[74] This suggests that, for populist leaders to emerge, there must be suitable historical circumstances that they can exploit to generate sentiments of crisis in their audiences and, using charismatic language, articulate an alternative message. Researchers must thus pay attention to both the conditions that facilitate the rise of populist or charismatic leaders and the distinct individual qualities that such leaders possess. Zambia's economic context between 2001 and 2006 presented conditions favourable to this very process of the 'discursive construction of an enemy'. As already shown in an earlier section of this chapter, much of this period was characterised by urban unrest resulting from a deteriorating economy inherited from the Chiluba era. The government's attempts to resuscitate the economy, amidst a crippling external debt, saw the implementation of severe austerity measures that gave rise to job losses, a wage freeze, a considerable rise in taxes, a shutdown on hiring public service labour, and reduced funding to social services.[75] The net result was worker discontent and increased poverty, particularly in the urban areas of the Lusaka and Copperbelt provinces, where many, as earlier discussed, had moved to in an attempt to make a living.

After the economy began to register signs of recovery in 2005, owing mainly to a positive turnaround in the strategic mining sector, criticism arose that the government was favouring new mine owners, mostly Indian and Chinese, while ignoring employees' concerns about unsafe and poor working conditions.[76] This situation was exacerbated by the absence of a more radical or militant labour movement that could check the excesses of the employers

---

74 Ernesto Laclau, 'Populism: What's in a Name?', in F. Panizza (ed.), *Populism and the Mirror of Democracy*, London: Verso, 2005, p. 39.
75 Interview with Leonard Hikaumba, President, ZCTU, Lusaka, 12 April 2011; Interview with Joyce Nonde, President, FFTUZ, Lusaka, 25 March 2011; Interview with Ng'andu Magande, Zambia's Minister of Finance (2003–2008), Lusaka, 23 April 2011.
76 Interview with Rayford Mbulu, President (2005–2011), Mineworkers Union of Zambia (MUZ), Kitwe, 24 March 2011.

and the government, and scrutinise the relationship between the two. As a somewhat belated response to this situation, a few months before the 2006 elections, an aggressive Mineworkers Union of Zambia (MUZ) team was ushered into office. All along, apart from the Federation of Free Trade Unions of Zambia (FFTUZ), the national leadership of the Zambia Congress of Trade Unions (ZCTU) and MUZ had remained fragmented and were viewed by most workers as compromised. The decision by the ZCTU leadership under their president, Leonard Hikaumba, to sit on a government-appointed Commission that was tasked to travel, at a huge cost, across the country from 2003 to 2005 to collect recommendations for a new national constitution, irked many workers at a time when they were being told to make sacrifices.[77] But more significantly, all the unions maintained their distance from politics and refused to endorse a specific party, not even the PF, whose economic policies were friendlier to workers' interests.

The reluctance of trade unions to formally back political parties highlights one of the main themes of Zambian political history, and one in which Sata's rise in urban centres must be understood. Historically, Zambian trade unions, radical as they have been, have resisted party political affiliation. This is principally because the radicalism of the rank and file has prevented the leaders from being able to sell out – they simply get replaced. But it is also because politicians tend to rely on trade union support when they are in the opposition, but then discard the trade unions once in power.[78] A case in point is that of Chiluba, a trade unionist turned opposition leader of the MMD, who came into power with the support of the labour movement and went on to fragment the very machine that had sponsored his rise, the ZCTU.[79] He introduced harsh economic policies that had devastating consequences for the union, with half of its members losing their jobs in the period between 1991 and 2001.[80]

The outcome today is that while workers may support party politicians for electoral office, trade unions as institutions have refused to affiliate to political parties in an attempt to protect their relative autonomy and interests. The contradiction, however, is that, while today's labour leaders are generally viewed

---

77 Brighton Phiri, 'Levy calls for sacrifice', *The Post*, 30 June 2003, pp. 1 and 6.
78 I am grateful to Miles Larmer for this point.
79 Trade unions also played a crucial role in the freedom struggle, as shown in an earlier chapter. After independence, however, Kaunda's government amalgamated all the unions and created ZCTU. The main objective of federating them was to turn the ZCTU into a pro-UNIP vessel that would further the development aims and objectives of the party and the government. See Azwell Banda, 'Default presidents', *The Post*, 12 September 2008, p. 17.
80 Friday Mulenga, 'Fighting for Democracy of the Pocket: The Labour Movement in the Third Republic', *One Zambia, Many Histories: Towards the History of Post-Colonial Zambia*, Lusaka: Lembani Trust, 2010, pp. 253–54.

as compromised, when Chiluba was ZCTU leader he was perceived to have been firm in resisting government pressure on the unions and rejecting appointments to serve on government corporations. In selected and random interviews I conducted with workers in Lusaka and on the Copperbelt in 2011, I found that, although workers retained pride in belonging to trade unions, they accused their leadership of having been compromised by capital and the government, and argued that the unions often did not speak for them.

It is in the context of this connection between declining economic fortunes, urban unrest, and a labour movement that not only refuses to align itself to any political party but also views its leadership as discredited, that Sata's emergence as a formidable opposition figure must be explored. Sata skilfully mobilised the support of the workers by championing their demands against foreign investment and the government. Beginning in 2003, he embarked on a series of public appearances in which he rallied the poor, the disadvantaged, and the workers, arguing that the labour leaders had been compromised.[81] Calling for mass demonstrations against unemployment, high taxation, and poor working conditions in the new mines, Sata aligned the PF with the workers and turned himself into their spokesperson. He articulated a populist message that resonated with many urbanites who, disillusioned with the MMD's economic performance, sought an alternative.[82] What also became clear is that Sata concluded shrewdly that it would not be strategic to ally with union leaders who were seen as compromised by their memberships. He derided them as utterly unlike the union leaders who had successfully fought for the country's independence, when he as a worker had taken pride in belonging to a union. Rather, he argued that the national union leadership had become part of the parasitic ruling elite that had allied with Eastern and Western capital:

> Today if workers try to protest or strike, their so-called union leaders are the very ones who appear at the factory gate with a message from the government or mine owners, telling them to go back to work, and that their grievances cannot be considered until they first go back to work ... After which, of course, their grievances are never addressed![83]

In July 2005, Sata claimed responsibility for inciting a wildcat strike at the Indian-owned Konkola Copper Mine on the Copperbelt, where miners were demanding improved wages and working conditions.[84] Justifying his actions,

81 Larry Moonze, 'Trade unions have let down workers, says Sata', *The Post*, 27 August 2003, pp. 1 and 4.
82 Webster Malido, 'Stage countrywide protests over high tax, urges Sata', *The Post*, 27 February 2003, p. 3; and Speedwell Mupuchi, 'Govt. killing its people through tax, says Sata', *The Post*, 18 November 2003, p. 1.
83 Interview with Michael Sata, Lusaka, 26 April 2011.
84 George Chellah, Stephen Bwalya, and Nomsa Michelo, 'I incited miners – Sata', *The Post*, 22 July 2005, pp. 1 and 4.

Sata argued that he was attempting to bring to the attention of President Mwanawasa the plight of workers in foreign-owned firms. His statement prompted a strong reaction from government. The Minister of Mines accused Sata of 'terrorism' and economic sabotage, while Mwanawasa threatened him with arrest.[85] In response, Sata dared the President to effect the arrest, charging that 'all workers will come to stand as my witnesses during my trial because we can't allow Zambian workers to be trampled upon'.[86] Seeking to defuse the tension, *The Post* newspaper's editorial put the issue in context:

> Why should President Mwanawasa's government be so excited by Sata's claim that he incited the miners to riot? Are these people so stupid that they can't see that Sata has no capacity to do that? These people can't see that Sata is just mocking them. He is taking advantage of their betrayal of the workers. Sata is an opportunist who never misses a political opportunity to shine. The miners have a genuine grievance with their employers which the government is playing down ... Sata is merely attempting to take credit for the workers' own efforts, initiatives and struggles. He had nothing to do with the industrial unrest that has rocked [the Copperbelt]. And this is indeed an insult to the trade union leaders of the miners. Sata did not start those riots. Even arresting him would be a stupid exercise and one in futility. What is needed is for the government to pay attention to the legitimate claims of the miners.[87]

Instead of addressing the legitimate claims of the miners as suggested by the newspaper, Mwanawasa turned his ire on Sata. A week after the riots, he personally ordered the police to arrest and prosecute the PF leader, warning that 'those who want to bring *Chachacha* (violent pre-independence campaigns) like Mr Sata have no place on the free streets of this country'.[88] Police subsequently charged Sata with espionage, incarcerating him for over two weeks before he was released on constitutional bail. The case dragged for the next five years before the government discontinued it in September 2010. By that time, however, especially in relation to the 2006 presidential election, Sata had gained what he sought to achieve: presenting himself as a fearless advocate of workers' interests at a time when the union and government leaders were seen as betraying a key electoral constituency.

More significantly, Sata 'appealed to the workers to reorganise themselves and chuck out their MUZ leadership because they are being compromised', arguing that what was needed was 'the same militancy that existed in the mine unions during the days of the late Lawrence Katilungu and Justin Chimba'.[89]

85 'Sata is a terrorist, charges Lembalemba', *The Post*, 23 April 2005, pp. 1 and 4.
86 Chellah, Bwalya, and Michelo, 'I incited miners', p. 4.
87 Editor, 'It's not Sata who incited the miners', *The Post*, 23 July 2005, p. 10.
88 George Chomba, 'Arrest Sata – Levy', *Sunday Mail*, 24 July 2005, p. 1.
89 Chellah, Bwalya, and Michelo, 'I incited miners', p. 4.

This suggests that Sata was aware that if he was to have any credibility as a spokesperson for the workers, then he would have to appeal to the workers directly, over the heads of the union leaders. Thus, although trade union leaders – not trade unions – partly undermined Sata's rise to power, they also enhanced it. If the union leaders had been effective advocates of workers' demands, Sata would have been left without a constituency. Instead, this gap provided Sata with the space to fully exploit his image as the representative of the workers, because the union leaders had abdicated from this role.

There is an impressive amount of academic literature analysing the economic conditions that resulted in the disconnection of the government from the voters during the 2001 to 2006 period.[90] Within this literature, Sata's ability to capitalise on dire economic conditions, and to articulate an alternative message that resonated with the grievances of urbanites, forms a core theme. These works also note Sata's populist skill. Larmer and Fraser put it aptly: '[Sata's] skill is consistently to identify the popular mood (or prejudice) of the day, to ally himself with it to his advantage, and to associate himself with mobilisations that demonstrate popular engagement with the issue.'[91] It is not my intention to repeat here what they have said about *how* he managed to do that. What I wish to demonstrate, rather, is *why* Sata – not any other political leader – was able to construct such a powerful populist message and increase his electoral appeal. Echoing Larmer and Fraser's conclusion that Sata is a product of 'specifically Zambian conditions',[92] I argue that Sata's populist strategy was not new, but an enduring legacy of his long and varied political career that finally met the needs of the moment, which at the time were a result of a severe socio-economic crisis.

From its inception, the PF slogan was 'For political and economic liberation', a general message that did not appeal to any constituency directly. Playing on the economic crisis, Sata, with the help of educated elites like Scott, changed the slogan in 2003 to 'For lower taxes, more jobs and more money in your pockets'.[93] This symbolic statement reflected urban discontent with the managers of the economy and appealed to the needs of the time, particularly the primary concerns of the workers, the unemployed, and the urban poor. The 2006 election results (I discuss them in detail later), which saw Sata emerge victorious in Lusaka and the Copperbelt, clearly suggest that

---

90 See for instance, Larmer and Fraser, 'Of Cabbages and King Cobra'; Cheeseman and Hinfelaar, 'Parties, Platforms and Political Mobilisation'; and Nic Cheeseman, Robert Ford, and Neo Simutanyi, 'Is there a "Populist Threat" in Zambia?', in Christopher Adam, Paul Collier and Michael Gondwe (eds), *Zambia: Building Prosperity from Resource Wealth*, Oxford University Press, 2014.
91 Larmer and Fraser, 'Of Cabbages and King Cobra', p. 624.
92 Ibid., p. 637.
93 Interview with Guy Scott, Lusaka, 8 April 2011.

the electorate found Sata's message attractive. How did a politician who had always been close to the levers of power recast himself as the spokesman for the common people and the workers? Since other opposition leaders had also pledged to address urbanites' concerns, what made Sata's campaign message more appealing? There are several answers to this question, and I discuss three in detail.

First, although Sata had resisted following Chiluba's more corrupt practices, largely because he desired political office as a means to power rather than as a way of capturing the state in order to loot it as Chiluba did, Sata's ability to recover after 2001 derived in part from what he learnt from Chiluba.[94] Despite his longer career in politics, he became Chiluba's student, and from Chiluba he consolidated his populist skill and learnt the key weapons in a populist's arsenal and how to use them. These include an ability to promise people what they want irrespective of whether it can be achieved, to identify oneself with the people and their needs, and to play the part of the ordinary citizen who can represent all disenchanted groups and suffering citizens. Thus, at the height of the economic challenges in 2004, and to project himself as an embodiment of the poor, Sata claimed:

> I am ready to die for [the poor]. I know what it means to suffer because I grew up suffering; my father was a cook for a colonial District Commissioner. I was born under a tree in Chitulika village while those in government now were born in a clinic, on a bed.[95]

Sata also claimed he understood workers' plight and that of the poor because he had once been a worker and poor himself.[96]

To illustrate how Sata drew on populist rhetoric to drive a political point, I give an ethnographic example from my fieldwork in 2011. On one occasion, I had arrived at Sata's office for one of several interviews with him to find a crowd of street vendors who had marched to his office in protest at perceived police harassment.[97] Sata walked to a street nearby and returned with four police

---

94 Van Donge, 'The Plundering of Zambia's Resources by Frederick Chiluba and His Friends: A Case Study of the Interaction between National Politics and the International Drive Towards Good Governance', *African Affairs*, 108, 430 (2009) pp. 69–90, p. 69; Interview with Roy Clarke, Lusaka, 17 April 2011.
95 McDonald Chipenzi, 'I was born under a tree, reveals Sata', *The Post*, 25 August 2004, pp. 1 and 4.
96 Michael Sata, Mufulira rally, 19 March 2011.
97 The government had argued against the sale of merchandise on the streets of the capital for sanitary reasons. This move by vendors to seek help over such grievances was not unusual. Chiluba had during his years as president set up a vendor's desk at State house – a populist move that gave informal traders direct access to the head of state.

officers from the Lusaka City Council. Choking with rage, he addressed them in front of the vendors:

> You see these people, they don't have jobs and are trying to make a living for themselves because of [President] Banda's uncaring government. Don't harass them; these are my Chinese investors![98]

As the officers nodded their heads in agreement, the vendors mobbed Sata: 'ba tata besu aba tusunga' ['our father who looks after us']! In this situation, Sata assumed a paternalistic role, which he also came to be identified with. By drawing on his multiple life experiences, and through his effective use of symbolic representations, Sata was able to articulate varied campaign messages for different audiences, to reflect local grievances and to project himself as a little part of everyone: the worker, the struggling and poor citizen, and the unemployed youth. Drawing on religious imagery, a few weeks before the 2006 general election, Sata cast himself as Zambia's saviour:

> simple life-saving drugs like panadol are not there in Zambian hospitals. Our people are running away to go to other countries. Zambia needs a redeemer, Zambians want a Moses to redeem [them] and I am the redeemer of Zambia! We want to bring confidence in Zambians. Zambians have never had a raw deal from me; they know me ... [and] what I did. [For instance,] when I was Minister of Health, there were no shortages of drugs in hospitals![99]

Sata's ability to reflect various local grievances on radio stations and at rallies was extraordinary. The time I spent travelling with him to different rallies and locations in both urban and rural constituencies in the run-up to the 2011 elections reinforced this point, and made me understand how he may have earlier mobilised urban poor and worker support. Before a rally, Sata would summon a local person (either a party official or an ordinary member familiar with the place) and ask: 'what are some of the problems that affect you and your community?', and the responses would become his campaign message for the rally. Several of my informants who attended his rallies claimed that they turned up because Sata articulated and understood their grievances, but also because they found him entertaining. Two journalists who covered Sata for most of the 2006 elections confirmed that he used similar strategies during the campaigns throughout the country.[100]

Like Chiluba, Sata had little few principles as far as winning power was concerned, and had no problem with promising anything if it secured him

---

98 Michael Sata, addressing members of the police, Lusaka, 27 April 2011.
99 George Chellah, 'I am Zambia's redeemer – Sata', *The Post*, 15 June 2006, p. 3.
100 Interview with George Chellah, Lusaka, 27 April 2011; interview with Thomas Nsama, Lusaka, 3 April 2011.

Figure 9 In the run-up to the 2006 election, Sata, a devout Catholic, declared himself as 'the redeemer for Zambia'.

Photograph 4   Sata traveling to a campaign rally in rural Zambia.

votes.[101] Suffice to say that Sata did not suddenly adopt a populist stance or forge an alliance with the grassroots when he founded the PF in 2001: it was a skill he had that stretched back to his days in the labour movement during the 1960s, as shown in Chapter 2. As District Governor under Kaunda, Sata had been one of the most popular officials in government after the President and developed his reputation as a 'Man of Action' who gets things done. In Chiluba's MMD, he was viewed as a pragmatist and, as demonstrated in Chapter 3, always identified himself with the workers and urban poor. It was only in the latter days of Chiluba, under the questionable title of Minister without Portfolio, that his manipulative, opportunistic, and violent traits came to the fore. After 2001, even when the electorate recognised this unpleasant part of Sata's persona, they supported him, partly because they felt Sata was someone they knew and understood, but also because they were fed up with an incumbent who had failed to meet

---

101   Many of Chiluba's most fundamental 'rule of law' promises were turned upside-down within the first few weeks of his gaining control of the government. For details, see David J. Simon, 'Democracy Unrealised: Zambia's Third Republic under Frederick Chiluba', in Leonardo A. Villalon and Peter VonDoepp (eds), *The Fate of Africa's Democratic Experiments: Elites and Institutions*, Bloomington: Indiana University Press, 2005, pp. 199–220.

Building an Alternative Political Force   165

their demands. Sata, portrayed as a 'Man of Action', appeared increasingly to a growing number as the only realistic alternative.[102]

Another possible explanation for why Sata gained moral respectability after having been seen previously as morally suspect may be that a good number of Zambian voters in 2006 were young people who were probably less conversant with Sata's earlier career. Also, in times of economic crisis, voters generally tend to look to stronger, more effective, and even authoritarian leadership.[103] Several interviews with urbanites in Lusaka and the Copperbelt reinforced this view and revealed that Sata was generally seen as that radical leader. To draw on a well-known example: if Hitler scapegoated the Jews for Germany's problems, Sata blamed foreign investors, most notably the Chinese, whom he claimed had allied themselves with the corrupt ruling elites, as the cause of urbanites' socio-economic ills.

In the months leading to the 2006 general elections, Mwanawasa and his administration came under renewed criticism for the growing number of Chinese engaged as traders in the local markets or working in unskilled or semi-skilled positions in the construction and retail sectors. These workers and the volume of cheap imported goods in the country only escalated the already existing ill feeling towards Chinese investment, which was characterised by low wages, poor working conditions and the general lack of safety standards that resulted in the death of forty-nine workers in an explosion at the Chambishi mine in 2005. Seeking to exploit this discontent to his political advantage, Sata promised to chase away the Chinese, and the Indians and Lebanese, if elected, calling them 'infestors', not 'investors'.[104] Claiming that the three Asian groups were taking away local jobs, he pledged to give more leverage to Zambians in the running of the economy, particularly those sectors where these foreign nationals were mostly involved: mining, construction, and retail trade.[105]

Sata articulated a nationalist discourse that has been a historically distinctive feature of Zambian politics and one that not only equates foreign investment with profit and exploitation but also places 'local benefit ahead of foreign investment profit'. Sata's 'Zambians first' idea first found expression during the country's First Republic (1964–1972) when Kaunda nation-

102   Interview with Roy Clarke, Lusaka, 17 April 2011.
103   Ian Kershaw makes this suggestion in his influential biography, *Hitler: 1889–1936* (London: Penguin Press, 1998) and partly attributes the rise of the Nazi leader to the severe economic conditions that characterised Germany in the post-First World War era.
104   George Chellah, 'Sata threatens to deport Chinese "infestors"', *The Post*, 24 August 2006, pp. 1 and 4; Brighton Phiri, 'Zambia needs a new order – Sata', *The Post*, 28 September 2006, pp. 1 and 4.
105   Larmer and Fraser, 'Of Cabbages and King Cobra', p. 628.

alised major foreign companies claiming that foreigners were benefiting more than locals. This discourse disappeared under the MMD's rule as successive governments, in line with the party's central policies of privatisation and economic liberalisation, sought to provide an economic and political climate that was conducive to profit and in which it was relatively easy to conduct business.[106]

A second reason for the appeal to urbanites of Sata's campaign message is that Sata's straight-talking and sheer rudeness to those in authority resonated with the disillusionment that had taken root in urban areas during the harshest years of economic crisis.[107] It was also compounded by Mwanawasa's lack of charisma and slurred speech, which made him a subject of ridicule rather than authority. Sata's persona, however, tended towards the authoritarian. This personality may have been shaped in part by his earlier career experiences as a constable in the colonial police and subsequently as a minor functionary (until the later stages) of the one-party state. These positions in organisations that supported a tendency towards an authoritarian view of institutions, and a top-down system where people do as the leader tells them, may have strongly influenced Sata's leadership approach.[108]

The prevailing dictatorial one-party system, by the time Sata was Governor of Lusaka, provided a grounding for and space in which to play up his maverick tendency. As shown in Chapter 2, it also gave Sata the chance to develop his own style of leadership, methods, and followers, including an ability to mobilise people from below while simultaneously paying homage to the notion of the supremacy of 'the Great Leader'.[109] By the end of his time as Governor of Lusaka, Sata was much admired as a 'no-nonsense' doer and a charismatic leader with the common touch.[110] This development had frightened Kaunda who, as noted earlier, 'promoted' Sata to the relatively innocuous position of Minister of State, a position without any significant power and that involved dealing merely with formal and ritual duties. In other words, Sata's experience, education, and natural inclination at this stage were towards a dictatorial form of organisation, which fitted in well with the one-party state system, in which he clearly prospered and rose surprisingly high.[111]

Sata's latter-day introduction to ideas of democracy arguably impinged less on his consciousness than authoritarian ideas did, except at the level of saying the right things to international development partners. This is illustrated by the

---

106 Interview with Miles Larmer, Oxford, 20 May 2011.
107 Interview with Neo Simutanyi, Lusaka, 7 April 2011.
108 Interview with Roy Clarke, Lusaka, 17 April 2011.
109 Interview with Simon Zukas, Lusaka, 8 April 2011; Interview with Roy Clarke, Lusaka, 17 April 2011.
110 Ibid.
111 Ibid.

way he related to his colleagues in government. Several ministers who served with him in the Chiluba government recalled that Sata was rude towards all but Chiluba and in fact forced Mwanawasa to resign as Zambia's vice-president in 1994.[112] Sata himself admitted:

> I don't believe that Levy [Mwanawasa] resigned in 1994 on account that Chiluba was shielding corruption. The issue is [that] ... Levy was very frustrated. Personally, I paid very little attention to Levy because he was not my appointing authority and he was not more competent in terms of Government work than I was. So, when he gave me instructions as Vice-President, half the time, I did not implement those instructions. I just looked at them. When I was working in UNIP as Governor, I was appointed by the President. And to me, a Prime Minister – who was an equivalent of Vice-President – was very irrelevant. So my attitude did not start with Levy Mwanawasa.[113]

Thus, the sheer insubordination that Sata demonstrated towards Mwanawasa after 2001, which 'allow[ed his] supporters to imagine in him potential for subversion and radicalism',[114] was simply a continuation of their earlier rivalry and a reappearance of a core part of Sata's persona – a rude attitude towards those in authority. While other opposition leaders moderated their criticism of Mwanawasa, as part of self-imposed political decency, Sata was unsparing, publicly berating the President as a 'cabbage',[115] a 'typical liar'[116] whose 'brain and mouth do not coordinate',[117] and whose 'intellect and rationality is the lowest among all presidents in Africa'.[118] To Sata, politics meant having a discursive enemy to attack and discredit.

A third reason for the success of Sata's campaign message in urban areas is that Sata was skilful at portraying the incumbent Mwanawasa as an ineffective leader, which he found a relatively easy task, and himself as the alternative, which was a little more difficult initially, but, in the absence of other strong opposition, became easier. Sata's success owed much to his abrasiveness, and symbolic

---

112 Interview with Rodger Chongwe, Lusaka, 25 April 2011; Interview with Akashambatwa Mbikusita-Lewanika, Lusaka, 15 April 2011; Interview with Katele Kalumba, Chiengi, 7 April 2011.
113 Amos Malupenga, *Levy Patrick Mwanawasa: An Incentive for Posterity*, Grahamstown: NISC, 2009, p. 68.
114 Larmer and Fraser, 'Of Cabbages and King Cobra', p. 613.
115 This was Mwanawasa's nickname arising from the alleged mental impairment suffered from the earlier noted accident.
116 Brighton Phiri, 'Mwanawasa is a typical liar – Sata', *The Post*, 24 July 2005, pp. 1 and 4.
117 YouTube, 'Michael Sata: His Mouth, His Greatest Enemy (Stand Up for Zambia)' <https://www.youtube.com/watch?v=peXcBfv3EJo> (14 November 2015).
118 Amos Malupenga and Brighton Phiri, 'Sata attacks Levy's intellect, rationality', *The Post*, 4 March 2005, pp. 1 and 3.

and brute language as well as to the shortcomings of the incumbent and his opposition colleagues. For example, Sata once famously tore apart a cabbage at a public rally. This was a brutal symbolic representation of how he claimed he would crumble the ruling party's candidate, Mwanawasa, at the polls.[119]

When, in 2005, an accident killed forty-nine miners at a Chinese-owned mine on the Copperbelt, Sata was the first political leader to appear at the accident scene, upstaging President Mwanawasa who was on the Copperbelt at the time the explosion happened. Mwanawasa later explained that he 'would have loved to have gone to the accident scene but he had to rush back to Lusaka because he had a meeting with a Dutch delegation at State House'.[120] The accident itself had confirmed the perception of the poor environmental and safety standards of Chinese-operated mines, as argued by Copperbelt workers and articulated by Sata, and Mwanawasa's explanation came to be seen as a confirmation of his collusion with foreign actors, investment, and capital. The public backlash against what was seen as Mwanawasa's insensitivity further reinforced Sata's position as pro-worker. A leading Zambian political commentator put it succinctly:

> This is the shallowest, least palatable reason for any president of Zambia, for not immediately rushing to the scene where so many Zambians have perished. The Dutch delegation must be truly pleased to note how important they are to Zambia that our President would first rush to meet them and not immediately attend, personally and directly, to so many of his own dead, dying and hurt people. There is a powerful symbolism for the reasons Mwanawasa chose to advance for not personally rushing to the explosion. Our donors now take precedence over us, poor Zambian workers. To our politicians, we must wait. Who the hell are our politicians pretending to be governing then?[121]

When Mwanawasa later appeared at the mass burial of the victims, miners booed him while Sata was received with loud cheers. The message was clear. Thus, in the task of (re)establishing himself as the alternative, Sata was ever active and indefatigable.

Sata's considerable charisma, responsible for huge crowds at his rallies and his party's message of 'lower taxes, more jobs and money in your pocket', resonated well with the unemployed, workers, and the poor. With a ready wit, he had something to say about everything and anything. Never at a loss for words, his language was colourful, appealing, discursive, and entertaining. He possessed an effortless command of illuminating and hilarious metaphors, and projected a

---

119 Larmer and Fraser, 'Of Cabbages and King Cobra', p. 630; Interview with Neo Simutanyi, Lusaka, 7 April 2011.
120 Azwell Banda, 'The Chambishi disaster', *Sunday Post*, 24 April 2005, p. 22.
121 Ibid.

sense of boundless energy that would not permit him to be inactive for long. His audience loved such attributes as well as his ability to draw multiple narratives and imagery that referenced the past with the present, a strategy that linked post-independence narratives of nationhood to his nationalist rhetoric. For example, attending a rally in Lusaka addressed by Sata in 2011, I heard him say:

> [Y]ou people are suffering. You have to liberate yourselves again. You liberated yourselves from Europeans, how can you fail to liberate yourselves from [President] Rupiah [Banda]? There is no water in schools and there are pit latrines. How can you use pit latrines forty-seven years after independence?[122]

Of particular importance was that, in Lusaka, Sata campaigned using the English language, a possible recognition of the multi-ethnic diversity of the capital city where only 17.6 per cent of its 2,191,225 population spoke Bemba in the 2000s.[123] His use of English may also have resulted from his inability to speak fluent Nyanja, a dialect from the Eastern Province that is, however, widely spoken in the capital city, with 61.9 per cent of the population using it as their first language of communication.[124]

The picture was different on the Copperbelt, where Sata mainly used the Bemba language throughout his rallies especially when giving illustrations or parables. His use of Bemba was meant to appeal to his audience, as 83.9 per cent of Zambians on the Copperbelt spoke it.[125] Bemba thus provided Sata with the language and rhetoric that he would not normally have had in English. His use of metaphors in Bemba at his rallies was relentless, and colourful criticism of the government poured out of him by the yard. Sata's campaign speeches were often earthy and lacking in any clear ideological framework, an approach that his audience considered refreshing and entertaining. He also often took a highly sceptical and critical stance on the state and its leadership, encouraging his listeners to do the same, and rallying them to cheers when he came to a punch line. For instance, drawing on graphic metaphors to make fun of the government's construction of hospitals and schools amidst a national shortage of health staff, drugs, and teachers, Sata remarked a few weeks before the 2011 elections: 'women, if you had a barn at home and there is no food in the barn but

---

122 Sata rally, Lusaka, 10 April 2011.
123 Central Statistical Office, 'Widely Used Language of Communication by Province', *2010 Census of Population and Housing – National Analytical Report*, Lusaka, 2012, p. 66.
124 Ibid.
125 Ibid. As of 2010, Bemba also remained widely spoken throughout Zambia, with about 33.5 per cent of the country's 13,092,666 people using it as their main language of communication. The rise of industrial employment on the Copperbelt mines during the colonial period and after independence, which saw Bemba emerge as the *lingua franca*, may be responsible for its spread to other parts of the country, as returning labour migrants carried it with them.

your husband starts building another barn, would you say he was sane?', and the crowd responded, 'no, no, RB [Rupiah Banda] is insane!'[126]

In another example I observed during the 2011 campaign outside the Bembaphone areas, Sata combined English and the local languages of the area. In the Western Province, for instance, Sata, responding to the government's promises to address the poor road network throughout the area, snapped in Lozi: 'When I was in parliament [more than ten years ago], MPs from here were talking about the Kalabo–Kalongola road. Is there a road from Kalabo to Kalongola?' [Sata asked as the people shouted,] 'No, no, no!' [Sata continued] 'Your problems are my problems. Within 90 days of PF, you will see change. The choice is yours. If you want change, don't look for change for Michael Sata, look for change for yourselves.'[127] Sata charismatically carried his audiences along in an interactive process that made them feel part of the campaign message and a general call for political change.

As in Bemba heartlands, Sata and his party received significant electoral support in the urban centres of Lusaka and Copperbelt in the 2006 presidential and general elections. He defeated Mwanawasa in eighteen of the twenty-two constituencies on the Copperbelt and secured 49 per cent of the total presidential vote in Lusaka province.[128] Of the two provinces' thirty-four parliamentary seats, the PF won twenty-five while the rest were shared between different political parties and independent candidates.[129] Sata's victories in Lusaka and the Copperbelt demonstrate the success of his populist strategy as well as the MMD's disconnection with urban constituencies, including those that had sponsored Mwanawasa's rise to power in 2001. Poor working conditions, high taxes, poverty, and unemployment later combined with economic growth rates, which did not translate into improved living standards, to construct an urban consciousness and generate social identities that Sata exploited and appealed to in a language that resonated with many urbanites. This was an iterative and incremental process. Other political leaders such as MMD's Chiluba had played on these conditions before, encouraging a sense of identity, which then made it easier for the next leader, Sata, to play on them and shape and reshape these conditions constantly based on economic factors and the agency of leaders.[130] Thus, as in Chiluba's case, it was the urban factor and the government's economic policies that failed to address the living standards of the majority, the decline in union militancy, and, more decisively, Sata's populist skill and charismatic language, developed over his

---

126 George Chellah, 'Western, Northern provinces are the poorest – Sata', *The Post*, 17 May 2011, p. 1.
127 Mongu rally, 24 August 2011.
128 Electoral Commission of Zambia, 'Past election results', <https://www.elections.org.zm> (3 November 2023).
129 *Ibid.*
130 Interview with Miles Larmer, Oxford, 20 May 2011.

long political career, that explain his success in urban areas between 2001 and 2006. Despite his impressive showing in Northern and Luapula (ethno-regional appeal) and in Lusaka and Copperbelt (populist strategy) provinces, Sata still lost the presidential election to Mwanawasa, as shown below.

Table 4   Results of the presidential election, 2006.

Candidate	Party	Total votes	Percentage of presidential vote
Levy Mwanawasa	MMD	1,177,846	42.98
Michael Sata	PF	804,748	29.37
Hakainde Hichilema	UDA	693,772	25.32
Godfrey Miyanda	HP	42,891	1.57
Winright Ngondo	APC	20,921	0.76
Total voter turnout		2,740,178	70.77

Source: *Electoral Commission of Zambia*.

Sata's loss resulted from his failure to broaden his campaign beyond four provinces, and beyond ethno-regional and urban economic grievances. This contrasted with Mwanawasa, who campaigned in all of Zambia's then nine provinces on governance issues ranging from economic recovery and increased food security to anti-corruption and constitutional reform. Sata's strategy of concentrated campaigns was worsened by his failure to win all his targeted constituencies. For instance, notwithstanding that he received 43 per cent of the presidential vote in Northern Province (a massive improvement from his 8 per cent five years earlier), Sata still lost to Mwanawasa, who polled about 50 per cent support in the area.[131] Even in areas where he (Sata) won, such as in the Luapula, Lusaka, and Copperbelt provinces, Mwanawasa generally lost by small margins. For instance, though Sata secured eighteen out of the twenty-two constituencies on the Copperbelt, his combined vote share there only represented 56 per cent of the total presidential vote.[132] Similarly, despite winning seven out of the twelve constituencies in Lusaka province, his total vote share was only 49 per cent.[133]

In contrast, where Mwanawasa won (such as in the Eastern, Central, North-Western, and Western provinces), he did so with huge margins and Sata

---

131   Neo Simutanyi, 'Zambia: Manufactured One-Party Dominance and Its Collapse', in Renske and Lia Nijzink, *One-Party Dominance in African Democracies* (London: Lynne Riener Publishers, 2013), p. 129.
132   Ibid.
133   Ibid.

was virtually absent from the ballot.¹³⁴ To illustrate, Mwanawasa won all the seventeen constituencies in the Western Province, representing 80 per cent of the total presidential vote.¹³⁵ Sata, by contrast, only polled 7 per cent. Similarly, in North-Western Province, Mwanawasa secured 72 per cent of the cumulative vote while Sata managed only a paltry 2 per cent.¹³⁶ This meant that Mwanawasa was easily able to recover the losses he suffered in Sata's strongholds. As a result, Sata, despite his impressive electoral performance between 2001 and 2006, still lost the presidency to Mwanawasa because of his failure to extend his campaign beyond Luapula, Northern, Lusaka, and Copperbelt provinces. To win the presidency, Sata needed to move from being seen as an ethno-regional and urban leader to a national figure who commands support across the country. As I demonstrate in the next chapter, this is exactly what the PF leader tried to do next.

134 Sata lacked popularity in the four provinces won by Mwanawasa mainly because he did not have any coherent alternative message to present to these constituencies and, as a result, spent little time campaigning there. As I show in the next chapter, this situation changed in subsequent years.
135 Electoral Commission of Zambia, 'Past election results', <https://www.elections.org.zm> (3 November 2023).
136 *Ibid.*

5

Winning the Prize

HALFWAY INTO the official count of the 2006 election results, with most votes from Lusaka, Copperbelt, and the Bemba-speaking Luapula and Northern provinces already tallied, Sata declared himself winner of the presidential election. Notwithstanding that results from the remaining five provinces were yet to be counted, the opposition Patriotic Front (PF) leader went on to announce that 'I have won the presidential race by 55 per cent followed by President [Levy] Mwanawasa at 25 per cent'.[1] So confident of victory was Sata that he moved to instruct the Cabinet Office to shift his inauguration from the Supreme Court grounds, the traditional venue, to the 30,000-seater Independence Stadium in order to allow the maximum number of his supporters to attend the ceremony.[2] He then went on to direct that Zimbabwe's President Robert Mugabe should be invited to the inauguration ceremony as the guest of honour.[3]

Sata's actions elicited strong criticism from the ruling party, whose campaign chief, Vernon Mwaanga, described them as 'premature'. Mwaanga argued that Sata's strongholds 'do not represent the total results of the elections for the whole country'.[4] As shown in the previous chapter, the results from the Electoral Commission of Zambia, which saw Mwanawasa of the Movement for Multiparty Democracy (MMD) the declared winner, demonstrated how hasty Sata's declaration was. Mwaanga's rebuke of Sata also highlighted the PF leader's limited understanding of the Zambian political landscape. In effect, the MMD campaign chairperson was making the point that, to secure the national presidency, a candidate needed to win their main electoral constituencies comfortably and perform well in the strongholds of their opponents. This was a consideration that Sata's campaign strategy had overlooked until then.

This chapter, building on the preceding one, explores the strategies of electoral mobilisation that Sata employed between 2006 and 2011 to establish

1   Larry Moonze and Bivan Saluseki, 'I've won by 55% – Sata', *The Post*, 1 October 2006, pp. 1 and 4.
2   *Post* Reporters, 'Sata forces his way into Cabinet Office', *The Post*, 30 September 2006, p. 1.
3   *Ibid.*, p. 4.
4   Kwenda Paipi, 'Sata's behaviour premature, says VJ', *The Post*, 1 October 2006, p. 1.

a national constituency as a response to his electoral defeat. It demonstrates that during this period, Sata managed to achieve his objective by targeting and appealing to non-Bemba ethnic groups through specific policy messages, such as decentralisation, which found an echo in several constituencies of the Lozi-speaking Western Province. The chapter further shows that the PF leader built coalitions of support with civil society groups around constitutional reform. As I show in greater detail below, this strategy weakened his opponents' position on the subject while enhancing his own, and portrayed him as a national leader. Sata's decision to reach beyond ethnic and urban constituencies reflected a belated acknowledgement of Mwaanga's earlier criticism about the narrowness of his campaign strategy. I argue that, together with his existing support in Bemba-speaking rural communities and urban Lusaka and Copperbelt provinces, Sata's expanded campaign strategy culminated in his victory on 23 September 2011.

The National Leader

After building his support base in the Bemba-speaking Luapula and Northern provinces and the urban constituencies of Lusaka and the Copperbelt, Sata set his sights on becoming a national political leader. Until early 2009, he had shown little interest in campaigning beyond the four provinces, believing that he could win the presidency by relying only on his core constituencies. Sata's defeat in the 2008 presidential by-election, occasioned by the death of President Mwanawasa, for which he mobilised the same electoral bases whose support he had cultivated between 2001 and 2006, appears to have persuaded him to rethink his position and campaign strategies.[5] Despite winning and increasing his appeal significantly in Bemba-speaking rural communities and the urban areas of Lusaka and Copperbelt, Sata still fell short of the electoral support that he needed to succeed. He lost the overall election to the MMD's Rupiah Banda, who, even with his deep losses in Sata's strongholds, secured a clear victory in Eastern, North-Western, Western, and Central provinces.

In the 2008 polls, just as in 2006, Sata barely campaigned in non-Bemba-speaking areas and accordingly performed poorly in them, failing to deliver any messages that resonated with voters in those regions.[6] Learning from his

5   For an excellent analysis of the 2008 poll, see Nic Cheeseman and Marja Hinfelaar, 'Parties, Platforms and Political Mobilisation: The Zambian Presidential Election of 2008', *African Affairs*, 109, 434 (2010), 51–76.
6   In a detailed discussion of the 2008 presidential election, Neo Simutanyi attributes the PF's poor performance in non-Bemba speaking areas to the boiling 'resentment for Sata by non-Bemba ethnic groups who completely rejected him in their areas, where [his] average votes were well below 10 per cent in the both the 2006 and 2008 elections'. The author identified these groups as 'the Lozi (Western province), the Lunda, Luvale and Kaonde (North-Western), the Nyanja-speaking people (Eastern) and the Tonga (Southern)'. For details see, Neo Simutanyi, 'The 2008 Presidential Elections in Zambia: Incumbency, Political Contestation and Failure of Political Opposition', paper presented to the CMI/IESE Conference on 'Election Processes, Liberation

electoral failures, Sata shifted his attention to building a national base and a genuine alternative political force with wider aspirations beyond ethno-regional and urban economic concerns. His first attempt to achieve this was through elite inclusion, a strategy that saw the appointment of 'ethnic big men and women' from areas outside Bemba heartlands to positions of influence in the PF.

Between 2001 and 2009, Sata had consistently made sure that there were no less than three Bemba-speaking figures in the party's four main leadership positions at any time. For instance, he appointed Edwin Lifwekelo (2001–2002), Guy Scott (2002–2007), Charles Chimumbwa (2007), and Edward Mumbi (2007–2009) to the position of Secretary General. The post of PF National Chairperson was given to Chitalu Sampa until April 2009, when he died. Apart from Scott, who was a white Zambian of Scottish descent who became Sata's deputy in 2007 when the position of vice-president was created, all hailed from Northern Province. This line-up meant that non-Bemba-speaking areas were not represented in the PF's most senior positions.

Seeking to address the persistent criticism that he was leading an ethnic political movement, Sata appointed Lusaka lawyer Wynter Kabimba, a Sala from Central Province, as PF Secretary General in April 2009. Another non-Bemba leader, Inonge Wina, was chosen as National Chairperson seven months later. As Kabimba recalled, Wina's appointment was, however, not without internal opposition:

> I remember that at the Central Committee meeting called to ratify Wina's appointment as National Chairperson, there was an uproar from the Bemba-speaking group, led by PF Chairman for Elections Samuel Mukupa, which protested against her appointment on grounds that the position was too senior to be given to someone who had just joined the party. Sata's response was: 'are you the only ones who don't know that we are viewed as a Bemba party out there?'[7]

Wina, a prominent Lozi politician whose late husband (Arthur Wina) was one of Zambia's foremost nationalists, had, between 2001 and 2006, served as the

---

Movements and Democratic Change in Africa', Maputo, Mozambique, 8–11 April 2010, p. 10. An online version is also available: <http.cmi.no/file/?1016> (28 September 2015). Simutanyi's argument about the resentment against the PF leader is, however, not substantiated by any empirical evidence and, as I later demonstrate, is weakened by Sata's victory, for instance, in several Lozi-speaking constituencies in the 2011 elections. It is highly unlikely that the Lozis' supposed antipathy towards Sata dissipated within a three-year period. This failure to explain the 2011 turnaround suggests that the real reason for Sata's previous poor electoral performance lay elsewhere. Another weakness of Simutanyi's work is that it undermines the effectiveness of Banda's campaign strategies, and presupposes that Sata should have won the support of non-Bemba ethnic groups, irrespective of whether his competitors positioned themselves as best placed to represent their interests. The fact that Sata lost the 2008 presidential election by a margin of less than 2 per cent suggests that Banda would have lost the poll if he and the MMD had not put up an effective campaign in their strongholds.

7   Interview with Wynter Kabimba, Lusaka, 12 May 2015.

Member of Parliament (MP) for Nalolo constituency in the Western Province under the United Party for National Development (UPND). In appointing her, Sata expressed hope that she would help the PF:

> [to] mobilise membership for the party in the [Western] province in the same way she mobilised for the United Party for National Development when she was Member of Parliament for Nalolo.[8]

Sata's comments on Wina should be put in context. In contrast to Kabimba's Central Province, where none of the several ethno-language groups enjoys dominance over another, most of the people in the Western Province are Lozi speakers.[9] Wina's appointment thus demonstrates the earliest show of Sata's attempt to secure the support of Lozi voters through elite inclusion, particularly at a time when he had no specific campaign messages that he could present to this electorate. However, the arrest in January 2011 of over a hundred Lozi-speaking protestors demanding the secession of Western Province from the rest of Zambia in protest at the area's neglect provided Sata with the opportunity and narrative to mobilise this electoral constituency more directly.

'The meaning of the Barotseland Agreement is power to the people': Sata, Decentralisation, and the 2011 Election

To understand how Sata, using the January political events, managed to create a foothold in the Western Province during the 2011 presidential election campaigns, a brief historical context of the evolution of Lozi demands for regional autonomy is required. Although events would not come to a head until early 2011, Lozi demands for secession have long roots, drawing in part on pre-colonial and colonial political formations. A full treatment of this complex subject is not possible here,[10] but two important points are worth a brief discussion: the signing of the Barotseland Agreement just before independence, and the consequences of its abrogation soon after.

Throughout British colonial rule in Northern Rhodesia, Barotseland, as present-day Western Province was then known, enjoyed a special status like that

---

8   Ernest Chanda, 'Inonge Wina becomes PF chairperson', *The Post*, 7 November 2009, p. 1.
9   According to official figures from the Central Statistical Office, 69.6 per cent of Western province's population of 902,974 people in 2010 were Lozi speakers. For more details, see Central Statistical Office, 'Widely Used Language of Communication by Province, Zambia 2010', *2010 Census of Population and Housing – National Analytical Report*, Lusaka, 2012, p. 66.
10 For a more detailed historical analysis, see Gerald L. Caplan, 'Barotseland: The Secessionist Challenge to Zambia', *Journal of Modern African Studies*, 6, 3 (1968), pp. 343–60; Gerald L. Caplan, *The Elites of Barotseland 1878–1969: A Political History of Zambia's Western Province*, Berkeley: University of California Press, 1970; Jack Hogan, '"What Then Happened to Our Eden?": The Long History of Lozi Secessionism, 1890–2013', *Journal of Southern African Studies*, 40, 5 (2014), pp. 907–24; and Robert Rotberg, 'What Future for Barotseland', *Africa Report*, 8, 7 (1963), p. 21.

of a 'protectorate within a protectorate'. Its hereditary ruler, known as the *Litunga*, was authorised to make laws for the area in relation to local government, native treasury, local taxation, native authorities, traditional and customary matters, native courts, land and natural resources, game conservation, and local festivals.[11] As the end of colonial rule loomed, the Lozi traditional aristocracy, unsure of its position in a free Zambia, demanded that the area be granted separate independence from Northern Rhodesia. Nationalist politicians, including several influential Lozis belonging to Kaunda's UNIP, strongly opposed the calls, creating a deadlock that threatened to derail Zambia's march to political freedom.[12]

After the British Secretary of State for Commonwealth and Colonial Relations, Duncan Sandys, hosted the Litunga and Kaunda for negotiations in London, a settlement that became known as the Barotseland Agreement was reached in May 1964.[13] In it, the Lozi King undertook to abandon his demand for secession in exchange for Kaunda's pledge to uphold Barotseland's semi-autonomous status in a new Zambia by preserving the Litunga's special powers and privileges on local government and customary law.[14]

The Barotseland Agreement was incorporated into the independence constitution of Zambia in 1964, but was repealed by the government in 1969 as the Zambian state, faced with the realities of managing post-independence tensions, became dominated by a tendency towards centralisation.[15] This unilateral action was to become in later years an intermittent wellspring of discontent for disaffected Lozi traditional elites and politicians seeking a greater share of state political power and resources. In other words, demands for secession arose whenever Lozi elites felt marginalised or excluded from preferential access to government positions and resources. As evidenced by the examples below, they accordingly attempted to regain their lost influence on the state by using the termination of the Barotseland Agreement as a strategic political resource to advocate an independent territorial entity.

Following a hiatus spanning nearly two decades of one-party rule, during which Lozi secessionism stayed at its lowest ebb thanks to Kaunda's strategy of appointing several Lozis including the Litunga to senior UNIP and government positions, calls for Lozi autonomy returned under Chiluba's presidency in the 1990s.[16] These were initially led by the Barotse Royal Establishment

11   Ibid.
12   Ibid.
13   Owen Sichone and Neo Simutanyi, 'The Ethnic and Regional Questions, Ethnic Nationalism and the State in Zambia: The Case of Barotseland, 1964–1994', in Owen Sichone and Bornwell Chikulo (eds), *Democracy in Zambia: Challenges for the Third Republic*, Harare: SAPES Trust, 1996, p. 182.
14   David C. Mulford, 'Northern Rhodesia: Some Observations on the 1964 Elections', *Africa Report*, 9, 2 (1964), p. 13.
15   Ibid., p. 184.
16   In 1989, for instance, Kaunda appointed Litunga Ilute Yeta to the ruling party's powerful Central Committee and placed him in charge of the Western province.

(BRE), who in July 1993 issued a series of threats to secede from Zambia if the Barotseland Agreement was not reinstated.[17] This was after Chiluba had refused to placate the Litunga in the manner of Kaunda. Later, Lozi politicians and former government ministers who had fallen out with Chiluba, such as Akashambatwa Mbikusita-Lewanika, picked up on these demands. In the run-up to the 1996 polls, for instance, Mbikusita-Lewanika's Agenda for Zambia party (AZ) campaigned on a pledge to honour the Barotseland Agreement if elected.[18]

A son of a former Litunga, Mbikusita-Lewanika only managed a paltry 2 per cent of the national presidential vote and was defeated by Chiluba even in the Western Province, where the President received 40 per cent of the total vote against the opposition leader's 27 per cent.[19] The outcome disproved earlier claims by the BRE and Mbikusita-Lewanika that most Lozis supported the demand for a reinstatement of the Agreement or the breakaway of the area. Frustrated by the failure to get the desired results through electoral politics, in the late 1990s a new group of radical Lozi separatists, led by Prince Imasiku Mutangelwa of the recently formed Barotse Patriotic Front (BPF), threatened armed insurrection against the Zambian state if Western Province was not permitted to secede. The government responded by arresting Mutangelwa on treason charges, and outlawing his organisation.[20]

Lozi demands for secession disappeared temporarily under the presidency of Mwanawasa, whose appointment of several Lozi figures to MMD and public and diplomatic positions, appeared to pacify both the traditional and political elites. Among the prominent beneficiaries of Mwanawasa's concessions was Mbikusita-Lewanika, who dissolved his small political organisation in July 2002 to rejoin the MMD before he was appointed as party spokesperson, the first of his many positions within the ruling core.[21] Mbikusita-Lewanika's sister, Inonge Mbikusita, also gained a top diplomatic job after she was appointed Zambia's Ambassador to the United States of America.[22] However, after Mwanawasa's death, calls for a Lozi nation were resurrected.

The latest demands arose after the Commission that was rewriting Zambia's constitution rejected submissions from the BRE in August 2010 to include the

---

The Lozi King was, however, not accorded any of the privileges that he had enjoyed under colonial rule.

17   Daniel Posner, *Institutions and Ethnic Politics in Africa*, Cambridge: Cambridge University Press, 2005, p. 189.
18   Hogan, 'What Then Happened to Our Eden?', p. 919.
19   Electoral Commission of Zambia, 'Past election results', <http.elections.org.zm/past_election_results.php> (3 November 2023).
20   Hogan, 'What Then Happened to Our Eden?', p. 919.
21   Ibid.
22   Ibid.

Barotseland Agreement in the final draft constitution.[23] Following this unsuccessful attempt to secure a permanent affirmation of their position as a semi-autonomous region, Lozi traditional elites warned that the dismissal of their proposals would result in revolt in the Western Province. Soon after, the previously banned BPF resurfaced and resuscitated its calls for the independence of the area on the grounds that it was underdeveloped in comparison to other parts of the country.

Mutangelwa's group was joined by three other covert and militant separatist formations: the Barotse Freedom Movement (BFM), the Movement for the Restoration of Barotseland, and Linyungandambo (meaning 'Alert your Kinsman' in Lozi),[24] which began to organise meetings 'to sensitise the people on the Barotseland Agreement of 1964'.[25] Several leaders of these organisations were arrested in late October 2010 after a meeting that was called 'to discuss the independence of Barotseland from Zambia' where the Barotse flag was to be hoisted, became violent when police threw tear-gas canisters to disperse hundreds of Lozis that had turned up.[26] The October events proved to be a dress rehearsal for January 2011 riots, which resulted in the death of two Lozi protestors and the detention, on treason charges, of over a hundred, including a 92-year-old former *Ngambela* (Prime Minister) of Barotseland, Maxwell Mututwa, who was one of the leading campaigners for secession.[27]

The BRE, reiterating its earlier position, warned in February 2011 that 'widespread lawlessness might be the order of the day in Barotseland unless the Barotseland Agreement is expeditiously restored ... during the lifespan of the current Parliament'.[28] Banda's administration responded to these demands by ruling out any chance of restoring the agreement and banning any discussion of the subject, citing the need to maintain peace. Sata, seeking to gain from this historical and political context, including the discontent arising from the killings and arrests, turned the Barotseland Agreement into an election campaign issue. In doing so, he reversed his earlier stance on the matter, which was not to support calls for the restoration of the Barotseland Agreement, arguing that 'the Lozis were cheated by the British when they signed the agreement'.[29]

In his turnaround, Sata started by promising that he would restore the Barotseland Agreement if elected and use it as a template for rolling out devolution

23   Henry Sinyangwe, 'BRE makes Barotse Agreement demands on draft constitution', *The Post*, 3 August 2010, p. 5.
24   Hogan, 'What Then Happened to Our Eden?', p. 921.
25   Mwala Kalaluka, 'Police question Barotseland Restoration movement leaders', *The Post*, 25 September 2010, p. 5.
26   Mwala Kalaluka, 'Police disrupt Barotse independence meeting', *The Post*, 24 October 2010, p. 2.
27   Mwala Kalaluka, 'Mututwa, 23 Lozis on Treason', *The Post*, 20 January 2011, p. 4.
28   Amos Malupenga, 'Chaos might grip Barotseland – BRE', *The Post*, 13 February 2011, pp. 1 and 4.
29   Bivan Saluseki, 'Barotseland Agreement won't be my election issue, says Sata', *The Post*, 13 July 2004, p. 6.

to the rest of the country. He presented the recurrent demonstrations around the issue as evidence of the Lozis' longstanding demand for decentralisation and a culmination of the failure of the MMD to implement the policy effectively:

> The meaning of the Barotse Agreement is power to the people. We shall implement that agreement within 90 days [of assuming office] because it will help us run other provinces. We are going to create provincial assemblies because Lusaka does not know what is happening in Barotseland. ... The British ruled this country for 70 years ... through village headmen ... [and] chiefs. If you give us the authority, government will start at the village level because a person in Kaoma [one of the six districts in the Western province] doesn't know how you suffer in the village. If the person in Kaoma does not know your problems, what about [President] Banda who is in Lusaka?[30]

Sata's campaign message secured him the endorsement of the leading advocates of Lozi regional autonomy, such as Mututwa, who was widely seen as the movement's godfather. In the wake of his release from prison in March 2011, the former Ngambela exalted Sata as a 'messenger' of Lozi demands on the state:

> The people of Western province are thirsty for Sata's message because he is speaking what they want to hear. [They] ... are attending Sata's rallies because he is talking about the Barotseland Agreement and [the need to release] those that are [still] detained. It would be through him that President Rupiah Banda would get the true feelings of the people of Barotseland over the matter.[31]

In addition to mobilising support on the contentious issue of the agreement, more specifically on the policy of devolution, Sata also identified the strategic constituencies in the Western Province where he concentrated his campaign. Out of the area's seventeen constituencies, he only visited and held public rallies in six. These comprised Mongu, the provincial capital and site of the January uprising; Senanga, home to many of the supporters of Lozi secession, including Mututwa; and Nalolo, where Inonge Wina, the PF National Chairperson, came from. The rest were Mangango, Kaoma, and Nalikwanda constituencies, which, despite their remote locations, all had high numbers of registered voters.

At his rallies, which attracted thousands of people as shown in Figure 10, Sata presented himself as having stood with Lozis during difficult times and reiterated his promise to reinstate the Barotseland Agreement if elected. He also tried to generate Lozi resentment against the MMD by parading several activists who were

---

30   George Chellah, 'Barotse visit an eye opener – Sata', *The Post*, 24 May 2011, p. 1; George Chellah, 'Rupiah can kill for power – Sata', *The Post*, 10 September 2011, p. 5. Also see YouTube, 'Sata making promises to restore Barotseland agreement in 90 days', <s://www.youtube.com/watch?v=tHjrGtF9P14> (14 November 2015).
31   Mwala Kalaluka', Sata message goes well in Western province', *The Post*, 25 May 2011, p. 1.

Figure 10 Media portrayal of Michael Sata's campaigns in Western Province.

injured in the January unrest as visible representatives of the brutality of Banda's administration and its failure to engage with a cause that was important to them.[32]

In his characteristic populist style and rhetoric, the PF leader accused Banda of neglecting a key constituency that had overwhelmingly supported him three years earlier:

> In 2008, Barotseland made Rupiah Banda to be President of Zambia with 35,000 votes. Banda has never come here to say 'thank you'. What Banda sent here are guns to kill your children. [Even after] … so many people were killed in Barotseland, Banda did not come to weep with you. The only person who

32 YouTube, 'Michael Sata issues Electoral Promise to Restore the Barotseland Agreement 1964', <https://www.youtube.com/watch?v=Jty2uPFdgcA> (14 November 2015).

came to Barotseland ... and mourned with you was Michael Sata. Where was ULP [the United Liberal Party], ADD and MMD.³³

Although Sata campaigned for electoral support mainly on the promise of devolution to chiefs, he also articulated other local grievances. For example, he made a case for the need to generate jobs for the youth in the region, increase rice production, establish cashew nut processing plants, and improve fish farming. He also pledged several infrastructure projects, such as building more canals, roads, schools, and health centres throughout the province.

Sata's campaign message clearly worked. The PF leader defeated Banda at the polls in Mongu and Nalolo, where his party also won at parliamentary level, and closely trailed the incumbent in the remaining constituencies. Most importantly, Sata both increased his share of the provincial vote from 9 per cent in 2008 to 23 per cent in 2011 and reduced Banda's proportion by a large margin. Although Banda still won the province, his cumulative vote fell to 33 per cent from 67.4 per cent in 2008, despite increased voter turnout in the area. The collapse of Banda's support among Lozi voters suggests that many of those who had earlier backed him may have either switched their allegiance to the opposition or simply stayed away.

As was the case in the Bembaphone areas of Lusaka and the Copperbelt, Sata's improved electoral performance in the Western Province resulted from the MMD's disconnect with another of its core constituencies. The election also highlighted the ineptness of Banda's campaign strategy, and the PF leader's ability to identify himself with the Lozis over a salient issue that united a significant number of them: the Barotseland Agreement. Through it, Sata successfully mobilised Lozi-speaking voters whose concerns coalesced around a growing sentiment of political and economic marginalisation that in turn found open expression in the demands for local autonomy, which he promised to deliver.

'Join me to get rid of Banda': Sata, Constitutional Reform, and Civil Society

Sata's final attempt at building a national support base drawing on specific policy appeals centred on constitutional reform. He was a latecomer to the cause, with civil society groups having led a campaign for the review of Zambia's national law since early 2003. A factor that may explain why he had shown no real interest in the subject relates to his past role as the champion of former President Frederick Chiluba's attempts to secure an unconstitutional third term in 2001, whereas the key leaders of the process of constitutional reform came from the influential

---

33   Chellah, 'Rupiah can kill for power', p. 5. The ULP (United Liberal Party) and ADD (Alliance for Democracy and Development) were small opposition parties led by Lozi-speaking leaders. By highlighting the absence of ULP and ADD leaders, Sata was strategically seeking to disqualify them for Lozi leadership and position himself as a fighter for Lozi interests.

Oasis Forum, a coalition of civic organisations that had opposed Chiluba's plans vociferously.[34] Another plausible explanation for Sata's late entry is that there had been hardly any political space for him to intervene as the working relationship between the state and civil society on the topic was initially close.

Sata's chance came when the Oasis Forum withdrew its participation from the constitution-making process in September 2007. The split in state–civil society relations was created after President Mwanawasa dismissed the Forum's key concern that the composition of the National Constitutional Conference (NCC) was biased towards government-appointed delegates.[35] Taking advantage of this political opening, Sata developed a threefold strategy aimed at undermining the MMD's commitment to the constitutional reform and presenting himself as the political ally that civil society needed.

To begin with, Sata attempted to re-establish relations of trust and solidarity with the Oasis Forum by playing to their demands. A week after the civic coalition announced its boycott of the NCC, Sata followed suit. He justified his party's position as 'in line with the Oasis Forum and other civil society organisations which have vowed to boycott the conference'.[36] In contrast, the UPND, the other main opposition party, chose to attend the NCC. Responding to a government request for his party to nominate representatives to sit on the NCC, the PF leader argued that he would do so only if the 'outstanding and unresolved matters' raised by civil society were addressed:

> PF would never subscribe to the NCC in its current state. You cannot expect a good document that is government-driven. In fact, President Mwanawasa should stop calling it a National Constitutional Conference because Zambians are not part of it. It is just a conference for MMD cadres (i.e. supporters). We want a people driven constitution as proposed by the civil society.[37]

The twenty PF MPs who defied the party's position on the NCC were promptly expelled in a move described by Sata as a sign of commitment to the civil

---

34 In addition to civic organisations that are mentioned in the text, the term 'civil society' is deployed loosely here to refer to the non-state actors that made up the Oasis Forum – the statutory Law Association of Zambia, the various women's organisations under the umbrella of the Non-governmental Organisations Coordinating Council and the three Christian mother bodies, that is, the Evangelical Fellowship of Zambia, the Council of Churches in Zambia, and the Zambia Episcopal Conference.

35 Lise Rakner and Lars Svasand, 'In Search of the Impact of International Support for Political Parties in New Democracies: Malawi and Zambia Compared', in Peter Burnell and André W.M. Gerrits, *Promoting Party Politics in Emerging Democracies*, London: Routledge, 2012, p. 204.

36 Lambwe Kachali, 'PF shuns NCC', *The Post*, 22 September 2007, p. 1.

37 *Ibid.*

society position on the constitutional reform process.[38] Sata's actions produced the desired results. Bishop Paul Mususu, the spokesperson of the Oasis Forum, recalled that 'Boycotting the NCC and even suspending the MPs who defied his directive made us believe that we were on the same page with him (Sata) when it came to the constitution-making process'.[39] Suzanne Matale, General Secretary of another affiliate of the Forum, the Council of Churches in Zambia, echoed Mususu's testimony: 'Sata's stance on the NCC had many of us start to gain confidence and believe that we had someone [a partner] who believed in us'.[40] The Law Association of Zambia representative, Musa Mwenye, revealed other forms of solidarity through which Sata expressed his support for civil society:

> He (Sata) was supportive of everything including demonstrations against the NCC. Whenever we organised public protests, he would say 'send three buses' and he would send people.[41]

Having secured the endorsement of the Oasis Forum, Sata then set his sights on frustrating the MMD-inspired constitution-making process in a way that consolidated his relationship with civil society. After Mwanawasa's death, the Oasis Forum reiterated its demands to Banda that the NCC be reconstituted. Like his predecessor, the new President rejected these calls. When the NCC concluded its work in August 2010, the fears expressed earlier by civil society that the government would hijack the outcome proved well founded. The majority of the NCC delegates scrapped from the draft constitution those provisions that were popular with civil society but that the MMD saw as disadvantageous to its electoral prospects. One such provision, which was endorsed by civil society, was that a winning presidential candidate should secure a minimum of '50 per cent + 1' of the total vote and another was that the vice-president should be elected alongside the president as a running mate.[42]

As a response to the outcome of the NCC, the Oasis Forum embarked on a nationwide campaign against the draft constitution, staging public rallies and lobbying opposition lawmakers to kill the proposed MMD-sponsored Constitution of Zambia bill, which needed the support of at least 106 (two-thirds) of the 158 MPs in parliament. At the time, the MMD only had eighty-seven MPs, including eight nominated ones, which meant that the ruling

---

38 Nearly all the expelled lawmakers obtained court injunctions that stayed their dismissals up to the 2011 elections. Six of those expelled later apologised to Sata and renounced their NCC membership. For details, see Laura Mushukwa, '6 MPs discontinue case against Sata, Mumbi', *The Post*, 28 November 2008. p. 5. Also see Neo Simutanyi, 'Expulsion of PF MPs', *The Post*, 24 March 2008, p. 12.
39 Interview with Bishop Paul Mususu, Lusaka, 13 April 2015.
40 Interview with Suzanne Matale, Lusaka, 22 October 2015.
41 Interview with Musa Mwenye, Lusaka, 22 October 2015.
42 Interview with Suzanne Matale, Lusaka, 22 October 2015.

party needed the support of at least nineteen opposition lawmakers.[43] Seeking to secure support for their position, representatives of civil society held a series of meetings with Sata, ahead of the crucial vote in parliament slated for March 2011. UPND leader Hakainde Hichilema, whose MPs had taken part in the NCC deliberations, was unsurprisingly overlooked in these discussions. Lee Habasonda, Patrick Mucheleka, Frank Bwalya, and Simon Kabanda, who, in the month leading to the vote, organised regular public protests outside parliament in an attempt to persuade opposition MPs to reject the proposed constitutional amendment, confirmed in separate interviews that Sata had committed PF MPs to voting against the bill.[44] Several MPs and party Secretary General Wynter Kabimba also recalled that Sata had called a party meeting a week before the ballot, at which he directed all PF MPs to vote against it.[45]

On 29 March 2011, the Constitution of Zambia bill failed to go through in parliament despite the MMD securing the support of a number of opposition UPND lawmakers.[46] As promised, Sata's PF MPs opposed the bill. Eager to cement his growing relationship with civil society groups, Sata hailed the defeat of the MMD-inspired constitutional bill as a vindication of the position of 'the PF, Oasis Forum [and other] civil society organisations over the failed National Constitutional Conference'.[47]

Having successfully frustrated the political programme of the MMD, Sata had opened up the space to make his own promises on constitutional reform. For a start, he undertook to enact 'within 90 days of assuming power' a constitution supported by civil society and containing the popular '50 per cent + 1' and running mate clauses – provisions that were responsible for the MMD's disagreements with the Oasis Forum.[48] Sata moved later to reflect this promise in the PF manifesto, which was released a few weeks after the defeat of the MMD-sponsored Constitutional Bill, before he appealed to civil society to help him defeat President Banda. As Simon Kabanda, Executive Secretary of the Citizens Forum, remembered:

---

43 National Assembly of Zambia, *Composition of Members of Parliament Between Ruling Party and Opposition Members since 2006*, Lusaka: Aquila Printers, October 2011.
44 Interview with Lee Habasonda, Lusaka, 21 October 2015; Interview with Patrick Mucheleka, Lusaka, 12 November 2014; Interview with Fr Frank Bwalya, Lusaka, 23 May 2013; Interview with Simon Kabanda, Lusaka, 21 October 2015.
45 Kabimba and PF vice-president Guy Scott also held a separate meeting with party lawmakers to reiterate the opposition to the bill; Interview with Wynter Kabimba, Lusaka, 12 May 2015.
46 Bright Mukwasa and Ernest Chanda, 'MMD loses vote on Constitution', *The Post*, 20 March 2011, pp. 1 and 4.
47 George Chellah, 'Sata calls for early polls', *The Post*, 31 March 2011, p. 5.
48 Interview with Suzanne Matale, Lusaka, 22 October 2015.

Sata told us that I have helped you to prevent the MMD from forcing through an unacceptable constitution that did not have the support of majority Zambians. Now join me to get rid of Banda so that I can give you the constitution you want.[49]

Sata's appeal fell on fertile ground as civil society organisations rose to back him, believing, in the words of then president of the Law Association of Zambia, that Sata 'seemed determined to deliver a new constitution'.[50] Although they never endorsed the PF publicly, the language and rhetoric of several leaders of civil society, especially the influential Oasis Forum, which was highly critical of Banda and the MMD, suggested an inclination towards Sata. Others, mainly outspoken Catholic priests, took their message of political change to the Sunday pulpit, where they urged the faithful to 'vote for a party that had shown genuine commitment on constitutional reform'.[51] Reflecting on this event a few years later, after Sata had ascended to power and refused to honour his promise, one prominent civil society leader involved in the constitution-making process admitted that the opposition leader had only told them what they wanted to hear:

> [On the constitution], Sata committed to everything we wanted. He did not raise any opposition or demands. For him, it was a done deal. Now we realise that it was too good to be true. We were sceptical about the 90 days promise, but we bought into his commitment actually.[52]

Given the segmented nature of the membership of civil society, it is impossible to break down by constituency the level of electoral support that Sata received for his position on constitutional reform. However, it is clear from the above discussion that many of the key civic leaders with the capacity to affect public opinion had supported Sata. Most importantly, Sata's demonstrated commitment to constitutional reform was part of a strategy of presenting himself as a national figure and allaying popular perceptions that he was only a leader of the Bemba-speaking communities and urbanites in Lusaka and the Copperbelt. As with the decentralisation campaign among the Lozis in Western Province, Sata's position represented a general reassurance to national voters that he was above ethnic and urban economic grievances, and had indeed become a national leader.

At the polls in September 2011, Sata defeated Banda and eight other presidential contestants as shown in Table 5.

---

49   Interview with Simon Kabanda, Lusaka, 22 October 2015.
50   Interview with Musa Mwenye, Lusaka, 22 October 2015.
51   Interview with Fr Frank Bwalya, Lusaka, 23 May 2013.
52   Interview with Suzanne Matale, Lusaka, 22 October 2015.

Table 5 Results of the presidential election, 2011.

Candidate	Party	Total votes	Percentage of presidential vote
Michael Sata	PF	1,170,966	42.24
Rupiah Banda	MMD	987,866	35.63
Hakainde Hichilema	UPND	506,763	18.28
Charles Milupi	ADD	26,270	0.95
Elias Chipimo	NAREP	10,672	0.38
Tilyenji Kaunda	UNIP	9,950	0.36
Edith Nawakwi	UNIP	6,833	0.25
Ng'andu Magande	NMP	6,344	0.23
Godfrey Miyanda	HP	4,730	0.17
Frederick Mutesa	ZED	2,268	0.08
Total voter turnout		2,772,264	53.65

Source: Electoral Commission of Zambia.

In addition to winning his four core constituencies with wide margins, Sata improved his performance in all MMD strongholds significantly (see Table 6), reflecting the effectiveness of his 'national' campaign strategy. As he was to note later, 'campaigning in your opponents' stronghold is not a waste of time; there are votes to be won there'.[53] Banda clearly did not understand this point. In contrast to Sata, he narrowed his campaign to the MMD's traditional constituencies, repeating the same mistake that the PF leader had made in 2008. Although the incumbent emerged victorious in the same four provinces that he had won three years earlier, it was with reduced margins as shown in Table 6.

Table 6 Sata's results in the 2008 and 2011 presidential elections by province.

Province	2008		2011	
	Sata votes	Percentage of total vote	Sata votes	Percentage of total vote
Luapula	82,418	69.95	151,822	73.54
Northern	134,244	64.69	242,455	64.18
Copperbelt	201,087	60.90	341,505	67.88
Lusaka	162,107	53.88	224,925	55.94
Central	37,656	24.25	63,890	28.28
Eastern	37,295	18.42	59,391	18.46
Western	11,891	9.77	43,579	23.12
Southern	11,866	4.73	24,609	6.59
North-Western	4,586	4.38	18,790	10.85

Source: *Electoral Commission of Zambia*

53 Interview with Michael Sata, Lusaka, 13 January 2013.

Table 7 Rupiah Banda's results in the 2008 and 2011 presidential elections by province.

Province	2008 Banda votes	2008 Percentage of total vote	2011 Banda votes	2011 Percentage of total vote
Eastern	148,197	73.18	233,528	72.60
Western	81,993	67.40	62,592	33.20
North-Western	59,370	56.75	86,994	50.21
Central	82,178	52.92	108,912	48.21
Northern	67,237	32.40	121,482	32.16
Copperbelt	105,225	31.87	131,897	26.22
Lusaka	90,057	29.93	123,653	30.76
Luapula	32,552	27.51	47,289	22.90
Southern	151,550	20.55	71,519	19.15

Source: *Electoral Commission of Zambia*.

Banda's failure to win his bases with large margins, alongside Sata's significantly improved performance in the elections, made Banda's defeat inevitable. Thus, Sata's victory and ability to retain the support of his traditional constituencies between 2006 and 2011 owed as much to the ineptitude of his political competitors, especially the incumbents, as to his extraordinary political skill. For instance, Sata's electoral appeal in Bemba-speaking areas increased ahead of the 2008 elections, in large part because of the MMD's decision to leave the field of ethnic politics. This departure was precipitated by Republican vice-president Lupando Mwape losing his parliamentary seat in Northern Province to a PF candidate in the September 2006 polls. Irked by this, President Mwanawasa, despite having defeated Sata in Northern Province, accused Bembas of being ungrateful, and appointed Banda, a Chewa-speaker from the Eastern Province, as Zambia's new vice-president in October 2006.[54] Mwanawasa's clumsy decision was meant to punish Bemba voters but resulted only in a significant drop in support for the MMD in Northern Province.

Banda, who succeeded Mwanawasa, did little to win back the Bemba votes. His appointment of George Kunda, a non-Bemba from Central Province, as Republican vice-president (2008–2011) fed into growing concerns about political exclusion among Bemba-speaking communities and further marked Sata as the only credible political leader for most Bemba voters. Sata, in turn, furthered his case by arguing that the MMD had shown little commitment to fulfilling Bemba interests. His message found an echo in the dominant ethno-regional group

---

54 Joe Kaunda, 'Rupiah is new Vice-President', *The Post*, 9 October 2006, p. 1.

that found itself increasingly marginalised from the corridors of state power and resources.

A similar pattern was in evidence in Lusaka and on the Copperbelt, where neither Mwanawasa nor Banda attempted to change the voting choices of the electorate in those places by addressing the noted grievances of the urban poor and workers. Their disconnection enabled Sata to hold on to these key constituencies until the 2011 elections. Sata was also careful to modify his image. In previous elections, his willingness to lash out at foreign actors made many Zambians fear that he would destabilise the country's international reputation and scare off foreign investment. In contrast to his rabble-rousing rhetoric and anti-foreign 'infestor' rhetoric of the mid-2000s, Sata modified his stance on China, and during a talk at Oxford University in May 2011 stressed the importance of maintaining healthy relations with Zambia's international partners.[55] The latter message constituted a core element of his altered image ahead of the 2011 elections.

This chapter taken together with the previous chapter shows that Sata's success as an opposition leader between 2001 and 2011 resulted in part from the MMD's failure to satisfy the demands and aspirations of the affected majority of Zambian voters, and MMD falling out of touch with its traditional constituencies, to which Sata then laid claim through an ethno-regional and populist campaign. He made a range of specific promises to different groups, some of which contradicted others. The segmented nature of Zambian society in the early 2000s, however, made it nearly impossible for this strategy to be uncovered and challenged because there was little overlap between the groups that he was addressing. To the Bemba-speaking rural communities in Luapula and Northern provinces, Sata became a Bemba, notwithstanding he was in fact Bisa; to the mineworkers on the Copperbelt, he appeared as a mineworker and a trade unionist; to the unemployed and urban poor in Lusaka, Sata promised to deliver 'more jobs, more money in your pockets' and appeared as one of their own because 'I know what suffering means'; to the Lozis in Western Province, he appeared and dressed as a Lozi; and to civil society groups, he became a constitutional democrat ready and willing to deliver a new national constitution. In short, Sata became what he thought diverse constituencies wanted him to be. It was this populist campaign – alongside the ethnic strategy – that delivered him to State House on 23 September 2011 – the point at which this book began.

---

55 Invited by the University of Oxford's African Studies Centre and the Department of Politics and International Relations, Sata was welcomed by prominent British academics of African politics including Professors Miles Larmer and Nic Cheeseman, who have both written extensively on his politics. His keynote address to the conference was titled 'Road to Presidency: How to be a successful opposition leader in Africa'. Sishuwa Sishuwa, 'Defying the Incumbency Theory: Explaining Sata's Victory in the Zambian elections', *Democracy in Africa*, 1 December 2011, <http://democracyinafrica.org/defying-the-incumbency-theory/> (14 November 2015).

Conclusion

A FEW weeks before Zambia's 2001 election, the then 65-year-old Sata rejected growing calls for him to leave active politics to younger people. Featuring on Radio Phoenix's *Let the People Talk*, a popular weekly programme that enjoys nationwide listenership, the leader of the recently formed opposition PF party insisted that he would do so only 'after serving as Republican president in State House. I am exiting politics from State House.'[1] His inauguration as President of Zambia a decade later, on 23 September 2011, represented the fulfilment of that ambition, one that started almost half a century earlier. Sata's strategy for gaining power, and the specific pledges he made to win votes, offer some criteria that can be used to assess not just how he attempted to deliver on his campaign promises but also the relationship between populism and political change in Zambian history.

Sata's Achievements and Legacy

It is a hard task to assess the legacy of Sata since he died in office on 28 October 2014, barely three years after his inauguration. In a sense, Sata's long road to the presidency involved almost his entire life. By the time he became president, he was an old man and, for much of his presidency, he was seriously unwell. His untimely demise prevents a definitive judgement about whether he would ever have fulfilled his many pre-election promises, but there are strong indications he would not have done so. For instance, once in office, Sata reversed his stance on the constitution, arguing that 'Zambia does not need a new constitution but only amendments to its existing one'.[2] He also reversed his position on decentralisation. Having campaigned on a promise to use the Barotseland Agreement as a template for devolution, President Sata argued that implementing

---

1   W. Malido, 'I will retire after being President, says Sata', *The Post*, 26 October 2001, pp. 1–4.
2   Post staff, 'Zambia does not need a new constitution – President Sata', *The Post*, 30 November 2013, p. 4; Kombe Chimpinde-Mataka and Godfrey Chikumbi, 'Sata warns nurses', *The Post*, 1 December 2013, p. 4.

the Agreement would lead to the break-up of Zambia.[3] These U-turns suggest that he never had a genuine commitment to honour his promises and that he adopted the ideas merely to win votes.

Having spent much time in the opposition criticising the poor working conditions in Chinese-owned enterprises, Sata in power became an ardent supporter of Chinese businesses in Zambia. His first task in office was to host a lavish state banquet for the Chinese community, where he urged them to forget his campaign rhetoric.[4] Over the course of the next few years, Sata forcefully defended Chinese investment from opposition criticism, such as in June 2014 when he declared that:

> if anyone who wants to kill China, they must kill us first … China and Zambia are Siamese twins. We don't look at the Chinese as foreigners. We look at them as our brothers.[5]

Sata, however, achieved the promise offered to Bemba speakers that they would enjoy more prominent positions within Zambia under his presidency. He appointed twelve Bemba speakers from Luapula and Northern provinces to Cabinet, out of the total nineteen ministerial positions.[6] The promotion of this kind of ethnic agenda led to criticism from the opposition that Sata was dividing the country on ethno-regional lines – divisions that continue to plague Zambia long after his death. Sata also risked undermining his support in Bemba-speaking areas when he got into a dispute with Bemba regents over the choice of the next Chitimukulu (Bemba king) following the death of the incumbent traditional leader. Refusing to gazette the candidate chosen by the regents, Sata attempted to impose his own choice, a Bisa speaker.[7] This move angered ethnic Bembas greatly and alienated many from Sata and the Patriotic Front (PF) until his death.

On the economic front, Sata increased both the wages of public sector employees by as much as 200 per cent and the income tax threshold by 100 per cent (from K1,000 in 2011 to K2,000 in 2012), exemplifying the fulfilment of his

---

3   Bright Mukwasa, 'Sata sees problems with Barotse deal', *The Post*, 24 February 2012, pp. 1 and 4.
4   Chibaula Silwamba, 'China congratulates Sata', *The Post*, 27 September 2011, p. 3; Interview with Wynter Kabimba, Lusaka, 12 May 2015.
5   Yande Syampeyo, Jimmy Chibuye, and Alvin Chiinga, 'Sata defends China', *Zambia Daily Mail*, 20 June 2014, p. 1; Joseph Mwenda, Roy Habaalu and Abel Mboozi, 'I have always been a labourer – Sata', *The Post*, 20 June 2014, p. 4.
6   'President Sata names Guy Scott as Vice president and reduces cabinet size by only 3 ministries', <https://www.lusakatimes.com/2011/09/29/president-sata-names-guy-scott-vice-president-reduces-cabinet-size-3-ministries/> (14 June 2016).
7   Email correspondence, *Chitimukulu* Kanyanta Manga Henry Sosala to the author, 28 May 2016.

pre-election pledge to 'put more money in people's pockets' once in power.[8] He also borrowed heavily from international sovereign bond markets to finance the construction of roads and physical infrastructure in the additional one province and thirty districts that he created after assuming power. These moves clearly led to huge budget deficits that outlived Sata, but the construction projects provided employment to many of his uneducated supporters who could not secure jobs in the formal sector.

Despite the broken promises, Sata's election nevertheless paved the way for reform in some areas. For instance, in the wake of his death, the PF under Sata's successor, Edgar Lungu, went on to deliver a national constitution containing nearly all the key proposals demanded by civil society groups, such as the clauses that a winning presidential candidate should secure a minimum of '50 per cent + 1' of the total vote, and the election of the vice-president as a running mate alongside the president.[9] Sata thus played an important role in moving Zambia forward. However, much like the rest of his career, Sata's time in power leaves a complex legacy and requires a more thorough assessment that builds on the work completed in this book.

After a decade in office, Sata's PF party was defeated by the opposition United Party for National Development (UPND) led by Hakainde Hichilema in the August 2021 election.[10] Many of the significant challenges that Hichilema's administration faced on assuming office, such as a crippling public debt, deep ethnic polarisation, and ongoing tension over the unresolved Barotseland Agreement in the western part of the country, can be traced back directly to Sata's time in power.

Populism and Political Change

Existing explanations for party politics and political change in Zambia, mainly from political science studies, have tended to focus largely on ethnic mobilisations, taking attention away from the fact that most ethnic politics has had a populist component.[11] As this book has demonstrated, populism has been

---

8   Chiwoyu Sinyangwe, 'More money in your pockets', *The Post*, 12 November 2011, pp. 1–4.
9   Chila Namaiko, Melbourne Mushitu, and Rebecca Mushota, 'Constitution fever ... as Lungu delivers', *Times of Zambia*, 5 January 2016, p. 1.
10 For an analysis of the 2021 election, see Sishuwa Sishuwa, 'The outcome of a historical process in motion in 1991: Explaining the failure of incumbency advantage in Zambia's 2021 election', *Journal of Eastern African Studies*, 16, 4 (2022), 659–80. For an analysis of Hichilema's political career, see Sishuwa Sishuwa, 'Multi-ethnic vision or ethnic nationalism? The contested legacies of Anderson Mazoka and Zambia's 2006 election', *Canadian Journal of African Studies*, 57, 2 (2023), 431–57.
11 See, for instance, Daniel Posner, *Institutions and Ethnic Politics in Africa*, Cambridge: Cambridge University Press, 2005.

a feature of party politics since the late-colonial period and is exemplified by Sata, who demonstrates the utility or effectiveness of populism as a mobilising electoral strategy in African politics. He was able to win elections in a one-party state, establish a power base in a dominant ruling party, and successfully build an opposition party by relying heavily on a populist strategy. Sata also showed an awareness of the extreme limits of populism as a governing policy. In opposition, Sata promised to nationalise the mines, among other measures, but in office he hardly governed as a populist. In a certain way, his early death – like that of Magufuli in Tanzania – makes it harder to provide a full analysis of how leaders who win elections as populists govern when in power for an extended period and when the contradictions of their pre-election promises become self-evident very quickly.

Although Sata became best known for the use of populism in party politics, he was not the only populist. Other political figures employed populist mobilisations with greater success. A notable example is Simon Kapwepwe and his United Progressive Party (UPP), discussed in earlier sections of this book, who gained popularity during the early 1970s by articulating diverse urban dwellers' economic demands and grievances using populist rhetoric. Another is President Chiluba, whose re-election in 1996 was secured against the backdrop of what might be regarded as the use of 'populism in office' two months before the general election. When it dawned on him that he had lost the support of urbanites, thanks in part to his administration's failure to build homes for the urban poor as promised in 1991, Chiluba embarked on a reckless nationwide sale of all council and 40,000 parastatal houses to civil servants, retirees, and sitting tenants, mostly urbanites, at ridiculously low rates, reflecting a desperate, if belated, attempt at honouring a key campaign promise and placating this key electoral constituency.[12]

Populism also provides a guide to understanding some of Sata's economic policies and actions in government, such as his U-turn on Chinese investment. Being in power required a balancing act. Ambitious plans for infrastructure, through which jobs were to be created for his political base, and raising the wages of state employees, needed finance. Having achieved near comprehensive debt relief in the 2000s, many lenders looked sceptically at Zambia. In this context, and in addition to raising the country's Eurobonds from private investors, Sata – and his successor Lungu – turned to China, who provided a wider array of finance, some of it hidden from the government's debt sheet.[13] Having railed against Chinese 'profiteers' when in opposition, Sata in power presided over significant increases in Chinese investment and loans.

12   Emmanuel Mutale, *The Management of Urban Development in Zambia*, Surrey: Ashgate, 2004.
13   Yuzhou Sun, *Kenya's and Zambia's Relations with China, 1949–2019*, Suffolk: James Currey, 2023.

Altogether, these examples reinforce the point that populism has been a significant part of political life in independent Zambia. Across different historical periods and party systems, individual leaders have employed the strategy to win elections and, once in government, maintain the coalition of disparate interest groups that supported their rise to power.

Sata, Party Politics and Political Change

In examining the growth in populism and its use in party politics through the career of an individual whose experiences cut across supposed turning points and disruptions, and the institutions that have come and gone with them, this book provides a clear understanding of the major themes of Zambian political history in each period, how the themes intersected with the life of an individual, and the broad continuities between them. Thus the book has intervened in several key debates, by historians and political scientists of late-colonial and post-colonial Zambian politics, regarding the interaction between the individual and wider society.

First, *Party Politics and Populism in Zambia* has demonstrated the endurance of late-colonial influences in the country's post-colonial political life. In so doing, the book builds on the insights of *Living the End of Empire: Politics and Society in Late Colonial Zambia*,[14] an edited collection that discusses the importance of the late-colonial period for what happens in post-colonial Zambia. Using the case of Sata, I have traced continuities between these two eras from the 1950s and early 1960s almost to the present, and shown that Sata's formative experiences during the late-colonial period had a significant, even determining, influence on the strategies that he adopted to mobilise political support in post-colonial Zambia. In other words, these experiences influenced his understanding of the world around him for the rest of his life and career, demonstrating the enduring nature of late-colonial political developments in independent Zambia. Existing studies of political life in independent Zambia lack appreciation of the deep historical roots of the country's contemporary politics and political actors. In this regard, this book is a contribution to remedying this sustained neglect.

Second, the book has demonstrated the significance of parliamentary elections and the nature of political change in the one-party state. In so doing, it rejects those studies that have argued that political life in the one-party state was static. On the contrary, the book argues that elections, at least at the parliamentary level, were surprisingly competitive and provided an outlet for opposition through the removal of sitting MPs. Patronage networks emerged, as shown by the funding that Sata secured for his successful election campaigns, using national public funds to procure political support.

---

14 Jan-Bart Gewald, Marja Hinfelaar, and Giacomo Macola (eds), *Living the End of Empire: Politics and Society in Late Colonial Zambia*, Leiden: Brill, 2011.

Third, the book contributes to the debates around the question of succession in Zambian politics. It has shown that, if we are to understand the outcome of succession contests, we should pay attention to the process of how they evolve or play out, especially in dominant parties. Using the case of Sata, I have shown that the real political dynamics in the 1990s were within the governing MMD, not outside it, where several budding successors attempted to establish power bases as early as 1992, highlighting the usefulness of studying internal party dynamics to understand succession outcomes.

Finally, the book contributes to the debate on the importance of individual political leadership to the mobilisation strategies of opposition parties in Zambian politics. Using the case of Sata and his PF in the early 2000s, it has demonstrated that the two – the individual and the institution – were inseparable. It is inconceivable to think of the PF mobilising voters and emerging as a credible political force without the personality and populist strategy of Sata. What this suggests is that, if historians and political scientists of post-colonial Zambian politics wish to understand political change, the mobilisation strategies of opposition parties, and the nature of political campaigning, then they should pay attention to the growing significance of individual political leadership.

The findings presented in this book also demonstrate the value of using biography to provide broader insights into the main themes of Zambian political history. Sata's experiences in late-colonial Zambia, for instance, were not unique. The broad contours of his life – migration to the Copperbelt and entering waged employment – were common to thousands of Zambians of his generation during the 1950s and much earlier. The ease with which he moved from colonial policeman to anti-colonial nationalist in the early 1960s was no barrier to his entry into political life in post-colonial Zambia, and is indicative of nationalism's lack of enduring importance in the political life of the country. Sata's trajectory and career under the one-party state was also not particularly unusual. Everyone involved in political life at the time shared the same party affiliation and was promoted, demoted, and moved sideways through the same structures and set of positions. Within the MMD, as the period of President Chiluba's leadership came to an end, Sata's faction was one among several built around prominent MMD members positioning themselves for power as Chiluba's successor. Like Sata, many of these disappointed budding successors founded small protest parties in the early 2000s.

Thus, in each of these eras of Zambian political history, the experiences and actions of Sata have much in common with those of many his contemporaries. Conclusions and arguments about the life of this individual therefore have wider applications, demonstrating the value of employing a contextualised biographic approach to understanding political change.

Political Biography, Party Politics, and Political Change in Africa

In understanding political change in Africa, the role of the individual generally remains neglected even for those individual political actors, such as Kizza Besigye in Uganda, Morgan Tsvangirai in Zimbabwe, and Raila Odinga in Kenya, who have played an outsized role in the opposition parties they founded and led, or whose personal experiences illustrate broader themes of their respective countries. This book makes two main contributions to the wider historical and political science debates on the broader processes of political change in Africa.

First, it demonstrates that the role of individual leadership matters in determining the strategies of political mobilisation and the success of political parties in Africa. It is not simply a question of institutions such as parties, for instance, setting political strategies. Individual leaders, as the book has shown using Sata's case, shape many of these strategies, significantly influence the style of political engagement, and are in many cases responsible for a party's success in political competition. Therefore, the importance of individuals rather than institutions in political life in many African states cannot be overemphasised. There have, however, been too few in-depth studies of major political figures showcasing this insight. This book provides one such study, but there are many other figures on the continent ripe for similar treatment. A serious historical study of Odinga, Tsvangirai, or Besigye may generate new and valuable insights into our understanding of dynamism and change in African political systems.

Second, the book demonstrates the value – and calls for increased use – of biography in understanding political change in Africa. The scholarship has tended to examine political engagement and change on the continent through the prisms of institutions such as political parties, trade unions, and civil society organisations, or supposed turning points like the beginning of one-party rule and the reintroduction of multi-party democracy. What Sata's case study tells us is the central role of individuals in African politics, and how we should study individuals: through a context-driven biography. It is gratifying that this book appears at a time when interest in the use of biography, as a methodological approach to understanding historical change in Africa, is growing. In this regard, I anticipate that this book will contribute to a burgeoning field of biography in African history, exemplified by the recent publication of an edited volume on the subject.[15]

---

15   Klaas van Walraven (ed.), *The Individual in African History: The Importance of Biography in African Historical Studies*, Leiden: Brill, 2020.

Bibliography

Primary Sources

Archives: United National Independence Party Archives (UNIPA), Lusaka

Chama, Moses, Acting General Secretary of NUBWMW to UNIP National Secretary, 16 May 1963, UNIPA 6/42.
'Programme of Unity of Action – Membership Drive Part 1', 13 June 1963, UNIPA/12/1/7–18.

Printed Primary/Unpublished Sources

Central Statistical Office, *2010 Census of Population and Housing – National Analytical Report*, Lusaka, 2012.
——, 'Formal Employment Trends in Zambia, 1991–2010', *Labour Force Survey Report*, Lusaka, 2012.
——, *1980 Population and Housing Census of Zambia*, Lusaka, 1985.
Erdmann, Gero and N. Simutanyi, 'Factionalism in an African Party System: The Case of Zambia', Unpublished paper, 2006.
Electoral Commission of Zambia, 'Nomination Papers for the 2011 Presidential Elections', August 2011.
——, 'Nomination Papers for the 2008 Presidential Election', Electoral Commission of Zambia, September 2008.
Fraser, Alistair, '"Don't *Kubeba!*" Beyond Patronage Politics in the Zambian Elections of 2011', unpublished paper presented to the African History and Politics Seminar, University of Oxford, 25 February 2013.
Hinfelaar, M., D. Resnick, and S. Sishuwa, 'Cities and Dominance: Urban Strategies for Political Settlement Maintenance and Change – Zambia Case Study', *ESID Working Paper No. 136*, Manchester: University of Manchester, 2020.
Miles Larmer, 'Historicising populism in late-colonial/post-colonial sub-Saharan Africa', paper presented to the Comparing Populism workshop, University of Sheffield, United Kingdom, 8–9 February 2013.
Larmer, Miles, 'Simon Kapwepwe: Zambia's greatest intellectual politician?', *Bulletin and Record*, November 2011, pp. 43–44.
Mung'omba Constitution Review Commission, *Report of the Mung'omba Constitution Review Commission*, Lusaka, 2005.

National Assembly of Zambia, *Composition of Members of Parliament Between Ruling Party and Opposition Members since 2006*, Lusaka: Aquila Printers, October 2011.

Rakner, Lise, 'Do Interest Groups Matter in Economic Policy-Making? Reflections from a Zambian Case Study', *CMI Working Paper 1994:4*, Bergen: Chr. Michelsen Institute, 1994.

Ranger, Terence O., 'Missionaries, Migrants and the Manyika: The Invention of Ethnicity in Zimbabwe', paper presented to the African Studies Institute, University of Witwatersrand, 2 April 1984.

Simutanyi, Neo, 'The 2008 Presidential Elections in Zambia: Incumbency, Political Contestation and Failure of Political Opposition', paper presented to the CMI/IESE Conference on 'Election Processes, Liberation Movements and Democratic Change in Africa', Maputo, Mozambique, 8–11 April 2010.

United National Independence Party, *The National Policies for the Decade 1985–1995: Aims and Objectives of the Third Phase of the Party Programme*, Lusaka: Office of the Secretary-General, 1984.

——, *The UNIP Manual of Rules and Regulations Governing the 1983 General Elections*, Lusaka: Zambia Information Service, 1983.

World Bank, *Zambia – Country Economic Memorandum: Policies for Growth and Diversification, Volume 1. Main Report*, Washington, DC: World Bank, 2004.

Newspapers

National Mirror (Lusaka), 1979–2005.
The Post (Lusaka), 1991–2016 (called *Weekly Post* until 1996, when it became a daily paper).
Zambia Daily Mail (Lusaka) 1964–.
The Northern News (Lusaka), 1958–1964.
Times of Zambia (Lusaka), 1965–.
The Telegraph (London), 1855–.

Interviews

Banda, Rupiah, Lusaka, 12 February 2013.
Banda, William, Lusaka, 23 October 2015.
——, Lusaka, 17 October 2012.
Bwalya, Frank, Lusaka, 23 May 2013.
Chellah, George, Lusaka, 27 April 2011.
Chikopela, Emmanuel, Lusaka, 5 April 2016.
Chikwanda, Chief, Mpika, 24 March 2016.
Chirwa, Alec, Lusaka, 21 March 2014.
Chitala, Derrick, Lusaka, 22 October 2015.
Chona, Mark Lusaka, 12 September 2016.
Chongwe, Rodger, Lusaka, 28 November 2015.
——, Lusaka, 25 April 2011.
Clarke, Roy, Lusaka, 17 April 2011.
Dunn, Colin, Lusaka, 28 November 2015.

Habasonda, Lee, Lusaka, 21 October 2015.
Hikaumba, Leonard, Lusaka, 12 April 2011.
Irwin, Carl, Lusaka, 14 May 2015.
Irwin, Joan, Johannesburg, 6 May 2014.
Kaliminwa, Fr Nicholas, Lubushi, 23 March 2016.
Kabanda, Simon, Lusaka, 22 October 2015.
——, Lusaka, 21 October 2015.
Kabimba, Wynter, Lusaka, 12 May 2015.
——, Lusaka, 16 January 2013.
Kalumba, Katele, Lusaka, 22 April 2014.
——, Lusaka, 11 March 2012.
——, Chiengi, 7 April 2011.
Kapwepwe, Chilufya, Chinsali, 12 December 2013.
Kaunda, Kenneth, Lusaka, 19 October 2015.
——, Lusaka, 29 April 2011.
Kavindele, Enoch, Lusaka, 29 April 2013.
Lafollie, Fr Pierre, Lusaka, 4 April 2016.
Larmer, Miles, Oxford, 20 May 2011.
Lifwekelo, Edwin, Lusaka, 18 October 2012.
Machungwa, Peter, Lusaka, 11 April 2013.
——, Lusaka, 3 April 2011.
Magande, Ng'andu, Lusaka, 23 April 2011.
Maine, Katongo, Chinsali, 17 December 2013.
Makhurane, Phinias, Bulawayo, 24 April 2014.
Malambo, Vincent, Lusaka, 19 April 2013.
Matale, Suzanne, Lusaka, 22 October 2015.
Mbikusita-Lewanika, Akashambatwa, Lusaka, 12 April 2014.
——, Lusaka, 10 January 2014.
——, Lusaka 15 April 2011.
Mbulu, Rayford, Kitwe, 24 March 2011.
——, Kitwe, 23 March 2011.
Miyanda, Godfrey, Lusaka, 3 December 2013.
Mucheleka, Patrick, Lusaka, 12 November 2014.
Mudenda, Lovemore, Lusaka, 27 November 2015.
Muneku, Austin, telephone interview, 17 July 2015.
Mususu, Paul, Lusaka, 13 April 2015.
Mwaanga, Vernon, Lusaka, 10 January 2014.
——, Lusaka, 26 February 2013.
——, Lusaka, 18 April 2011.
Mwanamwambwa, Amusa, Lusaka, 5 March 2013.
Mwanza, Regina, Lusaka, 26 February 2013.
Mwenye, Musa, Lusaka, 22 October 2015.
Mwila Jnr, Ben, Kitwe, 28 March 2014.
Nawakwi, Edith, Lusaka, 26 February 2013.
Nonde, Joyce, Lusaka, 25 March 2011.
Nsama, Thomas, Lusaka, 3 April 2011.

Patel, Dipak, Lusaka, 18 January 2013.
Sardanis, Stelios, Lusaka, 26 September 2014.
Sata, Michael, Lusaka, 13 January 2013.
——, Lusaka, 26 April 2011.
——, Lusaka, 14 April 2011.
——, Lusaka, 20 March 2011.
Scott, Guy, Lusaka, 18 March 2012.
——, Lusaka, 8 April 2011.
Sejani Ackson, Lusaka, 26 February 2013.
Shamenda, Fackson, Lusaka, 24 March 2014.
Silwamba, Eric, Lusaka, 19 March 2013.
Simutanyi, Neo, Lusaka, 13 January 2014.
——, Lusaka, 7 April 2011.
Soloti, Moses, Kitwe, 12 April 2016.
Wina, Sikota, Lusaka, 29 November 2015.
——, Lusaka, 12 April 2014.
——, Lusaka, 28 February 2013.
——, Lusaka, 16 December 2013.
Zimba, Newstead, Lusaka, 13 April 2014.
Zukas, Simon, Lusaka, 8 April 2011.
Zulu, Martha, Lusaka, 26 October 2015.

Secondary Sources

Books and Chapters in Edited Collections

Barkan, Joel D. and John J. Okumu, '"Semi-Competitive" Elections, Clientelism, and Political Recruitment in a No-Party State: The Kenyan Experience', in G. Hermet, R. Rose and A. Rouquié (eds), *Elections Without Choice*, London: Palgrave Macmillan, 1978, pp. 88–107.
Bates, Robert, *Unions, Parties and Political Development: A Study of Mineworkers in Zambia*, New Haven: Yale University Press, 1971.
Baylies, Carolyn and Morris Szeftel, 'Democratisation and the 1991 Elections in Zambia', in J. Daniel, R. Southall, and M. Szeftel (eds), *Voting for Democracy: Watershed Elections in Contemporary Anglophone Africa*, Aldershot: Ashgate, 1999.
Berger, L. Elena, *Labour, Race and Colonial Rule: The Copperbelt from 1924 to Independence*, Oxford: Oxford University Press, 1974.
Brelsford, W.V. *The Tribes of Zambia*, Lusaka: Government Printer, 1965.
Burawoy, Michael, *The Colour of Class on the Copperbelt: From African Advancement to Zambianisation Mines*, Lusaka: University of Zambia Institute of African Studies, 1972.
Butler, L.J., *Mining and the Colonial State in Northern Rhodesia, c. 1930–1964*, London: Palgrave Macmillan, 2007.
Bratton, Michael and Daniel N. Posner, 'A First Look at Second Elections in Africa, with illustrations from Zambia' in Richard Joseph (ed.), *State, Conflict and Democracy in Africa*, Boulder, CO: Lynne Rienner Publishers, 1999, pp. 377–408.

Caplan, Gerald, *The Elites of Barotseland 1878–1969: A Political History of Zambia's Western Province*, Berkeley: University of California Press, 1970.

Chan, Stephen, *Southern Africa: Old Treacheries and New Deceits*, New Haven: Yale University Press, 2012.

Cheeseman, Nic, Robert Ford, and Neo Simutanyi, 'Is there a "Populist Threat" in Zambia?', in Christopher Adam, Paul Collier and Michael Gondwe (eds), *Zambia: Building Prosperity from Resource Wealth*, Oxford: Oxford University Press, 2014, pp. 339–65.

Chitala, Mbita, *Not Yet Democracy: The Transition of the Twin Process of Political and Economic Reform in Zambia, 1991–2001*, Lusaka: Zambia Research Foundation, 2002.

Clayton, Anthony and David Killingray, *Khaki and Blue: Military and Police in British Colonial Africa*, Athens, OH: Ohio University Press, 1989.

Cooper, Frederick, *Africa since 1940: The Past of the Present*, Cambridge, UK: Cambridge University Press, 2002.

Crush, Jonathan and Charles Ambler (eds), *Liquor and Labour in Southern Africa*, Athens, OH: Ohio University Press, 1992.

De la Tore, Carlos, 'Populism in Latin America', in C. Rovira, P. Taggart, P.O. Espejo, and P. Ostiguy (eds), *The Oxford Handbook of Populism*, Oxford: Oxford University Press, 2017, pp. 260–84.

Epstein, Arnold Leonard, *Politics in an Urban African Community*, Manchester: Manchester University Press, 1958.

Ferguson, James, *Expectations of Modernity: Myths and Meanings of Urban Life on the Zambian Copperbelt*, California: University of California Press, 1999.

Gertzel, Cherry J. (ed.), Carolyn Louise Baylies, and Morris Szeftel, *The Dynamics of the One-Party State in Zambia*, Manchester: Manchester University Press, 1984.

——, Carolyn Baylies, and Morris Szeftel, 'Elections in the One-Party State' in Cherry J. Gertzel (ed.), Carolyn Baylies and Morris Szeftel, *The Dynamics of the One-Party State in Zambia*, Manchester: Manchester University Press, 1984.

Gewald, Jan-Bart, *Forged in the Great War: People, Transport, and Labour, the Establishment of Colonial Rule in Zambia, 1890–1920*, Leiden: African Studies Centre, 2015.

—— (eds), *Living the End of Empire: Politics and Society in Late Colonial Zambia*, Leiden: Brill, 2011.

——, Marja Hinfelaar, and Giacomo Macola (eds), *One Zambia, Many Histories: Towards a History of Post-colonial Zambia*, Lusaka: Lembani Trust, 2008.

Gould, Jeremy, *Left Behind: Rural Zambia in the Third Republic*, Lusaka: Lembani Trust, 2010.

——, 'Subsidiary sovereignty and the constitution of political space in Zambia', in Jan-Bart Gewald, Marja Hinfelaar, and Giacomo Macola (eds), *One Zambia, Many Histories: Towards a History of Post-colonial Zambia*, Lusaka: Lembani Trust, 2009, pp. 275–93.

Gupta, Anirudha, 'Trade Unionism and Politics on the Copperbelt', in William Tordoff (ed.), *Politics in Zambia*, Berkeley: University of California Press, 1974,

Hall, Richard, *Kaunda: Founder of Zambia*, Lusaka: Longmans, 1964.

Handlin, Oscar, *Truth in History*, Cambridge, MA: The Belknap Press of Harvard University Press, 1979.
Hinfelaar, Hugo, *History of the Catholic Church in Zambia*, Lusaka: Bookworld Publishers, 2004.
Kershaw, Ian, *Hitler: 1889–1936*, London: Penguin Press, 1998.
Killingray, David and David M. Anderson, 'An Orderly Retreat? Policing and the End of Empire', in David Killingray and David M. Anderson (eds), *Policing and Decolonisation: Politics, Nationalism and the Police, 1917–65*, Manchester: Manchester University Press, 1992.
Laclau, Ernesto, 'Populism: What's in a Name?', in F. Panizza (ed.), *Populism and the Mirror of Democracy*, London: Verso, 2005.
Larmer, Miles, *Rethinking African Politics: A History of Opposition in Zambia*, Surrey: Ashgate Publishing, 2011.
—— (ed.), *The Musakanya Papers: The Autobiographical Writings of Valentine Musakanya*, Lusaka: Lembani Trust, 2010.
——, 'Zambia since 1990: Paradoxes of Democratic Transition', in Abdul R. Mustapha and Lindsay Whitfield (eds), *Turning Points in African Democracy*, New York: James Curry, 2009.
——, *Mineworkers in Zambia: Labour and Political Change in Post-colonial Africa*, London: I.B. Tauris, 2007.
Lawrence, Benjamin., Emily L. Osborn, and Richard L. Roberts (eds), *Intermediaries, Interpreters, and Clerks: African Employees in the Making of Colonial Africa*, Madison: University of Wisconsin Press, 2006.
Lowndes, Joseph, 'Populism in the United States', in C. Rovira, P. Taggart, P.O. Espejo, and P. Ostiguy (eds), *The Oxford Handbook of Populism*, Oxford: Oxford University Press, 2017.
Lyell, Dennis D., *Hunting Trips in Northern Rhodesia*, London: Horace Cox, 1910.
Macola, Giacomo, *The Gun in Central Africa: A History of Technology and Politics*, Ohio: Ohio University Press, 2016.
——, *Liberal Nationalism in Central Africa: A Biography of Harry Mwaanga Nkumbula*, New York: Palgrave Macmillan, 2010.
MacMillan, Hugh, *The Lusaka Years: The ANC in Exile in Zambia, 1963 to 1994*, Johannesburg: Jacana Media, 2013.
Macpherson, Fergus, *Kenneth Kaunda of Zambia: The Times and the Man*, Oxford: Oxford University Press, 1974.
Makasa, Paul, *Sustainable Urban Areas: 1996 Zambia National Housing Policy*, Amsterdam: IOS Press, 2010.
Makhurane, Phinias-Mogorosi, *Phinias-Mogorosi Makhurane: An Autobiography*, Gweru: Booklove Publishers, 2010.
Malupenga, Amos, *Levy Patrick Mwanawasa: An Incentive for Posterity*, Grahamstown: NISC, 2009.
Mamdani, Mahmood, *Citizen and Subject: Contemporary Africa and the Legacy of Late-Colonialism*, Oxford: James Currey, 1996.
Mbikusita-Lewanika, Akashambatwa, *Hour for Reunion: Movement for Multi-Party Democracy: Conception, Dissension and Reconciliation*, Mongu: African Lineki Courier, 2003.

Mbikusita-Lewanika, Akashambatwa and Derrick Chitala (eds), *The Hour Has Come! Proceedings of the National Conference on Multi-party Option*, Lusaka: Zambia Research Foundation, 1990.

Meebelo, Henry S., *African Proletarians and Colonial Capitalism: The Origins, Growth and Struggles of the Zambian Labour Movement to 1964*, Lusaka: Kenneth Kaunda Foundation, 1986.

———, *Reaction to Colonialism: A Prelude to the Politics of Independence in Northern Zambia, 1893–1939*, Manchester: Manchester University Press, 1971.

Mhone, Guy C.Z., *The Political Economy of a Dual Labor Market in Africa: The Copper Industry and Dependency in Zambia, 1929–1969*, London: Associated University Press, 1982.

Mitchell, J. Clyde, *The Kalela Dance: Aspects of Social Relationships among Urban Africans in Northern Rhodesia*, Manchester: Manchester University Press, 1956.

Moffitt, Benjamin, *The Global Rise of Populism*, Palo Alto: Stanford University Press, 2016.

Molteno, Robert and Ian Scott, 'The 1968 general election and the political system', in William Tordoff (ed.), *Politics in Zambia*, Berkeley: University of California Press, 1974.

Morris, Collin, *Black Government? A Discussion between Collin Morris and Kenneth Kaunda*, Lusaka: Rhodesian Printers, 1960.

Mudde, Cas, 'Populism: An Ideational Approach', in C. Rovira, P. Taggart, P.O. Espejo, and P. Ostiguy (eds), *The Oxford Handbook of Populism*, Oxford: Oxford University Press, 2018.

Mulford, David C., *Zambia: The Politics of Independence, 1957–1964*, Oxford: Oxford University Press, 1967.

Mulenga, Friday, 'Fighting for Democracy of the Pocket: The Labour Movement in the Third Republic', in Jan-Bart Gewald, Marja Hinfelaar, and Giacomo Macola (eds), *One Zambia, Many Histories: Towards the History of Post-Colonial Zambia*, Lusaka: Lembani Trust, 2010.

Mususa, Patience, *There Used to Be Order: Life on the Copperbelt after the Privatisation of the Zambia Consolidated Copper Mines*, Michigan: University of Michigan Press, 2021.

Mutale, Emmanuel, *The Management of Urban Development in Zambia*, Surrey: Ashgate, 2004.

Mwangilwa, Godwin, *Harry Mwaanga Nkumbula: A Biography of the Old Lion of Zambia*, Lusaka: Multimedia Publications, 1982.

Mwendapole, Mathew, *A History of the Trade Union Movement in Zambia up to 1968*, Lusaka: Institute of African Studies, 1977.

Nyangira, Nicholas, 'Ethnicity, Class, and Politics in Kenya', in Michael G Schatzberg (ed.), *The Political Economy of Kenya*, New York: Praeger, 1987, pp. 15–32.

Nordlund, Per, *Organising the Political Agora: Domination and Democratisation in Zambia and Zimbabwe*, Uppsala: Uppsala University, 1996.

Ohannessian, Sirarpi and Kashoki, Mubanga, *Language in Zambia*, London: International African Institute, 1978.

Phiri, Bizeck J., *A Political History of Zambia: From the Colonial Period to the Third Republic*, Asmara: Africa World Press, 2006.

Posner, Daniel, *Institutions and Ethnic Politics in Africa*, Cambridge: Cambridge University Press, 2005.
Rakodi, Carole, 'Housing in Lusaka: Policies and Progress', in Geoffrey J. Williams (ed.), *Lusaka and Its Environs: A Geographical Study of a Planned Capital City in Tropical Africa*, Lusaka: Zambian Geographical Association, 1986, pp. 189–207.
Rakner, Lise, *Political and Economic Liberalisation in Zambia, 1991–2001*, Uppsala: Nordic Africa Institute, 2003.
Rakner, Lise and Lars Svasand, 'In Search of the Impact of International Support for Political Parties in New Democracies: Malawi and Zambia Compared', in Peter Burnell and André W.M. Gerrits (eds), *Promoting Party Politics in Emerging Democracies*. London: Routledge, 2012.
Ranger, Terence O., *The Invention of Tribalism in Zimbabwe*, Gweru: Mambo Press, 1985.
Rasmussen, Thomas, 'The Popular Basis of Anti-colonial Protest', in William Tordoff (ed.), *Politics in Zambia*, Berkeley: University of California Press, 1974.
Resnick, Daniel, 'Populism in Africa', in C. Rovira, P. Taggart, P.O. Espejo, and P. Ostiguy (eds), *The Oxford Handbook of Populism*, Oxford: Oxford University Press, 2018, pp. 140–64.
——, *Urban Poverty and Party Populism in African Democracies*, New York: Cambridge University Press, 2014.
Roberts, Andrew, *A History of Zambia*, London: Heinemann Educational Books, 1976.
——, 'Northern Rhodesia: The Post-War Background, 1945–1953', in Jan-Bart Gewald, Marja Hinfelaar, and Giacomo Macola (eds), *Living the End of Empire: Politics and Society in Late Colonial Zambia*, Leiden: Brill, 2011.
——, *A History of the Bemba: Political Growth and Change in North-Eastern Zambia before 1900*, Wisconsin: University of Wisconsin Press, 1973.
Rodney, Walter, *How Europe Undeveloped Africa*, London: Bogle-L'Ouverture Publications, 1972.
Rotberg, Robert I., *Black Heart: Gore-Browne and the Politics of Multiracial Zambia*, Berkeley: University of California Press, 1978.
——, *The Rise of Nationalism in Central Africa: The Making of Malawi and Zambia, 1873–1964*, Cambridge: Cambridge University Press, 1965.
Sardanis, Andrew, *Zambia: The First 50 Years: Reflections of an Eyewitness*, London: I.B. Tauris, 2014.
Sichone, Owen and Neo Simutanyi, 'The Ethnic and Regional Questions, Ethnic Nationalism and the State in Zambia: The Case of Barotseland, 1964–1994', in Owen Sichone and Bornwell Chikulo (eds), *Democracy in Zambia: Challenges for the Third Republic*, Harare: SAPES Trust, 1996.
Sikalumbi, Wittington, *Before UNIP*, Lusaka: National Educational Company of Zambia, 1977.
Simon, David J., 'Democracy Unrealised: Zambia's Third Republic under Frederick Chiluba', in Leonardo A. Villalon and Peter VonDoepp (eds), *The Fate of Africa's Democratic Experiments: Elites and Institutions*, Bloomington: Indiana University Press, 2005.

Simutanyi, Neo, 'Zambia: Manufactured One-Party Dominance and Its Collapse', in Renske Doorenspleet and Lia Nijzink, *One-Party Dominance in African Democracies*, London: Lynne Riener Publishers, 2013, pp. 119–42.

———, 'The Politics of Constitutional Reform in Zambia: From Executive dominance to Public Participation', in Danwood M. Chirwa and Lia Nijzink (eds), *Accountable Governments in Africa: Perspectives from Public Law and Political Studies*, Tokyo: United Nations University, 2012, pp. 26–42.

Spaita, James Mwewa (Archbishop), *They Answered the Call: Nyasa-Bangweolo Vicariates*, Kasama: Kalebalika Publishers Audio Visual Systems, 2012.

Sun, Yuzhou, *Kenya's and Zambia's Relations with China, 1949–2019*, Suffolk: James Currey, 2023.

Taggart, Paul, 'Populism in Western Europe', in C. Rovira, P. Taggart, P.O. Espejo, and P. Ostiguy (eds), *The Oxford Handbook of Populism*, Oxford: Oxford University Press, 2018.

Tordoff, William (ed.), *Politics in Zambia*, Berkeley: University of California, 1974.

Uwechue, Ralph (ed.), *Africa Yearbook and Who's Who 1977*, London: Africa Journal Limited, 1976.

Van Walraven, Klaas (ed.), *The Individual in African History: The Importance of Biography in African Historical Studies*, Leiden: Brill, 2020.

Van Donge, Jan Kees, 'Kaunda and Chiluba: Enduring Patterns of Political Culture', in John A. Wiseman (ed.), *Democracy and Political Change in Sub-Saharan Africa*, London: Routledge, 1995, pp. 193–219.

Vickery, Kenneth P., 'Odd Man Out: Labour, Politics and Dixon Konkola', in Jan-Bart Gewald, Marja Hinfelaar, and Giacomo Macola (eds), *Living the End of Empire: Politics and Society in Late Colonial Zambia*, Leiden: Brill, 2011.

Wanyande, Peter, 'Democracy and the One-Party State: The African Experience', in Walter O. Oyugi, E.S. Atieno Odhiambo, Michael Chege, and Afrika K. Gitonga (eds), *Democratic Theory and Practice in Africa*, Nairobi: Heinemann Educational Books, 1988, pp. 71–85.

Wright, Tim, *The History of the Northern Rhodesia Police*, Bristol: BECM Press, 2001.

Zukas, Simon, *Into Exile and Back*, Lusaka: Bookworld Publishers, 2002.

Journal Articles

Ambler, Charles, 'Alcohol, Racial Segregation and Popular Politics in Northern Rhodesia', *Journal of African History*, 31, 2 (1990), pp. 295–313.

Baylies, Carolyn, and Morris Szeftel, 'The 1996 Zambian Elections: Still Awaiting Democratic Consolidation', *Review of African Political Economy*, 24, 71 (1997), pp. 113–28.

———, 'The Fall and Rise of Multi-Party Politics in Zambia', *Review of African Political Economy*, 19, 54 (1992) pp. 75–91.

Branch, Daniel and Nicholas Cheeseman, 'The Politics of Control in Kenya: Understanding the Bureaucratic-Executive State, 1952–78', *Review of African Political Economy*, 33, 107 (2006), pp. 11–31.

Bratton, Michael, 'Zambia Starts Over', *Journal of Democracy*, 3, 2 (1992), pp. 81–94.

Caplan, Gerald L., 'Barotseland: The Secessionist Challenge to Zambia', *Journal of Modern African Studies*, 6, 3 (1968), pp. 343–60.

Cheeseman, Nic and Marja Hinfelaar, 'Parties, Platforms and Political Mobilization: The Zambian Presidential Election of 2008', *African Affairs*, 109, 434 (2010), pp. 51–76.

Cheeseman, Nic and Miles Larmer, 'Ethnopopulism in Africa: Opposition Mobilisation in Diverse and Unequal Societies', *Democratisation*, 22, 1 (2015), pp. 22–50.

Chikulo, Bornwell C., 'End of an Era: An Analysis of the 1991 Zambian Presidential and Parliamentary Elections', *Politikon*, 20, 1 (1993), pp. 87–104.

——, 'The Impact of Elections in Zambia's One Party Second Republic', *Africa Today*, 35, 2 (1988), pp. 37–49.

van Donge and Jan Kees, 'The Plundering of Zambian Resources by Frederick Chiluba and His Friends: A Case Study of the Interaction between National Politics and the International Drive Towards Good Governance', *African Affairs*, 108, 430 (2009), pp. 69–90.

Hogan, Jack '"What Then Happened to Our Eden?": The Long History of Lozi Secessionism, 1890–2013', *Journal of Southern African Studies*, 40, 5 (2014), pp. 907–24.

Hyden, Goran and Colin Leys, 'Elections and Politics in Single-Party Systems: The Case of Kenya and Tanzania', *British Journal of Political Science*, 2, 4 (1972) pp. 389–420.

Joseph, Richard, 'Zambia: A Model for Democratic Change', *Current History*, 91, 565 (1992), pp. 199–201.

Kapesa, Robby and Thomas McNamara, '"We are not just a union, we are a family": class, kinship and tribe in Zambia's mining unions', *Dialectical Anthropology*, 44, 2 (2020), pp. 153–72.

Larmer, Miles, 'Chronicle of a Coup Foretold: Valentine Musakanya and the 1980 Coup Attempt in Zambia', *Journal of African History*, 51, 3 (2010), pp. 391–409.

——, '"A Little Bit Like a Volcano": The United Progressive Party and Resistance to One-Party Rule in Zambia, 1964–1980', *International Journal of African Historical Studies*, 39, 1 (2006), pp. 49–83.

——, 'What Went Wrong? Zambian Political Biography and Post-colonial Discourses of Decline', *Historia*, 51, 1, (2006), pp. 235–56.

—— and Alastair Fraser, 'Of Cabbages and King Cobra: Populist Politics and Zambia's 2006 Election', *African Affairs*, 106, 425 (2007), pp. 611–37.

Lungu, John, 'Copper Mining Agreements in Zambia: Renegotiation or Law Reform?', *Review of African Political Economy*, 35, 117 (2008), pp. 403–15.

Melchiorre, Luke, 'Generational Populism and the Political Rise of Kyaluganyi – aka Bobi Wine – in Uganda', *Review of African Political Economy* (forthcoming).

Mulford, David C., 'Northern Rhodesia: Some Observations on the 1964 Elections', *Africa Report*, 9, 2 (1964), p. 13.

Paget, Dan, 'Again, making Tanzania great: Magufuli's restorationist developmental nationalism', *Democratization*, 27:7 (2020), 1240–60.

Prain, R.L., 'The Stabilisation of Labour on the Rhodesian Copperbelt', *African Affairs*, 55, 22 (1956), pp. 305–12.

Rotberg, Robert, 'What Future for Barotseland', *Africa Report*, 8, 7 (1963), p. 21.

Scaritt, James, 'The Strategic Choices of Multi-ethnic Parties in Zambia's Dominant and Personality Party System', *Journal of Commonwealth and Comparative Politics*, 44, 2 (2006), pp. 234–46.

Schlyter, Ann, 'Housing Policy in Zambia: Retrospect and Prospect', *Habitat International*, 22, 3 (1998), pp. 259–71.

Sishuwa, Sishuwa, 'Multi-ethnic vision or ethnic nationalism? The contested legacies of Anderson Mazoka and Zambia's 2006 election', *Canadian Journal of African Studies*, 57, 2, 2023), pp. 431–57.

——, 'Surviving on Borrowed Power: Rethinking the Role of Civil Society in Zambia's Third-term Debate', *Journal of Southern African Studies*, 46, 3 (2020), pp. 471–90.

——, '"A White Man Will Never Be a Zambian": Racialised Nationalism, the Rule of Law, and Competing Visions of Independent Zambia in the Case of Justice James Skinner, 1964–1969', *Journal of Southern African Studies*, 45, 3 (2019), pp. 503–23.

——, 'The outcome of a historical process set in motion in 1991: Explaining the failure of incumbency advantage in Zambia's 2021 election', *Journal of Eastern African Studies*, 16, 4 (2022), pp. 654–80.

Sishuwa, S. and D. Money, 'Defamation of the President, Racial Nationalism, and the Roy Clarke Affair in Zambia' *African Affairs*, Vol. 122, Issue 486, (2023), pp. 33–55.

Spear, Thomas, 'Neo-traditionalism and the Limits of Invention in British Colonial Africa', *Journal of African History*, 44, 1 (2003), pp. 3–27.

de la Torre Carlos, 'Trump's populism: lessons from Latin America', *Postcolonial Studies*, 20:2 (2017), 187–98.

Weyland, Kurt, 'Clarifying a Contested Concept: Populism in the Study of Latin American Politics', *Comparative Politics*, 34, 1 (2001), pp. 1–22.

Unpublished Dissertations/Theses

Garvey, Brian, 'The Development of the White Fathers' Mission among the Bemba-speaking Peoples, 1891–1964', Doctoral Thesis, University of London, 1974.

Larmer, Miles, 'Zambia's Mineworkers and Political Change, 1964–1991', PhD thesis, University of Sheffield, 2004.

Leenstra, Melle, 'Beyond the Façade: Instrumentalisation of the Zambian Health Sector', Doctoral Thesis, Leiden University, 2012.

Miles-Tendi, Blessings, 'Zimbabwe's Third Chumurenga: The Use and Abuse of History', DPhil Thesis, University of Oxford, 2008.

Piaget, Dan, 'The Internal Politics of the MMD, Zambia', MSc Dissertation, African Studies, University of Oxford, 2009.

Index

African National Congress, ANC 16, 33, 38–9, 40 50, 51, 59, 71, 72
age limit for presidency 41, 43, 46, 47
Agenda for Zambia, AZ 146, 178
alternative political force 31–2, 151, 156, 159–60, 189
   appeal of Sata's campaign message 161–70
      charisma 167–70
      insubordination to authority 166–7
      populist skill 161–6, 170
   Bemba-speaking rural support 136, 143
      ethnic strategy in Luapula and Northern provinces 56–7, 143, 144, 145, 151–5, 174, 189, 192
      prosecution of Bemba speakers 147–8, 151
      sidelining of Bemba politicians 150–1
   best option 158, 164–5, 167, 168
   civil society's ally for constitutional reform 32, 182–6
      Oasis Forum 183–6
      Sata's promises to reform the constitution 185–6
   elite inclusion 175–6
   Lozi vote 176, 179–82
      strategic constituencies 180
   national base 172, 174–5
   Sata's route to power
      alternative path 136
      context of anti-corruption 137, 140–1, 144, 147
      context of constitutional reform 142, 143
      context of economic hardship 137–40, 155–6, 160

   urban constituencies 136, 139, 143, 170–1, 189
      'Man of Action' populist campaign in Lusaka and the Copperbelt 24, 143, 155–6
      trade unions 139, 156–8
      urban worker unrest 158–60
Anglo-American Corporation 94, 137
austerity measures 105, 107, 120, 137, 139, 156

Banda, Dingiswayo 58
Banda, Rupiah
   2008 and 2009 presidential elections 180–2, 186–8
   acquittal of Chiluba 143
   appointments 188
   Barotseland Agreement 179–80
   civil liberties 143
   constitutional reform 142, 184–6
   economy 23, 24, 139–40
   expulsions 142, 143
   funding 81–2
   president, 2008–2011 1, 43, 135–6
   re-election 47, 143
   voters 87, 169, 170, 174, 187–9
Banda, William 58, 79–80
Barotse Freedom Movement, BFM 179
Barotse Patriotic Front, BPF 178, 179
Barotseland Agreement 176–82
   agreement, the 177
      secession demands abandoned 177
      semi-autonomous status 177
   Barotseland 176
      Litunga 177
      protectorate within a protectorate 176–7
   centralisation 177

Lozi demands for secession 176, 177–8
   Barotse Royal Establishment, BRE 177–8
   decreased 177, 178
   Lozi separatists 178, 179
   Lozi traditional elites and politicians 177, 179
   Lozi voters 178
  repeal of the Barotseland Agreement 176, 177
   used to influence the state to favour Lozis 177
  Sata's election campaign issue 179–82
   reversal 191, 193
  signing of the Barotseland Agreement 176, 177, 179
Bemba speakers 25, 50–5, 109, 112, 169
see also Chinsale *and* Malole
  advantages 56–7
  Kapwepwe and the UPP 10, 71
  marginalised by Mwanawasa 148–54, 188
  prosecution of Chiluba 26, 147–8, 151
  Sata 25–6, 31, 33–65, 75, 119
   becoming a Bemba leader 108–16, 143, 144–7, 151–5, 188, 189, 192
   claiming Bemba identity 56–7
   policeman 53–4
   scholar 56
biographical method 3, 6, 12–18, 19, 27, 30, 32, 35–6, 196, 197 *see also* sources
  autobiographies 20
  in practice in this book 54, 56, 58–9, 143 n.117, 107 n.57, 161–2
British South African Company, BSAC 37
Bukali, Henrietta Kabuswe 47
Bulaya, Kashiwa 147, 154
Bwalya, Frank 185
Bwana Mkubwa 58

by-elections, parliamentary 19
  1983 82
  1993 and 1994 108
   Bemba leader 99, 109, 110, 112, 113, 116
   importance for MMD 108–9
   importance for NP 109
   Sata 99, 109, 110–12, 114–16
  1993, Malole 109–12
   results 111–12
   Sata's successes 111–12
   strategy, Kasonde, NP 110
   strategy, Sata for Kalingeme, MMD 110–11
  1994, Chinsali 112–16
   Kapwepwe, Chilufya as an independent candidate 112–13
   Museba's challenges 114
   NP's divisions over candidate 112, 113–14
   results 116
   Sata's successes 116
   strategy, Kapwepwe, independent (NP) 113
   strategy, Maine, NP 113–14
   strategy, Sata for Museba, MMD 114
  1995 97, 120
  2008 25
  Mufulira West 75

campaign 196
  anti-corruption 148, 149, 151
  Barotseland 176, 178, 179, 180, 182
  Chinsali 109–16
  constitutional reform 182, 184
  electoral mobilisation 75–6
  funding 28, 78, 80, 81–3, 102, 104, 124, 125, 195
  government 23
  intra-party 20
   Chiluba 124
   Chiluba prosecution 147–8
   Chiluba succession 98, 99, 118, 123, 124, 125, 131

Chiluba third term 126, 127–8
Chinsali 112–14
Sata 92, 101
Kabwata 78–80, 87
Kaunda 9
ZANC 39
Malole 109, 110–11
Miyanda 120
multi-party democracy, for 90, 104
Mwanawasa 148, 149, 150, 155
nationalist 6, 7, 8, 9, 40
Cha Cha Cha 54
Oasis Forum 127
one-party parliamentary 68
opposition 8, 14, 27, 64, 143, 152–3, 187
anti-Federation 38–9, 40
party-controlled 17, 68, 75, 78
populist 4
promises 94, 96, 100–1, 191–3, 194
Sata 12, 27, 92, 126, 162, 169–70, 191–3
Bemba-speaking 57, 109, 119, 144, 152, 154–5
Chinsali 109, 114–16
constitutional reform 182
Copperbelt 64
ethnic 12, 152–5, 189
housing 86
limits 32, 171–2, 173, 174
national 122, 186–7
Malole 109, 110
Mpika 119
populist 12, 143, 189
presidency of Zambia 132–3, 135, 137
rural 57, 108, 152
strategy 26, 174
urban 68, 100, 143, 161, 162, 166, 167
Western Province 176, 180–2
without a plan 145–7, 169, 176
trade unions 104, 108

Central African Federation *see* Federation
Central Province 57, 131, 150, 174, 175, 176, 188
centralisation *see* Barotseland Agreement
Cha Cha Cha protests 40, 54, 159
Chama, Moses 60
Chambishi mine 138, 165, 168
Chibanda, Stella 147
Chikopela, Emmanuel 49
Chikwanda, Alexander 82
Chikwanda, Chief 48
Chilenje 79, 80, 83, 86, 102
Chiluba, Frederick 19, 73, 92, 105, 106, 107, 157–8, 161, 170
corruption 26, 96, 104, 108, 110, 139, 140, 143, 147–8, 151–2, 154, 167, 194
economic reforms 93–5, 97
populist housing measures 100–1, 194
retirement 95, 96, 98–9, 116
succession 20, 22, 99, 116–17, 124, 125, 130–1, 196
third term, bid for 21, 31, 123, 126–30, 146, 182–3
Chimba, Justin 159
Chimumbwa, Charles 175
Chinsali 109, 112–16, 120
Chipimo, Elias 187
Chipungu, Israel 84
Chirwa, Alec 106
Chitala, Derrick 20, 79–80, 83, 84, 97
Chongwe, Rodger 77, 96, 102
Chungu, Aaron 147
Chungu, Afrika 153
Chungu, Xavier 147, 152, 154
civil society
age limit for Zambian presidency 43
Chiluba's immunity from prosecution 147
Chiluba's third term 21, 129–30
constitutional reform 32, 141–2, 174, 182–6, 193
organisations 96
populist politics 10

colonial *see also* periods *and* white settlers
 anti-colonialism 26, 30, 38, 39, 40, 51, 57
  Sata 54, 59, 88, 106, 196
 criticised 7, 9, 60
 end of colonial rule 15, 34, 40, 67, 177 *see also* independence
 injustices 9, 86
 police 53, 54, 55
  Sata 11, 33, 37, 46, 49, 53, 54, 55, 58, 59, 66, 166, 196
 schools 52
 stereotype 54–5
constitution
 Banda's draft constitution bill 142
 Barotseland Agreement 177, 178–9
 Chiluba 12, 19, 21, 31, 96, 97–9, 116–17, 123, 126, 128, 129, 146, 182
 Constitution of Zambia Amendment Bill 46, 185
 Constitution Review Commission, CRC 141–2
 constitutional reform 178–9
  Lungu 193
  Oasis Forum 182–4
  Sata 185–6, 189, 191
 independence constitution 177
 Kaunda 90
 MMD's 98, 123, 126, 128, 129, 131–2
 Mwanawasa 141, 142
 National Constitutional Conference, NCC 142, 183–4
 new national constitution 157
 Nkumbula, Harry 39
 Sata 41, 43 *see also* constitution/constitutional reform/Sata
 UNIP 72
Coopers & Lybrand 74, 81
copper *see* Copperbelt
Copperbelt 33–4, 35–6, 55, 108, 136, 138
 anti-colonial struggle 51
 Bemba as lingua franca 25 n.63, 50, 51–3, 56, 58, 169
 Chiluba 124

copper
 boom 36–7, 53, 69, 81, 138, 139, 140
 mines 51, 69, 94, 138, 158
 revenue 6, 38, 69, 93, 94, 113, 137
 slump 37, 69–70, 93, 137, 139
 late-colonial period 1953–1964 33, 34, 36, 50, 60–1, 63–6
 migration from the Copperbelt 23, 76, 86
 migration to the Copperbelt 30, 33, 37, 50, 51–2, 196
 Miyanda 117, 119, 120, 122
 populist mobilisation 32, 35, 100, 143
  2000s 11, 22, 136, 146, 155, 156
  2006 election 24, 160, 165, 170–2, 173
  2011 election 174, 187–9
  second wave 10
 post-colonial period 71, 83
 Sata 26, 30, 33, 34–5, 41, 46, 49, 53–4, 58, 59, 60–2, 64, 65, 74, 76, 168
 unions 60–6
Corruption 113 *see also* Chiluba, Frederick/corruption
 anti-corruption 137, 139, 140, 144, 147, 148, 149, 151, 171
 Mwanawasa 26, 104, 140, 141, 143, 144, 147, 148, 149, 151, 167, 171
 prosecution of Chiluba and co-accused 26, 143, 147
  Sata to drop charges 154, 155
coups, attempted 72–3, 73, 89, 90, 92 n.98, 117, 122, 124
courts
 Chiluba 147, 154
 judiciary 77, 96
 MMD 129, 131–2, 148
 Mwanawasa 131–2, 140, 141, 144, 148
 Sata 47–8
 UNIP 72

debt   70, 93, 137, 139, 156, 193, 194
decentralisation *see* Barotseland
   Agreement
Dunn, Colin   46

Eastern Province   174
   Banda   188
   Chewa   55, 188
   Miyanda   122
   Nyanja   169
   Petauke   119
   Tembo   150
   UNIP   120–1
economy
   1953–1964   26, 36–7
   1964–1991   69–71
   1991–2001   93–5
   2000s   26, 137–40, 156–7, 160
   boom   26, 36–7
   Copperbelt   33–4, 36–7, 53, 56, 76
   decline   10, 57, 70, 76, 93, 94–5,
     100, 137, 139–40, 158, 161
   economic
     alternative   160
     change   13
     crisis   86, 160, 165, 166
     grievances   5, 10–11, 52, 64,
       143, 171, 182, 186, 194
     performance   6–7, 9, 10, 24,
       72, 158, 170
     policies   10–11, 70, 76, 137
     populism   5, 8, 10–11, 23, 27,
       71
     promises   11, 22
     situation   83, 88, 89, 97, 105,
       107, 137, 138, 170
     socio-   5, 6–7, 10, 22, 85, 160,
       165
   methodological approach, in   15,
     16–17, 20, 35
   recovery   139, 140, 171
     programmes   22, 70–1
   reform   69, 93–5, 97, 137, 139, 140,
     148, 156, 166, 192–3, 194
     trade unions   104–7, 138, 157,
       158–9

elections *see also* by-elections,
   parliamentary
   1958   39
   1962   40, 71
   1964   40, 67, 71
   1968   67, 71, 72
   1973   72
   1973 and 1978   67
   1978   77
   1983   41, 77, 82–3 *see also* Kabwata
     constituency
     increased number of
       candidates   78
     primary polls
       abolished   77–8
     results   84
     strategies   78–80
     UNIP control over
       candidates   78
   1983 and 1988   67–8
   1988   87, 89 *see also* Kabwata
     constituency
   1991, multi-party   11–12, 22, 73,
     90, 92, 93, 120 *see also* Kabwata
     constituency
     after the election   96
     before the elections   100,
       104–5, 124
     Kasonde   110
     Mpika   119
   1996   19, 20, 93, 97, 117, 118, 121, 178
     after the election   94, 123, 124
     Chiluba   21, 123, 194
     Kaunda excluded   19, 97
     MMD succession   19–20
     Mpika   119
     Mwanawasa   117, 145 n.45
     Mwila   124
     Petauke and Miyanda   119–21
     Sata   117, 118, 121–3
     UNIP   120, 121
   2001   12, 84, 135, 145–7, 150, 151
     Chiluba   98–9, 126, 129
     Sata   132, 135, 144–7, 191
   2006   24, 135, 171
     Sata   154–5, 159, 160–1, 162,
       165, 173

2008, presidential by-election 25,
    41, 43, 44, 135, 174, 182, 187–8
2011 174, 182, 186–9
    Barotseland Agreement as
        Sata's election campaign
        issue 179–82
    Sata's age 41–6, 47
    Sata's win 1, 2, 32, 41, 135–6,
        143, 176
    strategic constituencies for
        Sata 180
one-party 10, 13–14, 17, 31, 67, 68,
    194, 195
ethnic
    identity
        Bemba 10, 25–6, 52, 57, 95,
            136, 169
        language 26, 52–3, 56
        Lozi 114, 174, 175–82
        rural 4, 10, 95, 136
        Sata 40, 48, 56, 111
    marginalisation 10, 150, 192
    mobilisation 111, 113, 136, 143,
        151–5, 176, 193
    nationalist 3–4, 57–8, 113
    polarisation 193
    populist 3–4, 12, 22, 25, 26, 27, 95,
        136, 189, 193
    positions 108, 109, 119, 125, 128, 131,
        147, 150, 154, 175, 192
    power base 25–6, 32, 95, 111, 121–2,
        150, 174, 176, 186, 188
    stereotyping 54–5

factions 39, 128, 129, 196 see also party
    politics
Federation 37, 38–9, 40, 59
Federation of Free Trade Unions of
    Zambia, FFTUZ 157
Forum for Democracy and Development,
    FDD 98 n.21, 135, 135 n.1, 146, 150
Funkunta, Silva 84

Gore-Browne, Stewart 14–15
grievances
    Bemba 52, 57
    ethno-regional 171, 186

local 162, 182
rural 108, 122
urban 26, 71, 76, 103, 139, 143, 160,
    171, 186, 189, 194
workers' 60, 61–2, 63, 64, 65, 105,
    158
    unions 106–7

Habasonda, Lee 185
Hapunda, Frederick 118
Heritage Party, HP 98 n.21, 135, 146, 171,
    187
Hichilema, Hakainde 171, 185, 187, 193
Hikaumba, Leonard 157
Hlazo, Stanford 103
housing
    for voters 8, 88–9, 103, 139
    for workers 62
    Sata's construction company 76
    under Chiluba 100–4, 139, 194
    see also Sata, Michael/Minister of
        Local Government and Housing
    under Kaunda 86, 100–1
        Kajema flats 86–7, 88

impeachment
    Mwanawasa, unsuccessful 141
independence 69 see also Barotseland
    Agreement
    anticipated benefits 7, 8, 9, 69,
        86, 88
    'capital flight' 81
    disappointment 7–8, 9–10, 70–1,
        88
    nationalists 7, 88, 93
    struggle for 9, 14, 33, 37, 39–40, 51,
        59, 64, 65, 158, 159
International Financial Institutions,
    IFIs 25, 70, 106–7, 139
International Monetary Fund,
    IMF 70–1, 93, 107, 137
Irwin, Carl 84
Irwin, Joan 28
Irwin, Oliver 28, 74, 76, 80–1, 84, 85
    money transfer scam 81
    political protection 81–2

Jere, Siloni Paul 84

Kabanda, Simon   185
Kabimba, Wynter   175, 176, 185
Kabwata constituency   79
   1983 parliamentary
      elections   78–80, 82–4
   1988 parliamentary
      elections   85–9, 87, 89
   1991 elections   92
   Merzaf flats   102
   Miyanda   120–1
   Sata   77, 79, 80, 82–4, 85–6, 87, 89, 90–1, 92, 102, 119, 120, 143
Kabwe, Faustin   147, 154
Kajema flats   86–7, 88
Kaliminwa, Fr Nicholas   49, 51
Kalinda, Phillip   84
Kalingeme, Dismus   110, 111
Kalumba, Katele   120, 131, 146, 147, 152, 154
Kampemba, Katuta   151
Kantensha, upper primary seminary   48, 49, 51
Kapapa, Daniel   153
Kapwepwe, Chilufya   108, 130
   Chinsali by-election   112–16
Kapwepwe, Simon Mwansa   10, 39, 57, 71, 72, 73
   father of Chilufya Kapwepwe   112–16
   populist rhetoric for urban dwellers   194
Kasonde, Emmanuel   82, 101, 102, 103, 108, 112, 114, 117, 130, 150
   Malole by-election   109–12, 113, 114
Katibunga, lower preparatory seminary   48
Katilungu, Lawrence   50, 59, 159
Katyoka, Patrick   47
Kaunda, Kenneth
   Barotseland Agreement   177, 178
   economy   10–11, 69–70, 81, 90, 101
      IMF   70–1
   opposition to   9–10, 72–3, 67, 89, 104, 117, 112, 124
   patronage using civil service   93
   political challengers to   72
   politics   14, 15, 16, 57, 120
      independence   14, 15, 40
      nationalist   7, 9, 39, 83, 88, 165–6
      nationality   19, 97, 121
      one-party state   10–11, 17, 30, 67, 71, 73, 89–90, 96, 109, 113
   Sata   11–12, 30, 31, 66, 85, 86, 89, 90, 92, 100–1, 103, 120, 145, 164, 165–6
   undermining challengers   86, 89
   UNIP   9, 10, 16, 40, 67, 71–2, 73, 75, 93, 97, 120
Kaunda, Tilyenji   146, 187
Kavindele, Enoch   82, 130, 131, 141, 150
Kawambwa   124
Kayope, Valentine   148
Kazembe, Mwata   151
Konie, Gwendoline   146
Konkola Copper Mine   138, 158
Konkola, Dixon   15, 39
Kunda, George   188

labour   26, 51–2 *see also* trade union movement
   labour movement   34, 38–9, 65–6, 73, 156–7
   migration   33, 51–2
   Roberts Construction strike   61–3
   under Chiluba   73, 104–5
   see also Sata, Michael/Minister of Labour and Social Security
Liberal Progressive Front   96
Lifwekelo, Edwin
   Bemba-speaking Secretary General of the PF   175
   formation of the PF   132, 132 n.167
Linyungandambo   179
London School of Economics, LSE   48, 49, 50, 51, 74
Luanshya   121, 124, 125
Luapula and Northern provinces   25, 40
   Chiluba's prosecution   147–8
   Copperbelt   51–3, 71
   Sata   25, 56–7, 143, 144–7, 151–5, 173, 174, 189, 192

Luapula Province   52, 124, 151, 152, 153, 155, 171, 172, 187–8 *see also* Luapula and Northern provinces
Lubushi Seminary, Kasama   48, 49–50, 51
Lungu, Edgar   193, 194
Lusaka *see also* Kabwata constituency
   city   23–4, 100–1, 138
   migration to   23, 76, 86, 138
   Province   78, 170, 171, 187–8
   Sata's populist urban and worker mobilisation   22, 24, 30, 90, 143, 155–6
   urban riots   73
Lusaka City Council   102, 162
Lusaka Urban District Council, LUDC   86

Machungwa, Peter   146, 148, 150, 153–4, 155
Magande, Ng'andu   142, 143, 187
Maine, Katongo   108
   Chinsali by-election   112–16
Makhurane, Phinias   28, 65
Malambo, Vincent   127, 128
Malole   109–12
Matale, Suzanne   184
Maunga, Mwami   92
Mazoka, Anderson   135, 146, 150
Mbewe, Cheyani   84
Mbikusita-Lewanika, Akashambatwa   20, 96, 108, 112, 114–16, 178
Mbikusita-Lewanika, Godwin   38
Mbikusita-Lewanika, Inonge   108, 114, 146, 178
Mermigas, George   102
Merzaf   102–4
migration *see* Copperbelt, labour, Lusaka *and* Northern Province
Milupi, Charles   187
mineral royalties   37 *see also* British South African Company
mines *see also* Copperbelt
   employees   23, 24, 38, 51, 52, 55, 65, 62, 69, 74, 138
      Chambishi mine explosion   138, 165, 168

mining sector   22, 37, 65, 137, 139–40
   boom   11, 53, 69
   investors   23, 65, 69, 137, 138, 156, 165
   revenue   38, 53, 69, 140
   slump   69–70, 137
   nationalisation   69, 194
   new mines   36, 62
   other countries, in   51
   privatisation of mines   22–3, 94
   strikes   66, 158–9
      Konkola Copper Mine   158–60
Mineworkers Union of Zambia, MUZ   73, 104, 157, 159
Minister without Portfolio   100 n.24, 117, 118, 122, 130, 164
Missionaries of Africa *see* White Fathers
Miyanda, Godfrey   98, 116, 146, 171, 187
   career   117–18, 121
   Kabwata parliamentary seat   120–1
   'Mr Clean'   117, 118, 122
   Petauke parliamentary seat thwarted   119–21
      tenth anniversary of Samora Machel's death   120
   succession race   125–6, 128–9, 130, 146, 171, 187
      advantage   117, 118
      blocked from building power base   121, 122
      criticised by Sata   117–18
Movement for Multiparty Democracy, MMD   11, 67, 73, 196
   1991–2001   22, 26, 93–5, 96–9
   1993 and 1994 parliamentary by-elections   108–16
   2001–2011   135
   alliance with trade unions   104–5, 107
   anti-worker policies   105
   Barotseland Agreement   178, 180–1
   breakaway parties   19, 96, 97, 108–9, 125
   civil liberties   96
   coalition   11, 19, 20–1, 71

Constitution Bill 183, 184–6
defeat in 1995 parliamentary
   by-elections 97
delivery by politicians 99
democracy, consolidated 19, 96
formation 71, 73, 90
loss of voter support 188, 189
National Convention
   1991 92, 96, 101, 117, 124
   1993 96
   1995 97, 99, 116, 117, 118
   2001 98, 123, 125, 127, 128, 129
   2005 141
   2011 143
National Executive Committee,
   NEC 125, 126, 127, 130–2, 140
vice president 98, 116, 117, 118, 119, 120, 122, 130, 131
Movement for the Restoration of Barotseland 179
Mphande, Bede 147
Mpika 51
   Mpika Central constituency
      gateway to the Northern
         Province 119
      Sata 119
      Scott 119
   Sata's hometown 47–8, 51, 56, 119
Mpika Local Education Authority Native
   School 48
Mpombo, George 41, 43, 142, 143
Mubanga, Raphael 60
Mucheleka, Patrick 185
Mufulira 46, 53, 75, 117
Mugabe, Robert 144, 173
Mulemba, Humphrey 96, 108, 112, 114
Mulongoti, Mike 143
Mulwila, John 108
Mumba, Nevers 141, 146, 155
Mumbi, Edward 175
Mumbi, Potiphar Mwanza 121
Mung'omba, Dean 97
Museba, Charles 112, 114
Musonda, Samuel 147, 154
Mususu, Bishop Paul 184
Mutangelwa, Prince Imasiku 178, 179
Mutesa, Frederick 187

Mututwa, Maxwell 179, 180
Mwaanga, Vernon 91, 118, 128, 129, 130, 131, 173, 174
Mwanamwambwa, Amusa 128, 129, 130
Mwanawasa, Levy 23, 24, 43, 99, 103–4, 117, 146, 166, 171
   age limit of the president 41–3
   anti-corruption 26, 140–1, 144, 147–8, 149, 151, 155
      'stinking and dirty' 148–50, 151, 152–3
   appointments 141, 150, 154
      Bemba 148, 150
   constitution reform 141–2, 183
   economy 137, 138, 139, 140
   expulsions 148, 153, 155
   power base in MMD 118, 130–1, 140
   power base in Zambia 140, 141, 155, 171–2
      losing Bembas 148, 150, 151, 152, 153–4, 155, 188
      Lozi 178
      neglecting urban poor and workers 189
   President of the MMD, 2001–2008 135, 170
      pre-election deals 148, 150, 151
      presidential candidate 131–2, 141, 144
   President of Zambia, 2002–2008 135, 155, 168, 188
   Sata
      arrest 159
      insubordination 167, 168
      Merzaf 103–4
Mwango, Mary Kaluluma 79, 84
Mwanza, Regina 126
Mwape, Lupando 155, 188
Mwenye, Musa 184
Mwila, Ben 146
   against Chiluba's third term 123
   Luanshya MP 121, 124
   Minister of Defence 116, 122, 124, 125
   relationship with Chiluba 122, 124, 125

succession race 98, 116–17, 124, 125, 126, 130, 135, 146
suspended and expelled from MMD 124–5
Zambia Republican Party 98, 135 n.1

National Constitutional Conference, NCC 142
 age limit for presidential candidates 41–6
 objections 183–6
National Democratic Alliance 117
National Lima Party 97
National Party, NP 96, 97, 108–9
 1993 and 1994 parliamentary by-elections 108, 109
 Chinsali by-election 112–16
 Malole by-election 109–12
 MMD defectors 96, 108, 109, 112, 117
 multi-ethnic coalition 108
National Provident Fund 86
National Union of Building, Wood, and Metal Workers, NUBWMW 60–1, 63, 64–5
National Union of Engineering, Construction and General Workers, NUECGW 61–2, 64
nationalisation 69
 Sata's business 77
Nawakwi, Edith 187
Ngondo, Winright 171
Nkomeshya, Chieftainess 82
Nkumbula, Baldwin 96, 108, 114
Nkumbula, Harry Mwaanga 14–16, 38, 39 50, 59, 71, 72
Nonde, Boniface 147, 154
Northern and Luapula provinces *see* Luapula and Northern provinces
Northern Province 52, 108, 110, 120, 175, 187–8 *see also* Luapula and Northern provinces
 by-elections
  Chinsali 112–16
  Malole 109–12
 Kapwepwe

 Chilufya 112–13, 114–16
 Simon Mwansa 112–13
 Kasonde 110–12
 leadership positions 175, 188
 migration between the Northern Province and the Copperbelt 33, 51
 NP 108, 109
 Sata's campaigning 145, 153, 155
  2006 elections 171
  Chinsali 114–16
  Malole 111–12
  Mpika 119, 122
 Sata's early life 30, 36, 47–50, 56, 111
Northern Rhodesia African Congress *see* African National Congress, ANC
North-Western Province 108, 150, 171–2, 174, 187–8

Oasis Forum 127, 128, 129, 142, 182–6
obstruction of Miyanda by Sata 117–23
 altering Miyanda's parliamentary candidacy 119–23
 outcomes for Sata
  Bemba support 122
  rural power base denied to competitor 121–2
  standing in MMD power structure 122–3
 public criticism 117–18
ousting of Mwila by Sata 124–6
 accusations 124
 expulsion from MMD 124–5
  implications for Chiluba 126
  implications for Sata 125
 suspension from MMD 124

Pandani, John 84
party politics 22, 26–7, 31, 193, 196
 ANC 39, 59
 dynamics, party 20, 21–2, 26, 31, 130, 196
 ethnicity 3, 57–8, 111, 128, 147–8, 150
 MMD 20, 21, 31, 90, 95, 96–9
  factions 21–2, 92, 96–7, 127–8, 142, 143, 147–8, 151, 153, 155, 178, 196

succession *see* succession to Chiluba
third term for Chiluba *see* third presidential term, bid for, by Chiluba
transformed by Chiluba 97
multi-party democracy 4–5, 11, 18, 19–20, 21–2, 26, 67, 90, 104
nationalism 7, 8, 9, 36, 38–40, 50, 71
NP 113–14
one-party state 10, 17, 31, 73, 90
political change 3, 14, 19–20, 21–2, 26, 193, 195–6
populism 3, 4–5, 6, 8, 195
Patriotic Front, PF 108, 196
  Bemba-speaking leadership 175
  defeat 193
  electoral support 26, 31–2, 136, 144, 146–7, 151, 170–3, 182, 187
    Bemba-speakers 56–7, 151–2, 153, 155, 192
    civil society 174, 186
    Lozi 176, 180–2
    MMD members and MPs 31–2, 144, 146–7, 151–2, 153
    Oasis Forum 183–4
    urban 170
  ethno-populism 27
  Edgar Lungu's leadership 193
  formation 132, 132 n.167, 144–5
    Movement for Multiparty Democracy–Patriotic Front, MMD–PF 144
  manifesto 185
  NCC 183–5
  opposition 11, 22, 24, 135, 137, 108, 185
  populism 11
  rise 2001–2011 25, 27, 31, 135–6
  Sata 145, 196
  slogan change 160
  workers 108, 157, 158
    Sata 159

periods 3, 8, 13, 27
  late-colonial 3, 6, 9, 26, 34, 35, 57
    influences 195
  multi-party state 26, 67, 57
  one-party state 67, 195
    collapse 73
    elections 67–8, 195
  post-colonial 9, 34, 35, 57
    lead up to one-party state 71–2
Petauke
  influential rural constituency 119
  Miyanda 119, 120
  Mumbi 121
  Sata's interference 119–20, 121
  UNIP 119, 120, 121
Phiri, Nelson 84
political change
  biography 13, 14–16, 20, 27, 28, 196, 197
  blocked by
    Kaunda 72
    one-party state 19
  campaigning 27, 78, 94, 104
  ethnicity 22, 26, 150, 193
  individual leadership 1, 14–16, 18, 27, 196, 197
  institutional factors 13, 14, 16, 17–18
  one-party state 17, 195
    one-party state to multi-party state 92
  party politics 3, 14, 19–20, 21–2, 26, 193, 195–6
  populism 3, 22, 26, 27, 32, 191, 193–5
  state capitalism towards free market enterprise 94
  structural factors 16–17
  succession 20
  supporters 100, 186
Ponde, Jonas 60
populism 3–6, 8, 31
  Africa, in 4, 5–6, 8, 194
  definition 4, 24, 65, 156

ethno-populism   3, 22, 25, 26, 27, 193
   giving power to parties   11
   limits as a governing policy   194
   party politics   3, 4–5, 6, 8, 195
   political change   3, 22, 26, 27, 32, 191, 193–5
   response to economic situation   10–11, 22
   strategy   3, 5, 8, 24, 27, 194
   urban   4, 24
   Zambia, in   195
      1st wave, late-colonial   7, 9, 13
      2nd wave, post-colonial   7–8, 9, 10, 13
      3rd wave, one-party   8
      4th wave, multi-party   8
power base   21
   definition   95
   Miyanda's, prevented   121–2
   Sata's   22, 31, 68, 95, 99, 100, 111, 116
      labour   107–8
      MMD, in   95, 99, 107, 122, 123, 132, 194, 196
      rural   95, 108, 116, 174
      urban   95, 103, 108, 116
privatisation   22–4, 94, 105, 107, 137, 166
protests *see* unrest

Rakner, Lise   20, 107
riots *see* unrest
Roberts Construction   59–60, 61–2, 63, 65
role of individual leaders   1, 9, 13, 15, 16, 26, 27, 195, 197

Sakala, Richard   147
Sampa, Chitalu   104, 105, 130, 131, 146, 148, 150, 153, 155, 175
Sandys, Duncan   177
Sardanis, Stelios   82
Sata, Langford Juliano Mubanga   47
Sata, Michael
   aiming to be President of Zambia
      blocked by Kaunda   131
      court case against Mwanawasa's election   131–2
      discrediting Mwanawasa   145, 152
      formation of PF   1, 12, 61, 84, 132, 144–5
      loyalty to Kaunda   130
      MMD   116–17
      presidential elections 2001, 2006, 2008, 2011   135–6, 170–1
      rivals removed   130
      undermining Miyanda   117–22 *see also* obstruction of Miyanda by Sata
      undermining Mwila   124–5 *see also* ousting of Mwila by Sata
      victory against Banda of the MMD   1
   alternative politics *see* alternative political force
   Bemba leader   99, 108–116, 122, 143
      Luapula and Northern provinces   25, 56–7, 143, 144–7, 151–5, 173, 174, 189, 192
   Bisa   56, 119, 122
   businessman   76
      construction   76
      industrial consultant   74
   clerk   59–60, 61
   constable   37, 46, 53, 54–5, 58, 59, 66
   Copperbelt, on the   51, 53
   delivering on promises and rhetoric   191–3
      appointment of the next Chitimukulu (Bemba king)   192
      Chinese-owned businesses   192
      construction projects for jobs   193
      decentralisation and devolution using the Barotseland Agreement   191
      income tax threshold   192
      nationalise the mines   194

new constitution   191
positions for Bemba
   speakers   192
public sector wages   192
described by others
   campaigning   83, 115
   civil society   184, 186
   colleague   46, 60, 65, 104, 167
   constituencies   162, 189
   contemporary   66, 76, 80
   leader   165
   media   159
   minister   106
   opposition   80
   schooling   49, 56
   unpleasant traits   164
election campaigner   137, 92, 110
   1983 election campaign   80,
      81–4
   2001 elections   145, 146, 147
   2011   176, 187 *see also* Sata,
      Michael/political strategies/
      national base
   Barotseland
      Agreement   179–82
   buying beer for voters   83–4
   ethnic campaign   12
   fighter for Lozi
      interests   179–82, 182 n.34
   financing campaign   80,
      81–3, 195
   linking present to the
      past   169
   local grievances   162
   patronage   86–9, 195
   populist campaign   12
   spokesman for the
      common people and the
      workers   161–2
   supporters pretending
      to support another
      party   75–6
election strategies   75–6, 80, 83–4,
   87–9, 95, 111–12, 189
   concentrated campaign   180
   limits of campaign
      strategy   32, 171, 173, 174

ethnic mobilisation   136, 151–5, 193
   Chinsali   114–16
   Malole   111–12
   Mpika   122
ethnicity   55, 56–7
Governor of Lusaka Urban   85–6,
   89, 166
Irwin, relationship to   80, 82, 84–5
legacy   193
Lusaka, in   76
'Man of Action'   63, 88–9, 99–100,
   102–3, 105, 107, 143, 145, 155–6,
   164–5
Minister of Health   100 n.24, 116,
   118, 162
Minister of Labour and Social
   Security   99–100, 105–8
   garnering labour
      support   107–8
   improved dialogue with trade
      unions   105–6
   pace of economic
      liberalisation   105, 106–7
   privately stated
      positions   106, 107
   trade union concerns   105
Minister of Local Government and
   Housing   92, 99–100, 101–4
   experience in housing   101
   Merzaf housing
      empowerment
      scheme   102–4
   response to 1992 national
      budget   101–2
Minister of State   89, 90, 166
Minister without Portfolio   100
   n.24, 118, 122, 130, 164
   funds available   118
   Miyanda's previous posts   118
Mpika Central MP   119, 121
   rural Bemba-speaking ethnic
      mobilisation   122
national leader   174
   Bemba-speaking rural
      communities   74, 95, 136,
      174, 186
   civil society   182–6

Lozi voters 176–82, 186
Lusaka and Copperbelt urban
 voters 74, 186
non-Bemba
 appointments 175–6
National Secretary of MMD 12,
31, 98, 116, 118, 119, 123, 129, 132
 Chiluba's backing 122, 123,
 131
 consolidating MMD power
 base 99, 122
 obstructing Miyanda 119–22
 obstructing Mwila 124–5
 obstructing presidential
 competitors in the
 MMD 99, 117
 supporter of Chiluba's third
 term 126
 using Mwila to get closer to
 Chiluba 124–5
nationalist 6, 11, 65, 66
 claims 66
 transition to 65
party member 11, 31
 candidacy rejected 77
 central role in the PF 154
 forming PF as a fallback to
 MMD 30, 132, 144–5
 leaving UNIP, for MMD 30,
 31, 90–2
 MMD 11–12, 61, 90, 92
 PF 1, 11, 76, 196, 145, 154, 159,
 170, 173, 185, 196
 UNIP 65, 68, 70, 77, 89–90
 UPP 75
personal biography 11, 30, 51
 Africa yearbook, 1977 42, 48
 Bemba, becoming 50, 53–5,
 56–7
 contradictions 40, 41, 44–5,
 47–51, 54, 63–4
 date of birth 41, 42, 43,
 44–5, 46–7
 education 48–51
 family 47, 48
 name 48
 place of birth 47–8

political strategies 3, 26, 109, 169
 alliances 158, 183
 claims of being a
 worker 63–4
 coalitions of support 174
 constitutional reform 186
 delivery 88–9
 ethnic 25, 32, 95, 99, 111, 122,
 136, 143, 152–5, 174–5, 189, 192
 ethno-language 25–6, 31, 57,
 63, 95, 122
 ethno–populist 12, 26, 95,
 99, 136, 189, 193
 ethno-regional 25, 136, 152,
 154–5, 171, 172, 175, 188–9, 192
 gifts for voters 83–4
 limitations 155
 local grievances 162
 national base 137, 173–5,
 186, 187 *see also* alternative
 political force
 one-party state, under 68
 opposition party, as 27, 31–2
 party leader trust 92, 130
 party trust 92
 patronage 88
 populist 5, 8, 9, 22, 24, 25, 27,
 80, 95, 99, 107, 136, 160, 170,
 171, 189
 post-colonial 35–6, 56, 57, 64
 power base 99
 promise anything 162–4, 189
 roots of 13, 30, 35, 36, 41, 56,
 64, 164
 rural 95, 108, 122, 136
 strategies of other
 politicians 78–80, 86, 88,
 89, 121, 122, 139, 182
 urban 64, 68, 95, 136
politician 1, 11–12, 19, 22, 30–2, 84,
87, 146, 171, 187
 Bemba speaker, as a 56–7,
 115
 credibility 88–9
 elected 68, 77, 84, 87, 92
 finance 82, 194
 Kabwata MP 84, 87

MMD one-party state, in
    the   11, 26, 28, 31–2, 68, 85,
    87, 103, 166, 194, 196
opposition leader   143, 189
PF party, forming the
    breakaway opposition   61,
    95, 99
retire   1, 47, 132, 133, 191
rise 2001–2006   135, 136–7,
    151, 156
rise 2006–2011   135–7
urban areas, in   64, 88, 100
populist   6, 11, 12, 24–6, 189
    'enemy' rhetoric   65, 156
    financing populist
        projects   194
    labour movement   66, 107
    skill   160, 161–4
prisoner   48, 58–9
supporting other politicians
    Chiluba   92, 98, 146
    Kaunda   89
trade unionist   11, 26, 28, 30, 33, 37,
    60–1, 66, 189
    aligning with nationalist
        movement   64–5, 66
    NUBWMW member   60–1
    NUECGW, forming the
        breakaway union   61
    NUECGW, recruitment
        drive   61–2
    NUECGW, strike   62–3
    Soviet Union, training in   66,
    74
typical of his generation   196
United Kingdom, in the   74–5
    jobs   74
    outsider   74–5
    UPP representative   75
urban leader   143, 155–6, 160
    appeal of Sata's campaign
        message   161–70
    blame the Chinese (foreign
        investors)   165–6
    leadership style   166
    support in the 2006
        elections   170–2

worker mobilisation   158–60
worker, not   63–4, 158
Scott, Guy   97, 119, 145
    Minister of Agriculture   97
    MMD member   97
    National Lima Party   97
    PF member   175
        PF slogan change   160
        revealing Sata's role in the
        PF   154
Shamapande, Yobert   146
Shamenda, Fackson   105, 106, 108
Shansonga, Atan   147
Shikaputo, Paulo   50
Shimaponda, Luminzu   118
Sibongo, Maxwell   79, 83, 84, 87, 88
Silwamba, Eric   130, 131, 150
Simutanyi, Neo   77, 136
Sipalo, Munukayumbwa   39
Sokota, Pascal   50
Sondashi, Ludwig   105, 106
sources   28–30
Southern Province   55, 57, 108, 150, 187–8
state of emergency   37, 39, 96
strikes see unrest
subsidies
    agriculture   94
    food   70, 73
    for employees   138
    housing   87
succession to Chiluba   18–22, 31, 98–9,
    116–17, 126, 130–2
    ban on succession debate   98, 123,
    128
        call for expulsion of Chiluba
        from MMD   123
        Mwila declares his presidential
        candidature   123, 124
    decision by Chiluba, as a   98, 99,
    123, 126, 131
    early presidential ambitions   20,
    31, 99
    exit from MMD and formation of
    new parties   97, 125, 135 n.1, 196
        Sata   12, 31, 61, 99, 132, 135 n.1,
        144, 196
    expectation   98, 124, 125

MMD NEC meeting to elect
   presidential candidate   130–1
      Chiluba blocking Sata   131
      Chiluba's campaign for
         Mwanawasa   131, 140
      electoral rules   130–1
      nominees   130
      results   131
      Sata contesting result in
         court   132
   Mwanawasa   23, 32
   party dynamics, succession-driven
      affect succession
         outcomes   14, 22, 196
      central to Chiluba's rule   20,
         31, 98
      harm the party   18, 20, 97
   succession race   20, 31, 112, 117, 118,
      122–4, 125
   waiting for Chiluba's second term
      to end   31, 99, 116–17, 122 n.16
Tembo, Christon   118, 125, 126, 146
   Chawama MP   121
   opposed to Chiluba's third
      term   98, 128
         barred from the MMD
            National Convention   129
         expelled from MMD   98,
            129, 130
      presidential challenger   98, 116–17,
         121, 125, 128, 146
         formed own party, FDD   98,
            98 n.21, 135 n.1, 150
         non–Bemba speaking
            opposition   150
      vice president of Zambia   122
Tembo, Paul   126
third presidential term, bid for, by
   Chiluba   21, 96, 98–9, 123, 124,
   126–30
      Chiluba's actions
         appointment of DAs   126
         MMD extraordinary
            convention   127
         national tour funded to build
            support   126

      opposition excluded   129
      plan to change the Zambian
         constitution   129
      probing and canvassing
         support   128–9
      public stance   126, 127, 128,
         129
   support and opposition
      Chiluba's cabinet   126–7,
         127, 128
      MMD leaders   123, 126,
         128–9, 130
      MMD members   123, 126
      MMD National
         Convention   129
      MMD NEC   127
      MPs   128, 129, 130
      Oasis Forum   127, 128, 129
      Sata   98, 126, 127–8, 129, 146,
         182
      Tembo and Miyanda   128
      trade unions, diplomats,
         regional leaders   127, 150
trade union movement   10, 37, 38–9, 50
   autonomy from political
      parties   104, 157–8
   complaints   105, 127
   criticised   64, 97, 157–8
   Sata   26, 37, 33, 64, 74, 160
   split from nationalist
      movement   37, 59, 64
   unrest   37, 39, 73
United National Independence Party,
   UNIP   40, 67, 97, 120, 121, 135
   housing   86–7, 103
   leadership politics   72
   National Convention
      1969 and 1988   83
      1977   72
      1990   73, 89
   primary polls   77
   support for   71–2, 89
United Party for National Development,
   UPND   135, 146, 150, 176, 183, 185, 187,
   193

United Progressive Party, UPP   10, 11, 27, 71–2, 113, 194
    counterfeit UNIP membership cards   75
unrest   37, 38, 53, 59–60, 70, 71, 73, 137, 156, 180–1
    incited by Sata   62–3, 66, 158–9
    protests   10, 38, 40, 143, 153, 176, 179, 184, 185
    riots   65, 71, 73, 90, 159, 179
    strikes   37, 39, 62–3, 131
Western Province   51, 108, 150, 170, 171–2, 174, 187–8, 189
    secession   143, 176, 178, 179, 180, 181, 182, 186
    strategic constituencies for Sata   180
        Kaoma   180
        Mangango   180
        Mongu   180
        Nalikwanda   180
        Nalolo   176, 180
        Senanga   180
White Fathers   48, 49, 56
white settlers   14, 28, 36, 38, 39, 40, 60, 64, 74, 80–2, 175
Wina, Arthur   91, 92, 96, 108, 175
Wina, Inonge   175–6, 180
Wina, Sikota   115, 120
World Bank   22, 86, 93, 107, 137
Zambia African National Congress, ZANC   39
Zambia Congress of Trade Unions, ZCTU   73, 104, 105, 106, 107, 157, 158
Zambia Consolidated Copper Mines   94
Zambia Democratic Congress, ZDC   97
Zambia Federation of Employers   106
Zambia Republican Party, ZRP   98, 135, 146
Zimba, Newstead   104, 105, 107, 118
Zukas, Simon   59
Zulu, Martha   80, 82, 83